Planning Community Policing

Goal Specific Cases and Exercises

Victor G. Strecher

Emeritus, Sam Houston State University

WAVELAND PRESS, INC.
Prospect Heights, Illinois

For information about this book, write or call:
Waveland Press, Inc.
P.O. Box 400
Prospect Heights, Illinois 60070
(847) 634-0081

Illustrations by Mike Strecher

ISBN 0-88133-930-X

Printed in the United States of America

7 6 5 4 3 2 1

For Barbara
and our terrific kids
Vic, Mike, Jon, Chris and Matt

Acknowledgements

The notion for this book emerged from thirty years of teaching at Sam Houston State University and Michigan State University, some years of police management in the St. Louis Metropolitan Police Department, and many case presentations in the Texas Law Enforcement Management Institute and the Executive Institute of the Florida Department of Law Enforcement. I am indebted to my colleagues, students, and police managers for the countless fragments they contributed to the ideas and cases contained in the text. Profound thanks to Lou Radelet, Art Brandstatter and Ralph Turner, who first put "community" into policing long ago, in 1955. Special gratitude to Larry Hoover, Dick Stephens and Bill Bieck for their advice, and to Chief of Police Alan Philippus, San Antonio, for essential crime and service dispatch data. To Carol Rowe and Paige Force, humble gratitude for their superb editing. Finally, devoted appreciation to Barbara, my wife, who urged this project upon me and corrected my arithmetic, and to my son Mike, whose creative illustrations animated my words.

Victor G. Strecher
Professor Emeritus and former Dean
Sam Houston State University

Contents

Chapter 1

Reinventing American Policing

For many years following its 1950 publication, O. W. Wilson's *Police Administration* dominated the thinking of American policing. It was the first (and for a long time, only) police administration book. *Police Administration* was a giant step forward, but it was fatally flawed: it was a cookbook.

We have learned there are no cookbooks for American policing. Any cookbook is one chef's formula for personal success in the kitchen—ingredients, procedures, and equipment that work in one kitchen are selected to match one person's taste *and* success. The police administration books of the last generation fit this analogy: one chief's formula for success in a particular city, with its specific demography and political framework, personnel, organizational structure and management personality.

As we leave behind the police administration cookbooks, we are confronted by a new generation of books. Some of these are actually *public* administration textbooks decorated with some *police* administration terminology. With a few word changes, they apply to virtually all public agencies and do not address issues and operations which are specific to the police enterprise. Others seek to convert us to something called COP—community-oriented policing—or simply community policing. How are we to view this dual flood of new policing fashion? Is a public administration text, with a bit of bridging police terminology, an adequate replacement for the cookbooks? Is COP truly a snapshot of the future (as many claim, or as others criticize) or a sentimental journey to the past, a time when communities and social values were simpler? Is either approach an improvement over O. W. Wilson's "professional" model of policing? Have we shifted from one cookbook process (patrol) to others (community closeness)?

Without question, policing has long needed a reconciliation with its communities. It has taken over forty years for Louis Radelet's community-involvement message of the 1950s to gain a utilitarian foothold in the culture of American policing. There is, however, so much remaining to be done as the *ethos* of community policing searches for its methodology. Every community deserves policing which is responsive to its problems and goals, to its social and political environment, to its economy within which police departments must function. Cookbooks can't accomplish this transition. The purpose of this book is to provide a method by which local police administrators can take into account specific problems of their communities plus the social, political, and economic contexts that must be considered in planning police policies and operations. In attempting this, the book requires us to step away from some of our old habits.

Process Orientation: The Old Division of Work

Most modern organizations owe their structure to the traditional criteria of division of work: *purpose, process, time, location and clientele*. In addition, there have been two widely followed tenets of large-scale organizing: (1) the need to break the broad, general goals of large organizations into smaller goals for subordinate units and, eventually, into assignments for individual workers, and (2) the need to divide the total number of employees in the organization into manageable groups of subordinates (that is, a reasonable span of control for each manager). As a result of these two needs, most organizations are structured as hierarchies. It is rare for all the members of even a small organization to pursue the organization's overall goal—and unheard of for those in large organizations.

As many public administration theorists have observed, large, modern organizations are *complex* as well as hierarchical. This complexity is due mainly to the five criteria which serve to divide work.

These traditional means of dividing work will now be defined and illustrated.

Purpose, or *function*, is often the first criterion for dividing work. It is often used before the others to break down the most general goals of an organization. Following are some hypothetical examples.

In a manufacturing industry:

Goal: Maximize profits for investors (by)

Subgoals:

Manufacturing a product

Marketing the product

Distributing the product

Collecting income from product sales

Each of these subgoals is in turn divided into smaller subgoals, such as building or leasing factory space, obtaining raw materials and machinery, hiring and training workers, making the product, inspecting its quality, surveying demand for the product, advertising, packaging, shipping, billing, and so on.

In policing the most general goal could be stated as:

Goal: Preserve peace and security of community

Subgoals:

Contain crime

Preserve community order

Deliver order-related services

Subgoals of crime containment might be:

Prevent crimes

Intervene in crimes by arresting offenders

Clear crimes by identifying and arresting offenders

Recover stolen property, return to owners

To take one of these subgoals a step further:

Goal: Prevent crimes

Subgoals:

Change motivation of potential offenders

Change behavior of potential offenders

Reduce opportunity for potential offenders

To take one of the secondary subgoals a step further:

Goal: Reduce opportunities for potential offenders

Subgoals:

Reduce vulnerability of potential targets

Reduce attractiveness of potential targets

Induce uncertainty in potential offenders

Increase cost of committing offense

Put police between potential offenders and targets

Increase risk of arrest for potential offenders

Each of these subgoals has, in turn, a number of its own related subgoals (for example, reducing target vulnerability includes premise surveys and improved locks, high-intensity lighting for alleys for reducing attractiveness of targets).

Although rapid response to calls for service has been criticized as wasteful, there is evidence that some calls merit rapid responses, while others do not. Both extremes, responding rapidly to all calls or eliminating rapid response altogether, are unsatisfactory policies. Thus, a goal of crime intervention might involve the following subgoals.

Goal: Intervene in crimes to arrest offenders

Subgoals:

Determine rapid response cases by crime analysis

Screen incoming calls for rapid response status

Assign rapid response scene unit and backups

Assign perimeter cover units to escape routes

Get offender identifiers from scene unit

Broadcast identifiers to perimeter cover units

This goal moves beyond merely designating all serious calls as rapid response calls. Analysis determines which cases qualify as meriting rapid response. Planning for such calls means analyzing "what if" scenarios. For example, it is more likely that perimeter cover units will intercept fleeing offenders than scene response units, and proper planning will provide for that eventuality. Planned deployment of both scene and perimeter units should be part of every rapid response situation.

Goal: Clear crimes by identifying and arresting offenders

Subgoals:

Develop case-linking by crime analysis

Develop physical evidence leads

Develop known offender leads

Develop witness leads

Develop stolen property leads

Develop informant sources

These examples illustrate ways in which broad goals can be divided into smaller, related subgoals on the basis of *purpose*. The new subgoals can be differentiated from their parent goals and are often the entire purpose of a subordinate unit. Obviously, some of the subgoals are more difficult to achieve than others. It is essential, when dividing work, to conduct this analysis of goals and means so that feasible strategies and tactics are not overlooked.

Process differs from purpose but is often confused with it. This may be because general goals, after being subdivided to their smallest subgoals, often end up as processes, as will be illustrated. The clearest cases of dividing work by process involve specializations such as photography and computer operations.

Purpose and process are most clearly sorted out by the following statements:

- A single *purpose* specialization usually requires many *processes* to accomplish it.
- A single *process* is usually used to accomplish many *purposes*.
- A purpose-oriented workload is easily quantified, and so is the concept of successfully accomplished purposes.
- A process-oriented workload is hard to quantify, and it is hard to say when, if ever, it is successfully finished.

A typical case of process specialization which serves many purposes is photography, which may be employed to record:

- crime scenes
- visits of dignitaries to the department
- applicants for police jobs
- arrested persons
- documents in forensic labs
- community relations events
- illustrations for a department newsletter story

Another process specialization would be computer operations, which serve the needs of:

- field operations (name, auto license checks, Field Interrogation Reports [FIR], patrol planning)
- investigations (crime analysis, record checks, case assignments)
- administration (workload analysis, personnel records, payroll, budgeting, planning)
- technical services (inventory, auto service schedules, jail inmate status, telephone intake and dispatching, criminal records and identification)

The most easily confused divisions of work in policing are *patrol* and *investigation*, which are both specializations by process, rather than purpose. Each employs a process to accomplish many purposes. For example, a patrol force, in the doctrine of O. W. Wilson, should be able to perform any police task, if required. Patrol officers, traditionally, have been expected to prevent violent crime, control traffic, curb incipient delinquency, ameliorate abusive marriages, capture stray animals, heal neighborhood disputes, respond to medical crises and investigate crimes, serious and petty. Mid-century theorists went so far as to say a police agency could consist of a patrol unit alone.

Investigation, on the other hand, is a process employed to determine whether crimes have been comitted, to identify perpetrators of crime, to enhance criminal cases for prosecution after offenders have been identified, to determine the validity of citizens' complaints against police officers, and to determine the suitability of applicants for police work.

But even this process-oriented division of work is ambiguous: patrol officers investigate and investigators patrol. Thus the two primary work-division criteria do poorly at separating responsibilities.

Specialization by process certainly has its place in policing; however, its utility in dividing the primary functions of policing has been too passively accepted. Stated plainly: the work of policing has grown more complex since the days of foot patrol and the mystique of the "secret service" as detective bureaus were known in the late 1800s. The fundamental police organization has not been able to shed the basic structure it inherited from those times. We will return to this topic later in the chapter.

Time is abundantly used as a basis for dividing work in policing. Three shifts a day, plus overlay shifts, are ways time is managed. There are also tactical patrols and other directed operations aimed at peak crime hours as well as locations. Certain days of the week, weeks of the year and seasons are keyed into the schedule for special attention because of crime fluctuations or general workload. Resort communities are one example. The long-standing patrol plan concept is based on the interaction of time and the next criterion, location.

Location as a work-dividing basis is found in beats, supervisory areas, districts or precincts, and command sectors. Anything less than citywide or countywide is, in fact, a case of specialization by location.

Clientele specialization is seen most clearly in juvenile operations, help for geriatric victims, spouse abuse investigations, tourist and victim assistance, and truancy squads. Some would say that vice and dangerous drug enforcement programs are as much oriented to *clientele* as they are to specialized *purpose*. These are just two examples which mix the criteria for specialization.

Problems of Process-Divided Police Work

Most police departments divide their line work first by process and then by a combination of time and location. This produces a typical split of the primary police function into patrol and investigation, although the actual units have other titles, such as field operations, and detective bureau. Most patrol units are then divided into shifts, which typically cover all twenty-four hours of each day of the year. A patrol unit is then typically specialized by location: an area for each officer to patrol by foot or car, within a larger area in which six to ten officers are supervised by a sergeant. Although various mixes of these criteria have been used to divide the police mission since urban policing began 150 years ago, there is growing reason to believe this traditional division of work is no longer adequate.

Why Process-Oriented Policing Has Been Popular

Process-oriented policing has maintained its popularity mainly because it is so simple to do. Patrol and investigation are, after all, straightforward activities, easily defined, understood, taught and performed. Why, then, not simply keep it that way? Think of the argument against it this way: If policing were a competitive market enterprise, fighting for market share, our tax-supported law enforcement agencies would be the first to go bankrupt. Any agency that established clear goals and planned its strategic approaches and tactical operations on the basis of such goals would compete more effectively and efficiently than the best-run process-oriented department. In other words, its services would be better and its costs less.

Why is this the case? Because it is almost impossible to define "successful" and "unsuccessful" process operations. Is vehicle patrol better than foot patrol? Without defined, quantified goals it is impossible to say. Is specialized criminal investigation better than general assignment investigation? Again, the goals are unstated, unquantified and the quality of the process is not clear.

Not only are the process-driven police methods difficult to evaluate, but so are the quantity and quality of individual and unit performances. Most police administrators acknowledge it is difficult and often unfair to compare the performances of officers and units, even when they are doing the same kind of work. Admittedly, there are differences in the working environments of officers and units; however, the main impediment to performance evaluations and comparisons is the comfortable reliance on those good old processes: patrol and investigation.

Thus the broad processes (patrol, investigation) become the "everything" of policing, making for huge, ill-defined responsibilities which are never completed and whose quality cannot be ascertained. For example, the patrol might be quantified as miles covered, perhaps to be targeted as a performance level and compared from year to year. But to what purpose? What do we learn from year-to-year comparisons of the quality and productivity of patrol forces? Is Car A with 130 miles per watch doing better than Car B with 80 miles? Or are the differences simply attributable to the kinds of streets and highways patrolled by the two units? Or perhaps to a different number of hours consumed by answering calls for service by the two units? Then, why not compare miles patrolled per hour of uncommitted time? This returns us to different kinds of streets and highways, types of neighborhoods, speed of patrol. Fewer miles of patrol might indicate a more attentive patrol officer.

Similarly, is the number of investigations undertaken an index of efficiency for detectives? Is the number of crimes cleared? Or might that be attributable to greater solvability of cases in a detective's caseload?

As in the days of foot patrol, officers assigned to radio-dispatched patrol cars are expected to handle the full array of community problems, but with a difference: walking officers communicated continuously with their community, while intermittently dealing with problems. Placing officers in cars resulted in an emphasis upon the availability of cars for dispatch and rapid response, rather than upon officers' continuous community contacts and problem solving. This model, termed calls-for-service (CFS) police management, was fully implemented following World War II, and involved huge expenditures for communications systems, patrol deployment plans, and vehicles.

The new approach changed the nature of police work. With CFS patrol, ill-defined workloads contained even more unbalanced mixtures of duties which did not fit together into sensible, achievable workloads. Many commentators have pointed to the incongruous mix of social work and crime fighting, stress and boredom, which call upon officers to maintain contradictory mind-sets and which lead to many of the inappropriate responses of patrol officers to situations in the field. This is one of the major impediments to incorporating community-oriented policing into traditional calls-for-service patrol models.

Although process-oriented policing has these shortcomings, it is only fair to point out that goal-centered policing is more demanding to plan, implement and manage than the police processes model. What is it that makes goal-oriented policing somewhat more challenging?

The goals of policing are difficult to define and quantify because the problems and service demands are so comprehensive and general at the top of the organization. These goals encompass the protection of life and property and the preservation of community peace and order. This general obligation to handle everything from violent crime to minor interpersonal squabbles, traffic congestion and substance abuse, makes the definition of clear, achievable subgoals a complex undertaking.

For these reasons the general areas of responsibility are rarely subdivided by function. For instance, the first general goal might be divided between life and property protection (although this seems quickly to be a poor choice) or between protection from violent crime and protection from careless, disorderly but non-violent behavior. All crime control could be considered one division of work and maintenance of social order another.

It is easy to overstate the goals of policing. For instance, too many administrators (largely in the past) have ingenuously spoken of eliminating crime, keeping the community free of crime, or maintaining a peaceable community. Such objectives are, of course, impossible and guarantee the organization's failure. More modest goals, such as reducing crime to its minimum, or reducing crime ten percent, or clearing ten percent more of the serious offenses, are often based on flimsy assumptions about irreducible crime levels or solvability of crimes. Here the problem is that there is no baseline of irreducible crime (in any category), nor a minimum-optimum-maximum clearance rate (in any category). Thus, the quantification issue becomes more challenging—but not insoluble.

The past few pages have described some difficulties of measuring police workload and the success of police operations. This difficulty has been attributed to the long-standing *process* orientation of major police practices, such as patrol and investigation. The objection to process-oriented division of work may seem at first to be a quibble over nothing; however, it will be shown that effective planning, budgeting and administration cannot be accomplished if we continue to let process define police specializations. The division of work in policing will always involve the criteria described above, and process specializations will continue to result from technological advances. But as policing joins other public services in quantifying work demands and analyzing costs and benefits of its public safety programs, goal-oriented applications will greatly outnumber those based on process and clientele.

Mayors, city managers, city council members, county administrators and legislators no longer hesitate to ask how much product is being derived from law enforcement expenditures—nor do the media and voters.

Undefined Goals and Priority Default

There seems to be an unspoken assumption that all organizations have goals and that their members pursue these goals. This assumption makes intuitive sense, being rooted deeply in our belief in the rational basis of formal organizations. It is probably accurate to say that most organizations *did* have goals at the time of their founding. But numerous formal organizations, including those comprising the American criminal justice system, are *not* goal-directed in the present. The reasons:

1. Many formal organizations are so old that their original goals are no longer valid, useful or even recognized in the present time. Several factors can account for this. For example, the social context at the time of founding may have been displaced by social change. Such change might occur in any or all of the following:
    - the physical environment
    - economy
    - social institutions
    - social values
    - technological innovations
    - social structure
    - role definitions

    In any of these situations, continued focus on the old goals might be ritualistic rather than functional. For example, the goal of safeguarding public *morality* has been largely supplanted by attention to public *order*; for instance police no longer arrest adulterers. However, the police do continue to shine their flashlights into cars parked along Lover's Lane, inspect the degree of nakedness in burlesque theaters and topless clubs, interdict sexual activity in adult bookstores, and arrest nudists at public beaches.
2. Conversely, the original goals might continue to be valid and useful, but the organization's policies, practices and working culture may have drifted to the extent they no longer address the founding goals. For example, a primary goal of the colonial night watch was to arouse citizens to deal with trouble if it occurred. Modern

policing eschews calling upon the citizenry in this way, although community policing suggests a return to the practice in some form.

Other practices of the police were inspecting homes for fire hazards and requiring citizens to clean the streets in front of their homes. The goals driving these activities are still valid, but police rarely address them.

3. A third case is that a drift away from the original social context *and* a drift from policies, practices and organizational culture have occurred without an accommodation of a new goal and new approaches. In this case both forms of drift diverge from the objective policing needs of the community and leave the protectors further removed from the served. The drives to eliminate "politics" from policing and to professionalize policing represented movement away from the social context of the mid-1800s and toward an inappropriate emulation of the social mystique, isolation and self-regulation of medicine, engineering and the law. As this "professional" model of policing evolved, the community had little input to police policy. In some cases, institutional arrangements (for example, police commissions) were designed specifically to buffer the police from "politics," which was often interpreted to include legitimate community policy input or complaints.

All three of these cases occur commonly and explain the poor match in a given community between stated police goals, actual police practices, and policing needs of the community.

Drift can detach the work of a police agency from any valid and consistent goal orientation. In such cases the goals of a department become simply a reflection of myriad personal goals, the subjective interests of individual police officers on duty at any given time.

If clear, valid, achievable goals cannot be stated, there is no way to establish priorities (for example, whether to emphasize crime control, order maintenance or service delivery). James Q. Wilson's famous study of different policing "styles," *Varieties of Police Behavior* (1968), might more accurately be characterized as American policing without goals, resulting from its obsession with processes and a drift from its original social context.

Similarly, if valid goals cannot be quantified, there is no way of measuring the effectiveness of policing activities. For example, if no one investigates community levels of fear of crime, how can anyone evaluate to what extent police operations impact the fear of crime in those areas? Impossible as it may sound, it is possible, beforehand, that we do not know what we intend to do—and afterward, that we do not know if we have done it, or if we have done it, how it was done.

There is sometimes a gulf between what we know how to do and what we actually do in policing. Even when new methods, techniques, or goals offer a promise of effective results, resistance to changes works to keep the priority default active. The status quo is easier—it is easier to defend (people know it; they're more comfortable with a predictable, known quantity) and it is less risky. Just like the default settings on a computer, the "bases are covered" without having to exert any effort. For these reasons, practice lags behind the knowledge base. However, the lag is not equal among the 17,500 local policing agencies in the United States. There is a broad spectrum of capacity to perform ranging from primitive to sophisticated, state-of-the-art levels. Many police agencies operate as they did a century ago, while others are at the cutting edge of modern knowledge and performance. How can this be so in the most technologically advanced nation? It happens because the knowledge/practice gap is virtually invisible.

It is precisely for this reason that the knowledge/practice gap is so critically important. Few observers know much about it. Mayors know little about the quality of police performance, and they seldom have more than four or eight years to learn about it. Most mayors are satisfied with a police agency free of scandals which might threaten their political careers. Few chiefs of police lose their jobs because of their devotion to outmoded police practices, and few sheriffs lose elections because of it.

City managers tend to know more about policing because of their professional experience and networks. But even they have relatively little influence over the actual performance of police agencies. In most cases, they are stuck with officers who joined the local department some years before, competent or not. Most city managers have severe limits on their authority to reassign police managers or to replace them, below the level of the chief.

The important work of police accreditation will eventually have a positive impact on this situation, particularly to the extent that it concentrates on problem solving and goal setting.

Obstacles to Successful Police Administration

This section highlights some of the "cultural baggage" of policing which has blocked innovations in some departments. These are extensive and potent impediments to improving the police knowledge base and its applications to policies and practices, and must be eliminated.

Doctrines and Fixations

Some of the areas which have blocked forward progress of some departments are listed below. Improvements in the knowledge base of both police departments and observers will be impeded until these impediments have been removed.

1. *Eliminate politics from policing*. In its simplest, most pervasive form, this fixation of police culture has impeded many police administrators from rationally defining and maintaining their relationship with legitimate governmental officials, including city managers, mayors and city councils. At its worst it has inculcated a rigid, contentious mindset in some chiefs, and thus set the stage for inevitable antagonism between those chiefs and the political officials to whom they are accountable or with whom they must cooperate.

   The most serious effect of the no-politics doctrine is found in the general failure to develop workable boundaries between the *governance* functions of political officials and *administrative* functions of police executives. Although the latest issue of *Local Government Police Management* (Geller, 1991) contains some guidelines for the relationship between chiefs and city managers, there is not yet a formula for clear boundaries and policies which maintain the prerogatives and duties of chiefs and all other political officials with whom they have a working relationship.

2. *The police alone are capable of controlling crime*. This fixation includes expressions such as, "We are the professionals. Don't play policeman, leave crime to us. We are the thin blue line between good citizens and the barbarians." This aspect of the police culture for the first two-thirds of the twentieth century held most citizens at arm's length from policing. It resulted in the mutual alienation of police and community in the mistaken belief that policing should imitate the professional mystique and arcane knowledge of medicine.

3. *Blanket the jurisdiction with patrol*. An important part of this doctrine is the standardization of police operations throughout the jurisdiction. All parts of the community, even those at minimal risk, require police presence. Patrol plans calling for equal coverage and response times throughout the jurisdiction epitomize this doctrine. One result has been the failure of the police to concentrate sufficiently on trouble spots.

4. *Beat accountability*. Within the blanket of patrol, this doctrine makes an officer (and department) responsible for crime control everywhere in the jurisdiction. It dates from foot officers being

held to this standard by "roundsmen" (sergeants) who required them to be alert and to find every problem before the sergeants did. This pre-dated telephones, radios, cars and recent, passive police management based on responding to calls for service. A negative side-effect of this once useful idea has been a tendency for officers to neglect problems not on their beats.

5. *Investigate all crimes*. This fixation keeps detectives indefinitely responsible for all cases assigned to them. In particular, "important" cases remain active, regardless of their hopelessness. The fixation does not allow purging of cases. The effect has been to clutter up the caseloads of detectives and to imply that all cases are solvable.
6. *Patrol each beat randomly*. Another fixation urges, "Be omnipresent." Crime will be reduced because of criminals' impressions that the police are everywhere. The side-effect has been to institutionalize a lack of focus for individual patrol units—if crime is randomly distributed, then every spot on the beat is equally worthy of attention.
7. *Rapid response is good*. Promise it, deliver it, and spend on it. This fixation began long before the motorization of policing, with the installation of police telephone call boxes in the 1880s. By 1890 virtually all cities with a population over 100,000 had call boxes (Strecher, 1992). Since motorization, policing has spent billions on patrol plans, communications systems, high-speed vehicles, emergency lights and sirens, automatic vehicle locators, in-car computers, patrol car allocation models, and other rapid response-related components. One result has been the tendency to respond rapidly to all incidents, and a failure to analyze the difference between those calls which merit rapid response and those which do not.
8. *The big bust*. This mystique of investigative work sets detectives above the dog soldiers of patrol. It denigrates the value of crime deterrence, order maintenance, and service delivery. The images of uniformed guys bringing sandwiches to detectives at their important work, and the promotional stripes being pinned onto the heroic detective in his hospital bed (survived a shootout, you know) are still with us.
9. *Run the calls*. The institutionalization of the calls-for-service policing and management model has linked:
    - patrol plans devised by consultants, not patrol managers
    - dispatch by auxiliary unit outside the chain of command of the patrol force

- sergeants doing excessive paperwork in the station
- lack of active field supervision of patrol officers
- indirect means of assessing patrol performance

The end result of this doctrine has been the passive supervision of field forces. Sergeants don't supervise; they sign reports.

10. *Permanence and constancy of policies and practices.* Once adopted, procedures are forever kept active. This perpetuation happens with patrol plans, investigative practices, communications procedures, and even techniques. Some techniques (such as decoy operations and traffic enforcement) continue to be used even though their effects are about the same whether they're used intermittently or constantly.
11. *Single-idea obsessions.* Fixations dominate the consciousness of policing to the exclusion of alternatives. In the past it was random patrol, omnipresence, rapid response, standardization. It seems now to be community policing and perhaps a few allied ideas.

In addition to doctrines/fixations, there are two other prime obstacles to changing the status quo to a more responsive, goal-oriented institution.

Absence of a Database for Planning and Evaluating

A database such as the one in the appendix is essential to the systematic planning, implementation and evaluation of police policies and practices. Few departments have compiled such a database, despite having access to all of the information.

Lack of Systematic Policy Analysis

For ten years, beginning in the mid-1970s, the National Institute of Justice sponsored seminars in Managing Patrol Operations, Managing Criminal Investigations, and a hybrid of the two called Improving Police Management (Cawley et al., 1977). A primary thrust of these seminars, delivered to thousands of senior police administrators throughout the United States, was the systematic review and analysis of police policies. The intent was to institute planned policy across the board rather than the occasional, crisis-stimulated policy probes commonly done. It was recommended that departments routinely and methodically scan their policies over a broad range, including:

- workload elements
- priorities for enforcement and arrest efforts

- alternatives to dispatched responses to calls for service
- investigative case screening and purging
- resource allocation priorities
- patrol distribution criteria
- degree of investigative specialization
- interaction of patrol and investigative services
- focus and maintenance of community crime prevention programs
- liaison with prosecutors and courts
- use of paraprofessionals and volunteers
- summons in lieu of arrest
- systematic management of change (planning)

A survey of Managing Patrol Operations (MPO) participants indicated that a majority believed they were doing ongoing policy analysis; however, more detailed questions disclosed that most chiefs encountered serious setbacks, including inadequate data collection methods, irregularity of efforts, internal staff resistance, low priority of policy reviews, lack of managerial interest, fear of "spying" on operational units, line units' beliefs that such analyses were not directly helpful to the workforce, and lack of staff, expertise, and time.

The natural consequence of these factors is profound inertia and resistance to planned, deliberate change. What goes unnoticed amid these counter-forces is the unchecked impact of inherent change in the surrounding social and political systems.

Obviously police goals no longer include capturing escaped slaves or breaking labor strikes. What is not as obvious is that current patrol and investigative policies fail to recognize the ethnic Balkanization of America's cities and the specific, often unique, policing requirements of these diverse cultural pockets. We might ask: To which community does community-oriented policing relate? Hispanic communities have become fragmented into cultural microcosms of Cuba, Mexico, and the nations of Central and South America. Asian communities have grown beyond the old-fashioned Chinatown, to include Koreatown, Little Saigon, New Taiwan, Little Tokyo, and numerous other Asian and Pacific Islander components. The breakup of the Soviet Union has brought many refugees to the United States. Each of these cultural pockets, once ignored in police planning, confronts policing with culturally-specific forms of crime and disorder, including pervasive organized crime.

With the advent of expanded voting rights, city council members are now elected by large numbers of African Americans, Hispanics, Asians, Native Americans and other minority citizens. At various times policing has been under the control of dominant cultural groups, which were later displaced by newer immigrants (for example, English-Scots, by the Irish in the 1870s, who, in turn, were displaced by Germans, Poles and Scandinavians). Non-Hispanic whites dominated policing until the recent past, when African Americans and Hispanics entered policing in large numbers.

These demographic changes have yet to be fully recognized in police policy making and planning, but their impact will be profound. Beyond population changes, the erosion of the industrial base of cities, the absorption of dependent populations, tax-abatement referendums, the aging of the urban infrastructure, the emergence of police unions, the entry of women into policing, new modes of substance abuse and related crimes, and the emergence of potentially terroristic organizations call for police policy analysis and planning that is less passive and more creatively proactive. For an analysis of how social change affects police goals, see the final chapter of *Police Management: Issues and Perspectives* (Strecher, 1992).

What Needs to Be Done

Senior administrators who plan and manage police operations and the chiefs who approve these policies and plans need to begin by purging their thinking of long-standing policing obsessions.

1. *Forget* the wrong-headed idea that every police officer must be able to perform every operational assignment in the department. In this view, every officer is a standardized, interchangeable production unit, much like one of a hundred punch presses or lathes in a machine shop. This assumption, although it has never been true, has been the basis for virtually all police patrol deployment plans. It is a source of major distortion and needs to be eliminated from the thinking of police planners and administrators. It may be true that every sworn officer must be able to handle the initial response to any kind of call for service. But beyond that initial response lies an infinite variety of special capabilities not found in every law enforcement officer.
2. *Forget* the equally wrong-headed tendency to think of "patrol" and "investigation" immediately on confronting any service demand from the community. The first thought should be to question whether the demand represents a legitimate police "goal" and to proceed from there with systematic planning logic.
3. *Forget* the time-honored but mistaken imagery of an omnipresent "patrol blanket" ovcr the entire jurisdiction. There is no blanket.

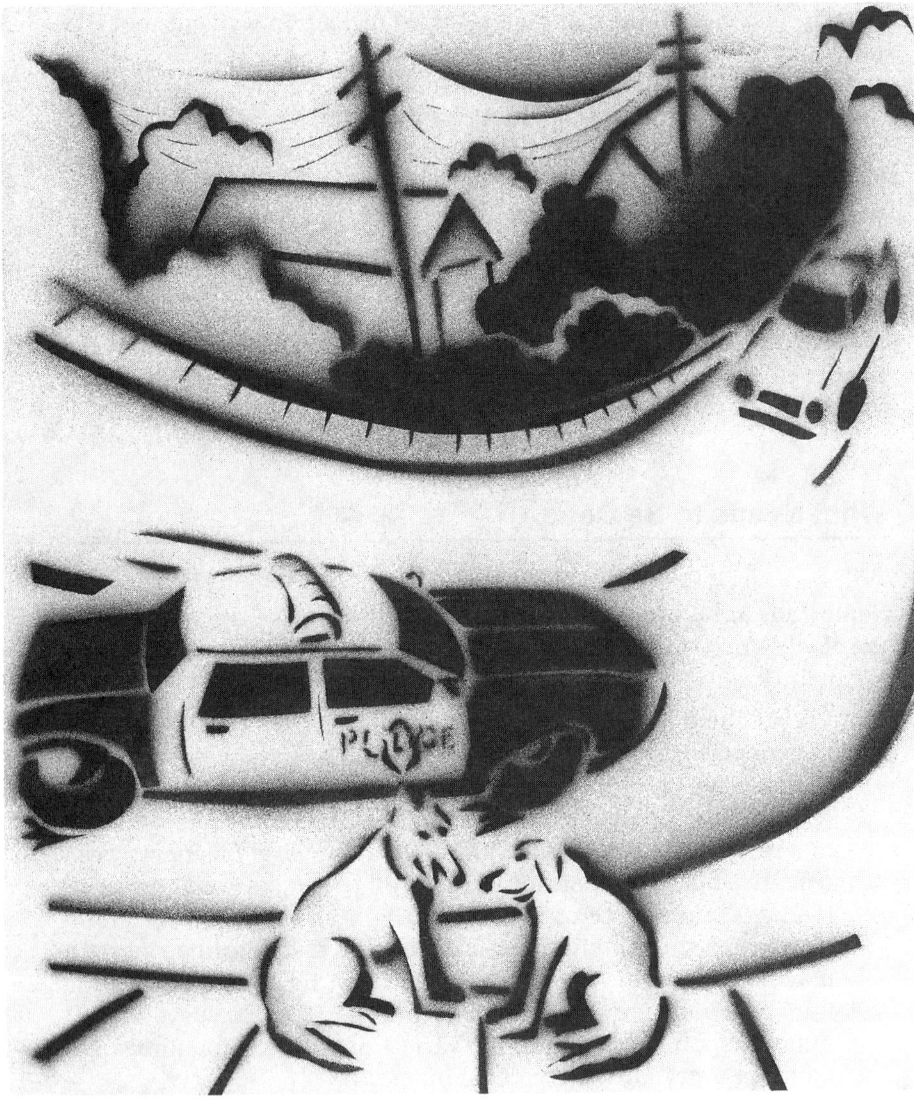

Hey, DPR says we're low priority. Life is GOOD.

There has never been a blanket. From the time of its enunciation by Vollmer, it has been an illusory doctrine which in recent years has revealed vast holes in its fabric.

4. *Forget* the simplistic notion that, to be fair and equitable, policies must be uniform throughout the jurisdiction. For example, patrol deployment is usually based on the geographic distribution of calls for service, whether or not this dimension serves the other purposes of patrol, such as crime suppression.
5. *Forget* the idea that programs and procedures, once originated, should continue indefinitely.
6. *Forget* the notion that all police operations must be active twenty-four hours a day, all year, even when they have little productivity.
7. *Replace your accustomed logic process: Start with a goal. What* you need to do, not *how*. If the goal is too big for a given unit or team of personnel, *divide* it into subgoals by *purpose*, not process. A suggested model of police systems planning is provided in chapter 2.
8. *Set priorities* among goals, and stick to them.
9. *Minimize low-priority* CFS functions and minimize resource allocation in proportion to their priority—get out of the stray dog business.
10. *Free up expensive patrol resources* by minimizing the number of cars needed to handle calls for service. Retain only these cars under the radio control of dispatch.
11. *Re-allocate patrol resources* to specific high-priority goals. This requires crime analysis to determine which offenses are suppressible by police strategies and tactics.

These eleven practices comprise an approach to policing called DPR—Differential Police Response. Management based on this model has a much greater likelihood of controlling priorities and resources in order to implement an effective style of policing that will service the needs of the community and the officers in the departments.

References

Cawley, D. F., J. A. Kelly, H. J. Miron, and V. G. Strecher (1977). *Managing Patrol Operations: Participant's Manual.* Washington, DC: National Institute of Justice, U.S. Department of Justice.

Geller, W. A. (ed.) (1991). *Local Government Police Management*, 3rd ed. Washington, DC: International City Management Association.

Strecher, V. G. (1992). "Current Perspectives on Policing," in *Police Management: Issues and Perspectives*, Hoover, L. T. (ed.). Washington, DC: Police Executive Research Forum.

Wilson, J. Q. (1968). *Varieties of Police Behavior*. Cambridge: Harvard University Press.

Wilson, O. W. (1950). *Police Administration*. New York: McGraw-Hill.

Chapter 2

Goal-Oriented Planning

Evolution, Environment, and Effects

There are three general requirements for the support of goal-oriented planning and management:

- A method of policy analysis, planning and budgeting
- Supporting concepts and models
- A local/regional database

A *method* of planning includes procedures for goal-setting, guidelines for making choices among strategic and tactical alternatives, and a means of implementing, monitoring and managing the planned operation.

Supporting concepts and models address the realities and limitations of planning; models of policies and operations which have been tested and evaluated in modern policing serve as proven examples to guide planning. Evaluations of policing methods must meet accepted standards of scientific testing in order to be considered trustworthy.

A *local/regional database* contains information about population, crime, service demands, government and policing itself, for the individual police agency and its surrounding environment. The appendix contains the elements of such a database for the policing agencies, governments and populations of a hypothetical metropolitan area. It was compiled from Uniform Crime Reports, U.S. Census Reports and other government documents.

Systems Concepts

Systems science has been applied in a number of disciplines, including physics, chemistry, biology, electrical engineering, psychology, the social sciences and military science. As a result, systems theory has taken on a huge burden of technical jargon. We all know in a general sense what *input* and *output* mean; however, *homeostatic* is an alien term to most of us (it means "steady-state"). At the other extreme, systems ideas are often *over*simplified because the word "system" itself has so many everyday uses. The ideas, for instance, that a system is (1) nothing more than an assembly line for processing criminal cases, or (2) any arrangement of parts in a larger structure are oversimplifications. Technically, a system is more than either one of these.

We will describe systems concepts in terms useful for our purposes of police policy analysis, planning and budgeting. The concepts will be as free of jargon as possible. There are, however, limits to what can be described in everyday terms. Einstein, criticized for presenting his concepts in unfamiliar language, responded, "Everything should be as simple as it can be, but not simpler." We'll try to observe his admonition.

Systems Concepts Defined

The following terms provide a bare-bones vocabulary essential to the clear presentation of thoughts about planning, budgeting and administration. Whenever the word *system* is used in this book, it should be assumed to have the following characteristics:

Goal-seeking: A system's purpose is clear and definable.

Goal is quantifiable: Its size is known or estimated.

A set of component parts: Sometimes called subsystems, these parts are describable units; for example, the human body system components include subsystems called circulatory, central nervous, autonomic nervous, gastrointestinal, muscular-skeletal, reproductive, and so on. In turn, the circulatory subsystem includes components such as the heart, arteries, capillaries, and veins.

The jargon of management makes simplistic approaches sound important and complex. If we dissect the terms, we're often left with no meaning.

Tony Mattera, a corporate communications officer at a Virginia bank, invented a "Jargon Master Matrix." Pick three numbers from one to 14 and use them to select words from the table below. For example, 7, 11, 3 give us "defined budget expectations." Try any combination you like. Does it sound reasonable? What does it mean? Could it be described more simply and meaningfully?

Perhaps the most important skills for any manager to learn are communication skills. The most meticulously devised plan will be rendered useless if those who must approve it don't understand it, and those who must execute it are bewildered by the description.

1	overarching	visionary	objectives
2	strategic	support	alternatives
3	special	customer-oriented	expectations
4	specific	stretch	mechanisms
5	core	planning	assessment
6	long-term	marketing	update
7	defined	service	model
8	technology-based	process	product
9	formal	fundamental	centralization
10	exceptional	sales	incentive
11	value-based	budget	initiatives
12	executive	operating	feedback
13	immediate	discretionary	infrastructure
14	interactive	tracking	proposition

Wall Street Journal, Aug. 1, 1996, p. B1

Interactive: The component parts work with each other, often in a complex fashion. It is often not merely a linear pattern of one component doing its work and then passing the job on to another component, but rather a complicated pattern of components coming in and out of action with the others at different times.

Consonant: The work of each component supports the work of all other components; they cooperate toward the same goal.

Synergistic: The interactive parts achieve a goal which is beyond the capability of any part to achieve by itself. Often the *product* is more than the sum of what the parts would achieve by themselves. In other words, synergy *multiplies* the effect of cooperation, much as in the concept of teamwork.

Steady-State (Homeostatic): Systems are set to run at a certain level, generally to achieve an expected amount of product. They continue to run at that level unless deliberately reset by policy. However, some systems are *adaptable* rather than steady-state; that is, they are designed to change their mode of operation in response to changes in their external environment.

Open or *Closed:* An open system can detect and respond to information from its external environment. A closed system runs steady-state on internal orders, regardless of what happens outside of it.

Self-Monitoring, Self-Correcting: A system has a component devoted to sensing whether it is working toward its goal. When the monitoring/correcting component finds the system straying off-course, it alerts it and redirects it back toward its goal.

Data-based: Everything about a system is measurable, including its goals, operations, productivity, and errors. While a system is running, these measurements form a database that is used to monitor and correct its goal direction, levels of effort, intended outputs, unintended outcomes, component breakdowns, and so on. A simple illustration from everyday life is the thermostat in our home. Its database includes the desired temperature, the actual room temperature, and whether the heater or cooler is on or off.

Note that our definition of *system* is more rigorous and demanding than the meaning of "system" used in everyday conversation. We are not suggesting that simpler uses of the word are less worthy, only that for purposes of this book, *system* will always mean the same thing, as described above. Less-defined uses of the word are best avoided in connection with planning, budgeting and administration.

A Model of Systems Planning

Diagram 1 presents the logic of planning a police system, implementing the plan and establishing its self-correction as it runs. Beginning with a problem may seem too limited a way to approach planning, so problem should be thought of as equivalent to a need or demand for some kind of police response. In designing police systems it is not too difficult to think of problems, needs and demands as synonymous. Most indicators of need and demand for police services *are* problems.

Diagram 1 Police System Planning Model

Define problem (need or demand for service)
Define service goal on basis of problem
Analyze service goal (appropriate police goal? Dimensions?)
Accept, refine or reject service goal
Commit agency to goal (policy, dimension of response)
Compile array of strategy alternatives
Analyze the cost of strategy alternatives
Select strategic approach
Convert strategic approach to action plan
Divide work of action plan
Assign tasks to unit(s)
Implement operation
Monitor operation
Feedback data to manage and retro-plan all stages:

- Operations output quantity and quality
- Assignment of tasks
- Division of work
- Action plan
- Strategic approach
- Analysis of strategic alternatives
- Policy, dimension of police response
- Definition and acceptance of service goal
- Definition of problem

Refine any stage in retro-examination
Manage system toward goal and productivity

This outline gives the logic but no substance with which to develop a police system plan. As the book progresses, examples and then case exercises will fill out this bare idea and lead to mastery of planning logic. Before proceeding with a mastery of police systems planning skills, it is useful to understand how systems ideas began, evolved, and became connected to budgeting and public administration. Systems thinking works better than previous methods of organizing and managing human enterprises. Simple, linear logic of "If A then B" cannot account for or predict the countless permutations possible when describing human activities. Systems theory—particularly the emphasis on interactivity and synergy—is better able to address human work.

Most large, complex business and industrial enterprises today incorporate systems methods in their structures, operations and evaluation techniques—although you will seldom find references to systems science. The main reason for this is that all "new" organization and management approaches have foundations in ideas from earlier approaches. The originators of these variations usually invent new titles for their efforts which make them appear to be innovative and independent ideas. This tendency will also be found in the invention and naming of budgeting systems which owe much to previous formats. There is, in actuality, no approach to planning, budgeting, organizing and managing which did not evolve from existing ideas. Virtually all knowledge grows incrementally, not explosively.

Following is a brief description of each element of the police system planning model shown in diagram 1.

1. *Define the problem.* Systems scientists emphasize "asking the right questions." What they mean is that the first impression of a problem may be superficial or based on a limited viewpoint. For instance, when response time was investigated in Kansas City, the true obstacle differed from what people expected would be the answer. Initial impressions were that quicker dispatch of vehicles or quicker travel time was necessary. However, the obstacle to intervening in crimes was found more often to be a problem of getting citizens to call the police sooner than a problem of reducing dispatch or travel time. The police response time interpretation, adhered to by administrators for decades, had led to a focus on (and many expenditures for) streamlining dispatch procedures and travel time. Bieck's (1978) citizen call-delay finding suggested that a citizen education and persuasion program could have done more to increase interventions.

   "Crime" is a virtually useless problem definition because it includes too many different phenomena (ranging from murder for revenge, murder for profit, forgery, selling stolen property, using an illegal drug, engaging in sex acts for money, to improperly disposing of dangerous waste). Even smaller categories, such as "sex crimes," are poor problem definitions for purposes of planning police policies and operations because they have so few elements in common (for example, what common features are found in categories such as random rape, date rape, prostitution, child sex abuse, child pornography, indecent exposure, and voyeurism?). Conversely, "street crime" may be a useful definition because strategic approaches and street tactics can be devised to deal with it, despite the fact that it encompasses many different criminal acts (mugging, drug sales, soliciting for prostitution, auto theft, stealing from vehicles, gang intimidation of pedestrians).

   "Disorder," and "public service needs" are also overly broad as problem definitions. They include social problems and services not within the sphere of policing. Lack of order in athletic facilities, for instance, may be a problem for the sports industry, not the police. And many services once delivered by the police (money escorts, funeral escorts, stray animal pickups) may now fall outside policing in many communities. *Remember:* There are many social problems which cannot be clearly defined.

2. *Define the service goal.* Just as "crime" is a useless problem definition for planning, "crime deterrence" is a service goal which includes too many different requirements. Some crime can be deterred, but much cannot be prevented by any means available to the police (including most murders, date rapes, family assaults, child sex abuse, incest, drug abuse, and embezzlement). A crime-related service goal would be to link all crimes committed by a single burglar to enhance prosecution, or to reduce burglaries of small businesses by "premise hardening," or to reduce victimizations by discouraging hitchhiking. *Remember:* There are many social problems for which there is no legitimate governmental service goal. Problems in which the government should not intervene include torts, or *civil* harms to citizens.
3. *Analyze the service goal.* Is it appropriate to policing? Achievable? American police departments have captured stray dogs, investigated welfare applicants, licensed taverns, taxis, bicycles, dogs, houses of prostitution and pharmacies, and lodged homeless men. These may no longer be police service goals, but what about providing security in subway cars and buses? What about patrolling the corridors and stairwells of housing projects, where so much crime occurs? Are these police service goals? How much patrol does a sheriff's department owe to the residents of small towns, which cannot afford full-time police of their own? Should police escort small business owners to the bank's night depository, or leave that function to commercial money couriers, such as Brinks and Wells Fargo? As the cases in chapter 4 will indicate, there are no simple formulas for making these decisions. They call for policy analysis. *Remember:* Even after a problem has been clearly defined, and a legitimate governmental service objective identified, it may not be a responsibility of the police or sheriff's department.
4. *Accept, refine or reject the service goal.* When a problem and its service goal have been defined, it still needs to be determined if the police department will accept responsibility for it as defined. This step has been consistently ignored throughout the history of American policing. The police have often deferred silently to the political leadership in accepting new functions. Is this appropriate? Is it professional? If there is political pressure to accept inappropriate functions, can the police ask the residents of the

community if they agree that the new functions should displace broadly accepted functions, such as crime control and order maintenance? Is there a framework for asking the community such a question? Certainly public opinion surveys can play a role in determining the preferences of the public if political tensions mount. Every university has the capability of conducting opinion polls.

5. *Commit the agency to the goal—policy, dimension of response.* Having decided to accept some version of the service goal, the department needs to decide upon the *size* of its commitment to achieve that goal. In the face of on-going workloads, any newly defined service goal must compete for resources with all other goals. This is the heart and soul of systems planning and budgeting.
6. *Compile an array of strategy alternatives.* A comprehensive list should first be prepared, without respect for values. This is hard for morally aware managers to do, even temporarily. However, evaluation of the morality, ethics and social values of the alternatives will be done in the next step. It's important to defer the ethical evaluations to increase the probability of a comprehensive list.
7. *Analyze the costs of strategy alternatives.* Everything costs. An hour of patrol time or a hundred hours of investigative time are not simply available in a grab-bag for a newly proposed function. Today's police administrator *must* view all functions as being in competition with each other; he or she is responsible for making priority decisions. To fail in this duty is to let priorities be made by custom, default or undue influence.
8. *Select the strategy.* On the basis of the informed judgment of a planning group, an approach is recommended to the administrative decision-maker. A decision is made to proceed or to review the plan.
9. *Convert the strategy to an action plan.* The words "strategy" and "approach" have been used interchangeably, because neither term spells out exactly what activities will be undertaken. Following are some problems, goals and approaches that require conversion to action plans:

   Problem: daytime shoplifting by children
   Goal: reduction of the crime
   Strategy: truancy squad or program

Problem: increase in repeat spouse abuse
Goal: reduction of recidivism
Strategy: mandatory arrest

Problem: mugging of pedestrians near train depot
Goal: increase risk to potential offenders
Strategy: victim substitution program (decoy squad)

Problem: untrusted, unpopular promotion system, using books and tests
Goal: make promotions more valid, trusted
Strategy: Assessment centers

In each of these cases there needs to be a specification of the number of personnel required, and what they will actually do on a regular basis.

10. *Divide the work of the action plan.* A truancy squad may consist of just a few officers who are targeted to high-incidence areas, while a truancy program might involve all patrol officers on the day watch. Assessment centers would require input from operational units as well as the human resources unit. A task group would probably have to be designated to move the project forward, with staff responsibility held by the human resources unit.
11. *Assign the task to unit(s).* If all patrol officers are to engage in the program in a large agency, there may be several district stations involved. In a specialized department, a juvenile unit might be given this task. A new truancy squad might be appointed.
12. *Implement the action plan.* Before putting an operation on the street, training needs of the personnel assigned have to be determined. Some time may pass between approval of a new program and the readiness of staff to perform the work. But at some point, management must "push the start button" to begin a new program.
13. *Monitor the operation.* Monitoring the operation should begin immediately. This should not be confused with the more rigorous term "program evaluation." Monitoring should be thought of as managerial oversight of the new activity, attention to the details of its daily action and productivity. Are the intended outcomes happening? Are unintended side-effects also happening? How are the staff taking to their new assignments? How are citizens reacting to the new police activity?
14. *Feed back the monitoring information.* This stage could be labelled retro-plan. Essentially, it involves working backward through the phases of planning—and re-examining the appropriateness of each phase. Was a sound action plan made? Was train-

ing adequate? Was the best unit assigned? Was the best strategy chosen? Was the work divided sensibly? Were costs reasonably estimated? Is the service goal still acceptable? Was the "right" problem defined?

15. *Refine any stage in the retro-plan.* This backward look can result in a fine-tuning of the program. In some cases it can result in radically modifying or scrapping the action plan or the entire program.
16. *Manage the system toward its goal and productivity.* This becomes the ongoing job of the department's managerial system. Management requires an extensive, sophisticated set of skills (an art based on science) which cannot be covered in this small text. The crux of management is the motivation of human beings to perceive and pursue agency goals as their own.

Systems science emphasizes that there are no automated decision formulas for public service policies. The model of police system planning presented here, in fact, is based on the idea that managers need to proceed through orderly steps in evaluating policy and strategy choices. As they do so, their awareness of the problem and its service context deepens, and the criteria for making choices among alternatives begin to crystallize. An excellent presentation of this process is found in "Principles and Procedures of Systems Analysis," by E. S. Quade (1982). One of his most striking assertions is that it is more important to select the "right" objective than it is to choose the "right" strategy from among the alternatives. The reiterative technique of looking back and forth between a goal and its strategy array has the effect of clarifying and perhaps modifying the goal definition. This procedure exposes conflicts among goals and operations, which need to be balanced in making choices. How is this done? Strategic choices should be evaluated based on two important criteria.

1. *Best-case and worst-case outcomes:* Professional managers and planners consider each strategic approach, list all of the possible outcomes, and arrange them in order of desirability. Then, on the basis of experience and their efforts to quantify the problem and goal, they attempt to recognize the most probable outcome. Some of the questions in performing this analysis are the following: What can go wrong? (See Robert Merton, later in this chapter.) What approach best fits the department? (See Chester Barnard, later in this chapter.) What approach best fits the community? (See the case studies and role-plays.) This procedure begins to weed out the less desirable approaches. A decision still has not been made; the economic issue must be considered.

2. *Costs and benefits:* This is not a precise accounting procedure, but rather a careful estimate. Every strategic approach requires human resources, equipment and supplies. These need to be estimated in the form of a zero-base budget "decision unit," which is described later in this chapter. In essence, a ZBB "decision package" includes estimates of several levels of the quantity of work to be done, the cost of the work at each level, and its productivity at each level.

Who Should Be Involved in the Sixteen Steps of Planning?

This will be fully discussed later. In brief, planning done by line officers alone will lack database support, expertise and top management validation, while planning done by staff technicians alone will lack validity at the street level. See the bi-level approach presented near the end of this chapter. Here again, the systems concepts of interaction and synergy are vitally important.

The Planning and Budgeting Connection

Formal budgeting originated about one generation before systems science, early in the twentieth century. The development of budgeting was prompted by the same groundswell of governmental reform which earlier had produced a limited Federal Civil Service (Pendleton Act, 1883) and the Progressive Era, which sought to improve American government from the 1880s into the 1900s.

Prior to the first reform period, there was little control over the collection and disbursal of public funds. By today's standards, the irresponsible fiscal practices of government agencies during the 1800s were shocking. Professional accounting standards had not yet been established, making it possible for public officials at the national, state and local levels to engage in every imaginable dishonest, unethical and inept financial practice. Efforts to impose ethical controls on the handling of public funds began about the same time as personnel reforms, but were somewhat slower to produce effective standards. It was not until 1909 that the first consolidated executive budget was adopted in New York City. Another ten years passed before the budgetary requests of all the departments of the federal government were submitted to Congress by the White House in the form of an executive budget. The changes in national budgeting were soon emulated by the governments of large cities and states. This phasing-in of the initial fiscal reform makes it difficult to set a single, precise date for it. The following summary of budgetary reform is based on Allen Schick's excellent conceptualization (1966, 1982).

First Era of Reform: 1920–1935

The purpose of reform was *control*, with an emphasis on fiscal integrity. The primary professional skill called into play was *accounting*, which would detail exactly how much tax money was collected, who controlled it, and for what it was spent. The *line-item budget* became the instrument best suited to accounting purposes. During the 1920s the line-item budget was adopted by numerous local governments. Also called *object of expenditure* budgeting, the line-item format adopted a scheme to segregate the items or objects to be funded or purchased. The most common accounts in a segregated line-item budget were personnel, equipment, supplies (or expendables) and contractual services.

Personnel accounts in the earliest days did not as clearly differentiate permanent and temporary employees as do modern line-item budgets, because local civil service and personnel administration standards and policies were still developing.

Some characteristics of the line-item budget are:

Advantages: Simple to prepare
Easy to understand and present
Straightforward accounting controls

Disadvantages: No sense of expenditure purposes
No planning of agency goals, programs, methods
No analysis of effort, productivity

Second Era of Reform: 1935–1960

The purpose of this reform movement was to improve *efficiency*, in the sense of producing the most public service for each dollar of expenditure. The professional skill most called for was *management*. Stress was placed on skill in directing the processes of the enterprise and getting the most out of the resources available. The budgeting format now became the *performance* budget, which emphasized efficient methods.

Advantages: Relates work methods to costs, efficiency
Sense of economy, basis of work management

Disadvantages: Increase in preparatory work, analytic complexity
Harder to present and understand
Stress on work quantity did not always recognize work quality

An Invisible Development

During World War II, largely unseen by the civilian world, military planners changed from operations research (OR) to systems science under the pressure of a new criterion: "efficiency." In the military, that meant reducing loss of life in battle. The main change was in the scope of questions asked by military planners. At the beginning of the war, a typical question asked of OR by a battlefront commander might be: "What form of air attack is best to take out this bridge that is carrying supplies to the enemy front?" Analysts in OR would prepare tables showing the tradeoffs between probability of success and probable losses (for example, 90 percent certain destruction, 120 planes lost; 80 percent certainty, 90 planes lost; 50 percent 30 losses, etc.). They would consider high-level bombing and dive-bombing from a variety of approaches. What the OR analysts were not asked early in the war was whether the bridge was best taken out by air attack, behind-lines attack, or down-river raft attack. Military personnel defined the questions; OR techs answered them.

That began to change as military planners began to perceive larger questions. The decision about what form of attack should be used to blow up the bridge became whether the bridge should be attacked at all. The question turned from how to destroy the bridge to how to stop the flow of supplies to the enemy front at the river. This new question opened consideration to blowing up ammunition, heavy weapons, fuel and food supplies, rear-area troop mobilization points, and similar links in the supply chain. A still larger question addressed the destruction of rail and road supply routes leading to the enemy rear area. Eventually, of course, the questions in this pyramid contemplated the destruction of the means of producing heavy weapons, fuel, ammunition and food supplies.

When this new scope of systems science reached the civilian world after the war, the tendency to raise larger questions produced new issues of decision-making and management control at tactical and strategic levels of business, industry and government. How big a question should be addressed at any level of the hierarchy? What about time-frames to get the job done? How about access to the equipment and personnel to get the job done?

Industry soon developed systems concepts beyond those of the peacetime Pentagon. President John Kennedy appointed Robert McNamara Secretary of Defense in 1960. He brought to the Department of Defense (DOD) a more advanced form of systems thinking: a paradigm that had transformed the Ford Motor Company.

The military's problems of dealing with open-ended questions with little concrete information (for example: How much defensive capacity is required to contain missile attack threats? How do we know when an enemy's submarine offensive capability has been contained?) were quite different than those of Ford, and the Pentagon went through some years of coping with McNamara's new way of analyzing and planning.

However, the open-ended missions of DOD later proved useful in thinking about the problems confronting civilian policing. For example: What is a baseline of crime below which it cannot be affected by police activity? What is an appropriate ratio of police to population? Which crimes are suppressible? The following section discusses these developments.

Third Era of Reform: 1960–Present

The purpose of this reform movement was *planning*, including a fresh examination and definition of the organization's goals. The professional skill called into play was *systems analysis*. Stress was placed on defining the goals of the enterprise, breaking down general goals into attainable subgoals, setting priorities among goals and subgoals, analyzing large arrays of alternative strategies for achieving these goals, and adopting strategic approaches which produced the greatest goal-impact for the cost.

Planning Programming Budgeting System. The earliest budget format of this era was the planning programming budgeting system, or PPBS. This system of planning and budgeting was brought to the national government by McNamara. One of his goals was the reduction of competition and duplication among the branches of the Department of Defense (Army, Navy, Air Force), and to cover gaps in their approach to military offense and defense. His observation was that the three services competed fiercely for the "glamour" programs (missiles, supersonic aircraft, nuclear weapons), but avoided "homely" systems, such as transport of troops and supply/logistics operations.

In essence, PPBS required that each of the services state its offensive and defensive objectives quantitatively, lay out five-year "time-horizons" and describe how the next year's budget advanced its programs toward the five-year objective. The characteristics of PPBS are listed below.

Advantages: Requires managers to define goals
Requires linkages of goals, programs
Requires timelines, long-term program costs
Sets extended (5-year) "time horizons" for plans

Disadvantages: Goals often difficult to define
Difficult to link goals and programs
Severe preparatory workload requirements
Massive documentation needs

Management by Objectives. During the Nixon administration, PPBS was replaced by a budgeting format organized around management by objectives, or MBO, a well-known approach to management. Mainly, this new format sought to reduce the massive paperwork and analysis required to maintain PPBS, and yet retain its goal-seeking orientation. In that sense, MBO budgeting may be regarded as an evolutionary step forward, rather than a rejection of PPBS.

Zero-Base Budgeting. While governor of Georgia, Jimmy Carter was impressed with a new budgeting concept originated by Peter Phyrr of Texas Instruments Inc. in the late 1960s. Carter adopted zero-base budgeting (ZBB) for the state of Georgia's 1973 fiscal year, and, after being elected president, installed ZBB in the federal government. This, too, may be regarded as an evolutionary stage in budget development, building on many concepts of performance budgeting, PPBS and MBO budgeting.

While MBO and ZBB were being introduced at the federal level, many states and major cities were experimenting with PPBS, lagging just a few years behind national government innovations. However, ZBB soon became identified as a major improvement over previous methods of budgeting. Often without adopting ZBB's title and terminology, many states and cities began using its essential reasoning, structure and methods.

Zero-base budgeting takes some of its best features directly from precursors: Performance Budgeting provided its focus on the relationship between resources and work output; PPBS, MBO and Program Budgeting lent it goal-setting and the breaking of large organizational objectives into quantifiable, achievable subgoals or "programs." ZBB originated two concepts: (1) annually placing each program ("decision unit") in competition for funding with all others, and (2) requiring each program to submit three to five levels of resource requests linked to expected work outputs. These "decision packages" from all "decision units" are reviewed by each level of management above the submitting units. Managers select their preferred combinations of "package" elements and forward them for reviews up the chain of command, with each level indicating its preferences (as well as those of its subordinates) to the ultimate decision-maker in the organization. The characteristics of ZBB are listed below.

Advantages: Requires managers to define goals, strategies, costs and expected outcomes
Requires managers to indicate preferred funding levels and achievement levels
Offers managers and legislators explicit goal-program-strategy-cost-outcome links
Raises level of debate from abstract funding to resource-outcome proposals

Disadvantages: Goals often difficult to define
Difficult to estimate costs/outcomes
Heavy preparatory and review workloads

In the first era of budget reform, *planning* was not a major concern and showed little evidence of systematic development. Public administrators generally examined the current and previous years' budgets and spending patterns and restricted their planning to estimating their needs in the four primary accounts: personnel, equipment, supplies, and services.

Successive periods of budget reform *did not* result in the replacement of the major purpose (control) and budget format (line-item) of the previous period. Rather, control continued to be an important purpose for the new period. In fact, for many agencies the line-item budget continued to be the most attractive and useful format, although newer formats surfaced as reform continued.

Public Administration as an Emergent Discipline

Budgeting was not evolving in a vacuum. The context of budgetary evolution was the concurrent development of public administration as a profession and academic discipline. Industrial engineering and management had been developing steadily from the second third of the 1800s and had eventually generated an interest in a governmental counterpart, the organization and management of public agencies.

By the 1960s most police departments employed line-item budgets because their governments did. The city or county requested the department's needs for personnel, equipment, consumables and contractual services. The agency budget generally listed these needs for the entire department, with perhaps some subheadings for the major units: patrol, investigation, administrative services. Some of the biggest jurisdictions employed performance budget systems, which required all agencies to show indications of productivity year-by-year. But a vast majority continued to use the line-item approach.

The real budgeting of a police agency was internal, once the overall department budget had been approved. This was accomplished by the allocation of personnel to the major units, and sufficient equipment, supplies and contract services to enable those personnel to perform their work. In many ways, this worked well enough, although it led to endless games played between agencies and the city councils and county commissions, which sought control over agency spending.

The huge, largely unrealized problem of line-item budgeting was that accountability was nearly impossible to establish for departmental heads. In a process-oriented agency, such as policing, productivity was impossible to estimate, much less measure. How could a mayor, city manager, council, county administrator or commission tell whether a chief or sheriff was doing a good job? All indicators were so indirect that they were meaningless. There was, however, little pressure to change methods of budgeting and evaluating performance for many years.

Cutback Management. This comfortable drift was rudely shaken by a new approach to budgeting called cutback management. Charles H. Levine, in November, 1978, presented the scope and significance of this new phenomenon to the American Association for Budget and Program Analysis (Levine, 1979, 1982). He cogently recognized the complacency of endless economic growth and government expansion through the 1960s in the United States. Cutback management, he said, resulted from international competition, general economic contraction, inflation, erosion of economic bases of cities, and the widespread taxpayer revolts launched by Proposition 13 in California, which in 1978 rolled assessed values on property back to the 1975 level.

Levine correctly predicted a hard future for public managers, who would be required to accomplish a growing workload with reduced or stabilized resources. He outlined tough choices among strategies for doing so.

For policing, the significance of cutback management is found in new demands for chiefs and sheriffs to demonstrate they are doing all that is possible with current funding before increases will be approved by city councils and county commissions. As we have pointed out several times, this is almost impossible to do with line-item budgeting and process-oriented division of work in policing.

The timing was perfect for zero-base budgeting (ZBB) to make its appearance; it was clearly an improvement over previous budgeting formats, when it came to allocating scarce resources among competing local agencies. The reasoning, structure and methods of ZBB required departmental managers to show exactly what they planned to do with different levels of funding. While many cities and counties did not adopt ZBB by name, they began pressing its logic on agency heads. Chiefs and sheriffs reasonably believed everyone already understood what their goals were, but they carried a great burden of low-priority functions and were unable to eliminate them. Their predecessors had sold the public and local government on these functions during times of unlimited growth. Now they were expected to employ the hard logic of business managers; for the first time, there *was* a bottom line in public management.

Police Systems Budgeting. Most of the elements of ZBB are included in the following format, which we will entitle police systems budgeting. In police systems budgeting, internal managerial evaluations of unit budget requests and subsequent political evaluations of the department's budget request are based on the analysis of programs ("decision units" and "decision packages"), rather than individual items to purchase, such as cars, computers, pistol cartridges and first aid kits. In this sense, the purpose of the department, broken down into achievable goal units, can be clearly seen by local government administrators and legislators.

For the following section, assume you are in charge of a mid-level program or "decision unit." For example, imagine yourself as the manager of *one* of the following programs:

- Community crime prevention
- Street drug interdiction
- Major crimes clearance
- Auto theft apprehension
- Anti-fencing operations
- Jail custody
- Juvenile gang interdiction

Proceed through the system planning logic presented earlier in this chapter. Eventually you will have an array of strategies to evaluate. Taking community crime prevention as our model, we might break it into the following strategies:

- Decreasing vulnerability of premises to burglary
  - Premise security surveys and recommendations
    - Businesses
    - Residences
    - Public facilities
  - Improved street and area lighting
  - Defensible-space presentations to citizens

- Vacation/vacant house checks by patrols
- Neighborhood watch and citizen patrols
- Apartment corridor monitors
- Location-oriented foot patrols
- Decreasing vulnerability of citizens to attack
  - Personal safety presentations in schools
    - Dangerous locations
    - Crimes resulting from hitchhiking
    - Recent crime patterns
    - Known offenders and their crimes
  - Personal safety presentations to the elderly
    - Con games currently targeting elderly
    - Personal safety as a pedestrian
    - Dangerous driving/parking locations
    - Daily phone checks of the elderly
  - Media public service spots and features
    - Anti-hitchhiking
    - Current con games
    - Dangerous parking areas
    - Pedestrian routes receiving emphasized police attention ("safe walkways")
  - Location-oriented patrols
    - Schools
    - Neighborhoods of the elderly
    - Known trouble spots
  - Known offender operations
    - Con artists
    - Molesters
    - Victimizers of children, elderly
    - Rapists on parole
    - Professional burglars and fences

After evaluating the strategy array, list them in order of cost-productivity. Estimate costs of personnel, equipment and supplies for each strategy at an estimated level of effectiveness (for example, school personal safety presentations: Two officers, $72,000; vehicle/expenses, $22,000; videos, props, pamphlets, $6,000. Productivity at this level of resource: Present safety message to approximately 22,000 children in 300 school classes and assemblies).

Prepare a "decision package," which consists of the following elements:

- Several (3–5) levels of funding, including present or beginning level for combinations of the most cost-productive strategies
- Description of each strategy and its funding level

- Estimate of expected impacts for each combination of strategies

These elements are to be presented in a format similar to that illustrated in table 1. Mid-level might include three strategies, Level +1 four or five, and Level +2 five or six. Level −1 might include two strategies, and Level −2 a single strategy. In some cases, higher and lower levels of programming might represent an increase or decrease in one or more of the strategies (for example, assign two teams of personal safety officers to schools and geriatric centers, rather than one team).

Table 1

Police Systems Budget Request

Title of Major Departmental Unit ____________________

Title of Decision Unit ____________________

Problem to Be Targeted ____________________

Service Goal of Decision Unit ____________________

	Costs	Quantified Inputs of Action Program	Resource Levels Personnel, Equip. Supplies, Contracts	Expected Impacts Quantified Outputs
Level +3				
Level +2				
Level +1				
Previous/ Mid-level				
Level −1				
Level −2				
Level −3				

Now assume you are a *major* unit manager; for example, you are responsible for *one* of the following:

- Crime control
- Order maintenance
- Calls for service response
- Civil division
- Jail

Each of these units would include a number of "decision units" which would submit "decision packages" for your consideration. For example, the jail might consist of decision units named "custody," "inmate services," "booking," and "inmate transportation." Crime control would probably consist of the largest number of decision units, such as community crime prevention, violent crime clearance, property crime clearance, repeat offender operations, decoy squad, auto theft apprehension, street drug interdiction, and so forth. Your task as a major unit manager is to:

- Evaluate each decision package in competition with all other departments. Mark up the submissions from all decision units, indicating which levels of support and impact you prefer.
- Send your marked-up decision packages to the chief of police or sheriff.

Now assume you are the chief or sheriff.

- Evaluate the marked-up decision packages, beginning with the preferences indicated by the major unit managers. Mark up your own preferences, indicating where they differ from those of the major unit managers. Balance the decision packages from all units into an executive budget by indicating your final choices on a master copy which also contains the preferences of your subordinate managers and where they differ from yours.
- Have the departmental executive budget prepared in final format, with your preferences and those of subordinate managers. Send this budget document to your superior in the local government (mayor, city manager, county administrator, etc.).
- Your superior will analyze your department's budget and place your preferred decision packages into competition with those of all city or county government services. From this competition will emerge a city or county executive budget, which will be sent to the city council or county commission for evaluation and formal consideration. Most city councils and county commissions will similarly place all decision packages in competition with each other in fashioning a budget bill, which is eventually passed as a city or county ordinance.

Enabling Theory

The vast literature of public administration deals largely with organizing and managing governmental agencies. There is a dearth of discussion and advice relating to creating and executing plans. For purposes of realistic planning and management, the essential qualities of a plan are its *grounding in reality* and its *cultural validity* in the organizational and community settings. Most of us, when devising a plan, visualize some sort of objective—and almost immediately visualize an action to reach the objective. We may weigh the likelihood of achieving the objective, but we seldom consider all of the consequences of the action. Our pairing of the action and its intended result often obliterates other possible or even likely consequences of the action. We also fail to see our intended plan/results as a small raft of deliberate activity thrown into a stream of ongoing, inherent social change. We know our little corner of the world, after all, and can change things in that little corner. But can we really do that? The following ideas are intended to connect planners with aspects of the changing world and its organizations which have, potentially, great influence over the fate of a plan and its implementation. It may be fair to claim that planning which ignores these aspects of the real world and organizational culture risks failure.

The Plan as Deliberate Change in a System of Inherent Change

Any plan, unless it proposes that *nothing* be done (not much of a plan!), is (1) a statement about the future, and (2) a proposal to change the future which will occur in the absence of the plan. In a discussion of planning, it seems prudent to ask whether deliberate planning by human beings is the primary source of social change. Observation shows that deliberate, planned change is only a small part of actual social change, and a relatively weak force within the very large, restless, churning maelstrom that is social change. It is more affected by intrinsic social change than a major influence on it.

> *As a general principle, every plan should be considered an attempt to interfere in inherent social change.*

If this sounds ominous, it is important to understand that plans come in many sizes and that their capacity to disrupt intrinsic social change is proportional to their dimensions. But size is not the only factor which determines the disruptive power of a plan. Intrinsic social change occurs because of the behavior of human beings as individuals and interaction in groups of all sizes, from pairs to nations.

Understanding intrinsic social change is essential to knowing the possibilities and limitations of organized planning. Understanding social change requires a context of some kind. After all, people do not behave randomly; they usually follow the patterns that make up our culture. While we do have choices, observation generally reveals that these choices form patterns. The context of social change gives us a number of arenas of individual and group behavior that make it possible to analyze some of the social churning which produce intrinsic, ongoing change.

Police Culture

Policing is in one of its more intensive periods of change, and all of us have opinions about the causes and directions of this change. We are all entitled to our opinions, but the opinions of police administrators cannot be formed casually or simplistically. Police officials plan, and every plan is a statement about the future—presumably about a *preferred* future, rather than the future that would occur without the plan.

The evolution of policing and of its management are forms of social change; more particularly, they are forms of institutional social change. Policing is merely one of the many institutions that has emerged in our complex social system to sustain some of our more compelling and durable values. Community safety is a social value, while policing is one of the instruments to achieve this value. In our complex society, with its minutely detailed division of work, the crystallization of values into social institutions (for example, policing, schools, churches, labor unions, charities, retirement systems, and research hospitals) gives continuity to the fulfillment of the social values which gave rise to them.

But policing is more than just another social institution; it has been aptly termed a subculture, which implies for its membership more than a mere paycheck. This subculture, often simply referred to as "police culture" has been thoroughly discussed in other sources, and requires no additional presentation here. (See Kappeler, 1995.)

Environment of Social Change and Deliberate Change

All forms of ongoing social change involve one or more of the following variables.

- physical environments or habitats of daily life

- technologies
- institutions or organizations
- beliefs or social values
- social functions
- knowledge base of the culture
- economy
- social structure
- social roles

When one variable changes, it induces change in some of the others. It is a truism that new technology causes changes to ripple through other sectors of life.

The assembly line, for example, created new roles for workers, new kinds of factories, different kinds of neighborhoods near factories, a new layer in the social structure, a need for still newer technologies, and increased the creation of new social institutions, such as labor unions and associations of industrialists.

The automobile changed the physical environment (probably more than any other recent technology): streets, roads, expressways, parking lots and ramps, oil refineries, and ocean tanker spills occurred as a result of the new means of transportation. It also introduced new modes of recreation, occupations, institutions (for example, AAA Motor Club, insurance firms, retail dealerships), and a personal freedom of movement unrivaled in history. A whole configuration of new social values, institutions, social roles, economic behaviors and environmental adaptations radiated from the automobile.

The automobile is only one example. After thousands of years of living on the surface of the earth and using what they found there, humans thought to poke down into the earth, where they found coal, metal ores, gems, and terribly poisonous things, such as radioactive cobalt ore—good and terrible things which changed the world forever. Pope Gregory (A.D. 590–604) decreed that only the human voice and plucked string were godly; pipes and horns were pagan. His decree barred the use of the pipe organ in churches for hundreds of years. In this case social belief and institutional policy impeded technology. The pertinent point for policing is that new technologies introduce new crimes, forms of disorder, needs for police service, and potential law enforcement responses.

Beyond technology, change may be induced by value shifts:

- Birth control methods could not have become widespread without an earlier social value shift toward smaller families.
- Political conservativism resulted in reduced funding for social programs and more funding for police.
- Liberalized legal doctrines produced tougher search and

seizure laws, with more restrictions on interrogations.

- Social value shifts led to institutional policies to restrict chases and to hire female officers and minorities.
- Suburbanization of cities reduced pedestrian traffic while it embraced strip malls, convenience stores, ATMs, and limited access highways—all of which dismembered neighborhoods.
- Public schools produced new social classes, a new economic base for education, a massive market for teachers, school buildings, textbooks, school supplies, sports and band equipment.

Deliberate change by the police (planning) is acted out within these variables. Each new plan introduces change in one or more of these categories, changes which may then ripple outward into others. If it is a very small plan, confined to a single operational unit of the department, it may not escape the agency and may cause no external ripples at all (for example, a new scheduling method for a unit). A large plan—affecting more of the department and perhaps the community, as well—with a long time-frame may set in motion huge waves of social change rolling outward from the department (a field interrogation program, a new policy on traffic enforcement, or an effort to organize the community against residential burglary).

It is not possible to describe all the kinds of changes which might occur because interactions are both intricate and generally unexpected. We often do not recognize massive changes in these variables until they are upon us, and then we think of them as recent history rather than the present. The next section of the book is intended to alert you to the probability that significant ripples will be created within the police agency or sent out into the community as a result of police plans and their activation.

The next section considers what can go wrong with plans within the police agency and in the community. Although these problems apply to other administrative concerns, they have particular relevance to plans and their implementation.

Environment of Decisions

In his book, *Administrative Behavior* (1957), Herbert Simon referred to the formal organization as "an environment of decisions." The heart of his concept is that decision-making is not reserved to the upper administrative reaches of an organization, as many theorists state or imply, but is inherent in the work of organizations at all levels, including the base activity levels.

Although Simon wrote about organizations in general, his idea applies graphically to police agencies, because their primary function is to obtain information, to make decisions about the information and to send their information and decisions forward in the criminal justice process. When examined in detail, police work consists almost entirely of receiving, collecting, evaluating and making decisions about information and sending it to others. The police continuously monitor human behavior, decide whether the behavior is disorderly or criminal, and then decide on a course of action. All follow-up activities similarly involve obtaining information, evaluating it and deciding what to do with it. Police management, similarly, consists of obtaining, processing and making decisions about information. In this important sense, policing and police administration differ sharply from many businesses, industries and other public service agencies that process raw materials into products or deliver more tangible services.

Despite the information/decisional nature of policing and police administration, the kinds of information/decisions differ greatly between the operational and administrative levels of a law enforcement agency. At the street level, officers and detectives tend to obtain their information directly and make decisions primarily about individual incidents, situations and persons. This might be termed *logic of the street*.

At the top of the management pyramid, the executive obtains most information indirectly. He or she makes two types of decisions. One type is categories of incidents, situations and people. The other is abstractions, such as policies, strategies and time-frames. These activities might be termed *executive logic*.

Diagram 2 Hierarchy of Decisions

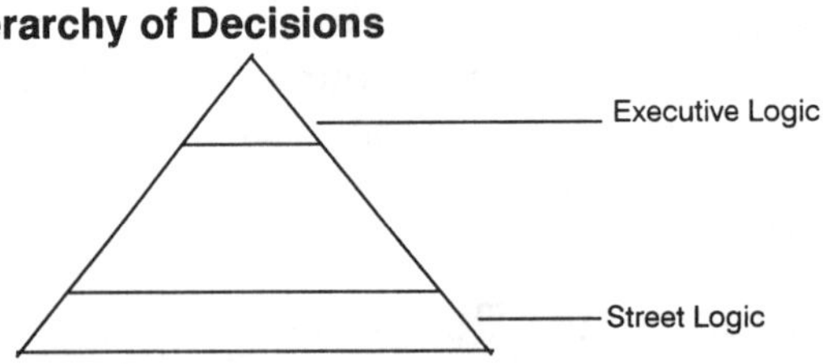

If a police agency is visualized as a pyramid, one of the most vexing issues of police administration is responsibility. The chief executive is accountable to his/her political superior and makes decisions that are large-scale and abstract—intended to maintain accountability. However, the performance (accountability) of the entire agency is actually evaluated on the basis of the aggregate of decisions made by police officers and detectives. It would not be correct to say the chief wants all officers to make decisions with the same logic as the chief, merely at the street level, because the decisions are so different in scale and level of abstraction. It is, however, accurate to say the chief would wish that all officers' decisions were consonant with the chief's. *Consonance* means in harmony with rather than clashing with executive decisions.

It is not exaggerating to say the entire chain of command between the chief executive and the line police officer has two main purposes:

1. Reducing the span of control to a manageable number.
2. Maintaining consonance between the top and bottom of the organizational pyramid.

Supervisors make their decisions a step away from the street level; middle managers are several steps removed from the street and make decisions a step below the executive. However, the decisions of supervisors and middle-managers differ in important ways from the decisions of their subordinates and their executive superiors. They must convert the abstract, categorical decisions above them to concrete, case-by-case guidelines for those below. This incredibly difficult task—translating executive logic into street logic—is left largely to their ingenuity. Similarly, the risks inherent in translating also fall on them.

Maintaining Consonance in an Environment of Risk

The most significant factor affecting planning and implementing plans is consonance. As discussed earlier, a police chief's decisions and those of subordinates down the chain of command to the operational levels of the organization must work in harmony. Every time a police administrator sets out to plan or to put a plan into action, he/she enters an environment of high risk. The main risk factors can be described as unintended consequences of the activated plan due to:

- police organizational culture
- political culture
- cultures within the community
- ongoing social change outside the department

Unanticipated Consequences of Plans

One of the classics of administrative literature is Robert Merton's "The Unanticipated Consequences of Purposive Social Action," (1936) which not only originated the concept, but also a framework for analyzing the troublesome side-effects which so often diminish, interfere with or nullify the desired effects of planned actions. Merton wrote that deliberate social action often produces alternative or additional results to those intended because of ignorance, error, habit and, to use his phrase, "the imperious immediacy of interest." His scheme involves (A) the planner's assessment of the present condition, (B) the planner's imagined, preferred future condition, and (C) the planner's intended means of getting from A to B. The following discussion is based on our interpretation of Merton's ideas and is not presented as a paraphrase of them.

Diagram 3 Merton's Model

C

A ———————— B

Ignorance. Rather than stupidity or lack of education, ignorance is defined here as "incomplete information." Systems analysts commonly speak of working in an "environment of uncertainty," which expresses the same concept. The incomplete information can be about A, B, or C in Merton's model.

Example of ignorance in assessing the present: New Chief Jonah of Apex City believes the department is managerially top-heavy (A), and intends to achieve a leaner organization (B) by eliminating subexecutive positions (C). The department loses effectiveness because of the chief's lack of information about his department's requirements of management resources. The command structure was not, in fact, top-heavy.

Example of ignorance about the preferred future condition: Observing that most officers work more than their assigned eight hours each shift (A), a task force recommends that the Apex PD convert to four ten-hour workdays each week (C). Some months after the recommendation is adopted it is discovered that officers report greater job fatigue and dislike the new arrangement (B). They now find themselves working twelve or more hours per shift, rather than the former nine-plus hours. The task force had insufficient information to accurately visualize the outcome of their preferred future condition, the 4–10 schedule plan.

Example of ignorance about the means of accomplishing the goal: This kind of ignorance is most often due to a failure to gather sufficient evidence to evaluate alternative strategies aimed at the same goal. Chief Jonah is distressed by the animosity between the patrol force and detective bureau of his department (A). In an effort to improve working relationships (B), he transfers the detective bureau to the bureau of field operations, bringing both patrol and investigations under the same manager (C). The animosity worsens and the field operations commander complains of "sabotage" by the former chief of detectives. The chief's visualization of patrol-investigation harmony may have been a valid concept, but his method did not achieve it. He did not consider alternative approaches.

Error. Reasoning incorrectly about information that may be correct is defined as error. Error in the assessment of the present situation (A) could be, for instance, deciding that a decrease in the incidence of a certain crime resulted from a police patrol strategy. Chief Jonah then increases resources for that strategy because of his erroneous linking of the crime decrease (which was real) and the patrol strategy (which did *not* produce the crime decrease).

Error in assessing the preferred future condition is often hard to distinguish from ignorance about future conditions. Since information about the future is inherently incomplete, errors become highly probable. However, administrators are constantly required to reason and to make decisions in this environment of uncertainty. Some administrators err less often than others, seeming to require fewer cues to arrive at the correct conclusion. Two chiefs, for example, faced with similar efforts to unionize their departments and having access to the same information might reach different conclusions about the futures of their respective departments. One might be essentially correct and the other essentially wrong on the basis of very different reasoning from the same information.

Earlier we described ignorance that can result from the planner's failure to consider alternative strategies to achieve a visualized goal. Assuming that the planner has assembled a set of valid alternatives, there is still the possibility of error if the planner reasons incorrectly about the alternative strategies and chooses one that is *not* most likely to achieve the goal with fewest side-effects. This type of error is probably the most frequent kind in police administration, because police culture is predisposed to apply a familiar technique to a problem, rather than to evaluate alternatives patiently and systematically. The common rationalization for this tendency is that the police must act *now*—that delay allows situations to deteriorate. While this reasoning is sometimes true of field situations, it is almost never valid for police planning. It is simply brought into the culture of police administration from the culture of street policing by officers who are promoted into management; they do not leave behind ingrained patterns of thought and action.

Habit. Patterned behavior, whether individual or organizational, is called habit. Certain behaviors become habitual because they are found by experience to be both effective and efficient, consistently delivering the sought-after results with less effort than known alternatives. Think of how you begin each day. Are there clear patterns for a time of waking, a way of grooming, dressing, eating, getting to work, beginning the workday, and other behaviors? Organizations are similarly patterned: structure, lines of communication, contacts among workers, initiating and adopting policies and procedures, making decisions, responding to issues, and so on.

But *habit*, that reliable standby of proficiency, can change into a destroyer of both effectiveness and efficiency, if external conditions change. For an individual, the morning timetable can be upset by a snowfall that requires clearing a driveway. The customary, efficient route to work can, overnight, become the worst possible route on the start of a road construction project.

At the organizational level, we find a greater variety of external challenges to patterned effectiveness and efficiency. Size and complexity make organizations even more dependent on deep-seated patterns than individuals. The sheer size and interdependence of their structures often masks the significance of external change and organizations continue in their accustomed patterns of functioning. These patterns become dysfunctional and require organizational adaptations, but the inertia of existing patterns is difficult to overcome. Unanticipated, sometimes disastrous consequences, often follow.

Consider the conduct of the American automobile industry in the years following the introduction of small, inexpensive European and Asian cars to the American marketplace. American cars continued to be large, heavy and fuel-inefficient. At first a novelty, imported cars steadily grew to comprise about one-third of all new car sales in the United States. During this time, manufacturers of domestic vehicles ignored the trend and went through several new-car design cycles without a reduction in size, weight or fuel consumption. This reliance on previous patterns enabled foreign autos to gain a long-term foothold in the domestic market. The same lack of adaptation pattern occurred with the labor-intensive steel industry of the United States. Japan, for instance, could import the iron ore, produce the steel in automated plants, ship it to the United States and still sell it profitably for less than American steel.

The examples in policing are more subtle, because we do not have a profit-loss indicator as in commerce. Observation and analysis, however, can provide our examples. In criminal investigation, for instance, most agencies assigned cases to detectives more or less permanently. That is, they did not have a standard case-purging policy, which would shelve cases on which no progress had been made for a specific period of time (for example, six weeks, two months, or six months). Many detectives had file drawers crammed with "active" cases on which they were periodically required to submit perfunctory "progress reports." The resulting accretion of paper cluttered the files, the minds of investigators and their supervisors, and destroyed any sense of productivity in case clearance work.

Similarly, dispatching all calls with equal priority, regardless of seriousness, often resulted in the depletion of patrol units at busy times. When that happened, the only choices were to delay sending a car to a critical situation or to send supervisors from the station. The advent of personal radios has improved this situation somewhat, but the concept of *differential police response* (prioritizing calls for alternative responses) has had an even greater impact on the problem in larger jurisdictions.

With community policing going through its difficult birth, the police habit of keeping tight control of all operations from a central, high-level point will come under severe strain. It is virtually impossible to have both strong centralized control and neighborhood operations under local management.

The habit of city- and county-wide standardized policies will also stand squarely in the way of implementing COP. These and many other long-standing police patterns of behavior—habits—will either be expunged or will impede the realization of COP.

Obsession. The fourth factor, which Merton called "the imperious immediacy of interest," is obsession. It refers to a fixation on a desired outcome or a method of producing it that is so compelling that it brushes aside all indications to the contrary, all signals of risk, all obstacles, all advice, and all opposition.

Examples from the operational world include the need to end every chase with a capture, regardless of the danger. Another common obsession is the new chief's or sheriff's wish to reorganize the department. An obsession of many first line supervisors and middle managers is to exercise total control over their subordinates. Whole agencies share obsessions about being first into the field with every innovation, being the best in the state or nation (as if this were scientifically verifiable), or in some cases, being the toughest department (for example, a former commissioner of police in Philadelphia boasted his department "could retake Cuba"). Control, secrecy, comradeship, cynicism, partner loyalty, stand-up toughness—all have been obsessions of law enforcement.

Can an entire organization be obsessed? Actually, it is the culture or management of an organization that becomes obsessed and carries its obsessions into organizational action. Cultures and members of management can, indeed, be obsessed.

There are no routine stops for police officers on patrol.

Authority and Communication

Chester Barnard, educated in business administration at Harvard University, rose through the managerial levels of a major communications industry to become its chief executive officer. Barnard's talent was of a rare kind in that he not only succeeded as a manager but also observed keenly what was happening around him on the way up. He later described what he had observed in his celebrated book, *The Functions of the Executive* (Barnard, 1938). This book was rich with accurate portrayals of complex organizational life but was particularly useful in casting a new light on the nature of administrative *authority*. Barnard's view of authority ran hard against the current of its time. For more than a generation ideas about bureaucracy and the nature of bureaucratic authority were dominated by Max Weber, the German sociologist. Weber, who observed a variety of large organizations in Europe, believed that each level or rank in a hierarchy carried with it both responsibility and authority appropriate to that level and that members of the organization recognized the inherent authority based on rank and were obedient to it.

Barnard observed organizations in the United States and concluded that authority is not automatically inherent in rank or position. Conversely, he found that authority is an on-and-off quality of managerial *communication*. In Barnard's view, the authority of Sergeant Jones in diagram 4 might exist for Patrol Officers A, B, C and D, but not for Officers E and F. Max Weber would have had difficulty accepting this disparity in the authority of Sergeant Jones. For Weber, a sergeant was a sergeant.

Diagram 4

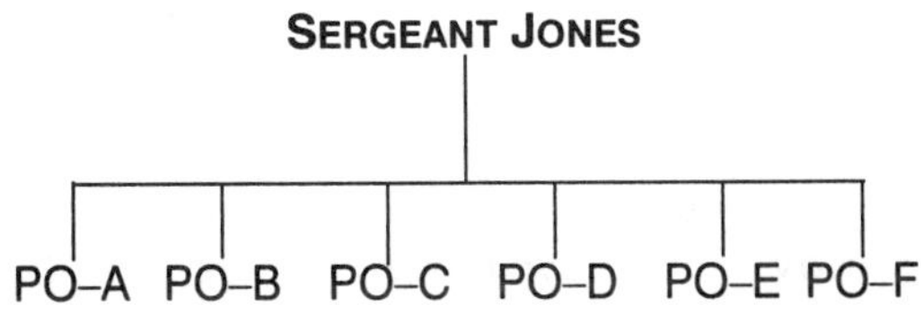

For Barnard, however, Sergeant Jones's authority depended on his communications to his subordinates. To paraphrase his position, he believed that authority is the character of a communication (order, directive) by which it is accepted by its recipients as governing their behavior. He went on to describe four characteristics of orders which must be present if the orders are to be authoritative. These four characteristics are summarized below.

1. *The order must be received and understood by its intended recipients.* This seems so self-evident that it hardly needs to be stated. However, during the 1960s the St. Louis Police Department discovered that a significant number of its general and special orders were not reaching officers in its nine districts and many divisions, despite a thorough distribution system. That discovery led to still another order: that all orders be read at four successive roll calls and that hard copies of the orders be issued to all officers, to be kept in a department-issued notebook. Further, a copy of each order was posted on district and division clipboards for a lengthy period, with the requirement that all officers returning from vacations or extended absences of any kind read the clipboard and sign off on its contents. Despite these efforts, some officers were still found to have missed some orders.

   Beyond simply *receiving* the order is the more complex expectation that the order will be *understood*. It was found at the annual in-service classes for all St. Louis officers, supervisors and managers that many orders were not, in fact, understood. In some cases the multiple interpretations of orders were so far scattered as to be comic and at times diametrically opposed. The main source of this problem was found to be in a conceptual and linguistic gulf between those who wrote the orders in planning and research, and the officers and managers on the receiving end. The planners and officers/managers employed different vocabularies and patterns of thought. This is a prime example of "street logic" and "administrative logic" not connecting. This obstacle to authoritative communication was partially alleviated by having all drafts of orders reviewed by classes of in-service officers and supervisors and then signed off by all major bureau commanders before publication.

2. *The recipients of the communication must be able—physically and mentally—to comply with it.* Law enforcement officers are generally sturdy physically; however, it is possible to issue an order that will not be executed because of fatigue or stress. Orders which are not understood are much more common than those which present a physical challenge. Some orders are so complex

in detail that they simply cannot be retained. It is generally—and mistakenly—assumed that a *written* order will assure comprehension, retention and implementation. The old "avoid verbal orders" signs posted in business offices were evidence of this common assumption. Written orders avoid claims of "I didn't hear you"—they do *not* promote the ability of subordinates to carry out confusing, poorly phrased directives.

3. *The communication must, in the view of the recipient, be consistent with the purpose of the organization.* Problems occur if an organization clings to traditional beliefs in its purpose and teaches its officers accordingly but then introduces different purposes when addressing issues created by social change. It is also difficult if new officers are taught a set of purposes in accord with executive logic and are introduced to a different set by street logic. The challenge for management, in either case, is to bring the street logic and executive logic into consonance.
4. *The communication must, in the view of the recipient, be consistent with the recipient's self-interest, taken as a whole.* Officers ordered to do something utterly foreign to their morals, sense of decency, or sense of mission as police officers, will find a way to evade the full impact of the order.

Does Barnard mean that officers will routinely screen orders and directives against these criteria and reject those which fail the test? Will insubordination inevitably follow? Not at all. The action of these four factors is largely invisible, often below the level of consciousness or open discussion.

Barnard does say that the consistent satisfaction of these four criteria in a manager's orders will establish a "climate of authority." With a robust climate of authority, there will be a very large "zone of indifference," in which employees automatically accept and carry out orders. The indifference refers to challenging authority—not indifference to orders and authority.

Criticism from traditionalists takes the form that this kind of thinking abdicates the authoritative leadership role and caves in to the "democratic management" school of thought (as in, "Let's take a vote on the orders, people").

Is this a valid criticism? To the contrary, deeply embedded in Barnard's concept is a blueprint for responsible management. Each of the four required attributes of orders, if found lacking, can be secured by managers who analyze the problems and improve communications with their subordinates. This, again, is a matter of management, a topic far too extensive to be adequately considered in this book. For planning, however, the lesson is that plans which ignore Barnard's principles will lack authority.

Organizational Locale of Planning: A Bi-Level Approach

Where to locate planning is a dilemma in all larger police agencies. Compiling and maintaining the kind of database that serves planning requires access to all parts of the department and to external governmental sources, as well. This speaks well for locating the planning function near the top of the police organization, probably in an administrative support unit.

Conversely, nearly every empirical study shows that plans that originate far from their units of implementation fail. Current thought is that those who will carry out plans should have a direct hand in their development.

An obvious arrangement to accommodate these somewhat oppositional elements is to create a bi-level structural approach to planning:

(1) A staff unit high in the organizational structure to maintain the wherewithal for agency-wide planning (database, technical expertise, liaison with resources, management authority, and so on). This unit would also serve as a strategic policy planning unit.

(2) Ad hoc planning task forces within the operational units of the department, assigned to participate in strategic plans involving those units, and also to perform actual tactical plans for those units, with assistance from the staff unit.

Ideally, a planning group or task force should include officers who will probably work in the program under consideration, plus their immediate supervisors and at least one level of management. This hierarchic task force should be as close to the future work level as possible. Its members bring to the planning process an intimate knowledge of the working situation and represent the police culture. But these line officers are not professional planners and have not compiled the databases necessary to perform the phases of planning described above.

For the technical expertise and database access, staff personnel from planning and other support units should be assigned to the planning group. They should not direct the task force as much as assist it in analyzing problems, goals and strategic alternatives. Being external to the line work group, planners can also provide an objective filter for the social perceptions of the line officers. However, their primary role is to provide the main resource for policy analysis and planning—information.

In the small policing agency, planning is best performed by a task group consisting of line officers, supervisors, and the chief's or sheriff's staff assistant.

Database Development and Use

Data needs are determined by decision needs. Too often police decision making has been limited to the use of available information. Rather than use, and be limited by, information which is easy or "natural" to accumulate as a result of police activities (for example, crime and service reports), the gathering of information for planning and management purposes must be based on clear thinking about the kinds of decisions and evaluations involved in those administrative duties.

The utility of a database in planning and learning to plan hinges on observing limits in planning. Any policing official who works at the upper management and policy levels sits in numerous meetings that pass for planning sessions. In most cases these meetings are blue-sky sessions, where the managers and planners kick around the possibilities of an unknowable future. Such sessions can be fun, because they have no real consequences. Everyone present knows they can't be taken seriously, because there is no penetration of reality, no limit on areas of speculation, no reduction of the uncertainty throughout the room. Anybody's guess is as good as the next guy's. The database in this book (the appendix) has two purposes:

1. It provides a set of limits for teaching police planning and policy analysis. A class of students or police managers should not sit around and stab wildly at the dimensions of problems, or toss out unrealistic goals, or propose unaffordable or politically ruinous strategies without understanding where errors of judgment are likely to occur. Everything costs, and every action has unintended consequences. Instructing police managers and students in the art of planning and policy analysis requires the discipline of real-life limits and consequences. Oceana, Exurbia, and Americus County provide reality-based limits for this purpose.
2. It is a minimal example of the database every police jurisdiction should compile for itself. Rather than relying on police reports and dispatch records for resource allocation, departments should assemble the census, UCR and other data sources to inform their policy and planning decisions.

Table 2 Planning Framework

	Strategic Goals	Tactical Goals
Operational Functions	Agency mission; major unit goals and major unit approaches to work	Street goals and approaches to work
Management Functions	Agency philosophy, structure, resource allocation	Field supervision, inspections

Summary

Action without planning is one of the reflexive habits of policing—an example of Merton's institutional habits that eventually cause problems.

The corollary—planning without action—means nothing happens. Endless talking about plans accomplishes nothing. Action does achieve goals if well planned.

The other necessary ingredient is monitoring: How do you know what happened if you do not monitor actions? The first stage of monitoring is goal achievement: Did the job get done at an adequate level within cost estimates?

The second stage looks for unintended consequences: Were the side-effects serious enough to detract from the intended outcome? Did the side-effects make the outcome too costly?

References

Barnard, C. I. (1938). *The Functions of the Executive*. Cambridge: Harvard University Press.

Hudzik, J. K. and G. W. Cordner (1983). *Planning in Criminal Justice Organizations and Systems*. New York: Macmillan Publishing Co.

Kappeler, V. E. (1995). *The Police and Society: Touchstone Readings*. Prospect Heights, IL: Waveland Press.

Levine, C. H. (1979). "More on Cutback Management: Hard Questions for Hard Times." *Public Administration Review* 39, No. 2. Reprinted in F. J. Lyden and E.G. Miller (eds.), *Public Budgeting: Program Planning and Implementation*, 4th ed. Englewood Cliffs, NJ: Prentice-Hall. 1982.

Merton, R. K. (1936). "The Unanticipated Consequences of Purposive Social Action." *American Sociological Review*, No. 1.

Phyrr P., "The Zero-Base Approach to Government Budgeting," *Public Administration Review*, No. 1 (Jan–Feb 1977), reprinted in Lyden & Miller, *Public Budgeting*, 4th ed. Prentice-Hall, 1982.

Quade, E. S. (1982). "Principles and Procedures of Systems Analysis." In *Public Budgeting: Program Planning and Implementation*, 4th ed., eds. F. J. Lyden and E. G. Miller. Englewood Cliffs, NJ: Prentice-Hall. Chapter 12.

Schick, A. (1966). "The Road to PPB: The Stages of Budget Reform." *Public Administration Review*, 26, No. 4, 243–58. Reprinted in *Public Budgeting: Program Planning and Implementation*, 4th ed., eds. F. J. Lyden and E. G. Miller. Englewood Cliffs, NJ: Prentice-Hall. 1982.

Simon, Herbert A. (1957). *Administrative Behavior: A Study of Decision-Making Process in Administrative Organization*, 2nd ed. New York: The Macmillan Co.

Chapter **3**

Linking Research, Policy Analysis and Planning

The emphasis in this text is on policy analysis and planning. This focus requires a concise presentation of police research findings as a basis from which to explore alternatives available in the planning process. It also requires a definition of terms which are used in the planning process (for example, "team policing," COP).

The intention here is to supplement the material commonly presented in police administration and management books. While familiarity with organizational theory and design, channels of communication, human resource management, leadership, labor relations, legal aspects of police administration, financial management and evaluation methods for programs are essential prerequisites to becoming an effective administrator, that background knowledge must be applied effectively. The purpose of this text is to simulate conditions and problems administrators will face. Management by objectives, time management, and labor management are requisite tools, but without some idea of how to apply them they remain another set of jargon.

In science, all knowledge is provisional. The essence of science is the verification and advancement of what is already known with repeated and refined research. The value of most police research findings is limited by a lack of both replication and refinement of the research. All but a few of the following research findings resulted from single studies and suffer this limitation. Nonetheless, all of the following to varying degrees add something to the knowledge base of policing and should be known to police administrators. Respectful interest and skepticism are appropriate.

In addition to problems of replication, there has often been a gulf between research conducted by academic institutions and the practice of police departments. Program development and project implementation can benefit enormously from multiple ideas, examples, and ongoing inquiries. When theory, research, experimentation and practice intersect, the final product should be more effective policing. Cooperative ventures between police departments and universities can have reciprocal influences. Police departments may find that habitual responses to problems through a paramilitary organizational structure are not ideal; university faculty members may be alerted to new areas and methods to target for research. Training and education issues for police personnel could also benefit from dual input. Changing practice and procedure is never easy—from either side of the equation. Starting from the same side of the ledger can help both parties. Continuing professional development and education should be the goal of enlightened parties—whether practicing professionals or academics.

Planning is a partnership process that ideally should involve academics/practitioners, multiple public/private agencies, citizen groups and individuals. If we hope to bring substantial changes in the quality of life, reduction of crime, and seeds for future change, cooperation of many diverse elements is essential. Joint efforts between police departments, public housing authorities, the Department of Housing and Urban Development, the National Institute of Justice, and universities can help planned programs address a wider range of concerns—and perhaps avoid unintended consequences.

This chapter will present a number of concepts that have inspired, challenged, and intrigued researchers to date. As mentioned above, the studies are not presented as final answers. They are intended to stimulate thinking about alternative ways to perform police functions. The studies represent how policing has evolved to this point and give us thumbnail sketches of how concepts change or originate. The studies have been included because it is important that you understand the existing research to put the exercises in chapter 4 to effective use.

When you begin the exercises or cases in chapter 4, try to imagine why a particular study was undertaken. Did it result from a decision to test a habitual response? Was it an attempt to discover a more effective response to a recurring problem? What motivated the researcher? Were there errors in pinpointing the activity to be studied? Were the conclusions drawn reasonable or subject to errors of interpretation? Was there a preferred future effect? Concise descriptions sometimes strip these elements from the presentation, but they are important factors when planning. If you hope to be an effective planner and manager, the processes that contributed to the research summarized below* must be a familiar and accessible part of your background. The goal of this text is to help you make informed decisions; this research offers one basis for decision making.

Assessment Center Screening for Promotion (O'Leary, 1995)

Hundreds of police agencies use assessment center techniques to screen their officers for promotion into management. The techniques were first used by the Office of Strategic Services to select intelligence agents during World War II. Written tests are often employed to reduce the number of candidates because of the high costs of assessment centers ($500–$3,000 per candidate). Job analysis must precede the assessment of candidates, because the assessment procedures are intended to produce job-related behavior in candidates. Job simulation exercises may include problem solving, employee counseling tasks, leaderless group discussions, self-profiling presentations, "in-basket" exercises, and other elements of a supervisory or managerial role. A panel of assessors, generally assembled from other agencies, evaluates the performance of the candidates to avoid the biases of local managers. A good discussion of this technique is found in the article by O'Leary in the *Encyclopedia of Police Science*.

Calls for Service Policing (see Traditional Policing)

Career Criminal Program (see Repeat Offender Program)

*More general research resources include those listed below. The *Encyclopedia of Police Science* (Bailey, 1995) is an excellent summary of authors, books and articles on a large variety of subjects. Other major sources are the monthly TELEMASP bulletins published by the Police Research Center, Sam Houston State University; National Institute of Justice monographs published by the U.S. Department of Justice; and books and mongraphs published by the Police Executive Research Forum (PERF).

Community Crime Prevention

Community crime prevention refers to a variety of titles such as "community organization," or "community self-help." Popular program elements include:

- *Neighborhood Watch* (or *Block Watch*): Citizens volunteer to observe their neighborhood during certain hours of the week and report crimes or suspicious conditions to the police.
- *Citizen Patrol:* Volunteers patrol their neighborhoods in groups to report criminogenic conditions to the police. They are unarmed and trained to take no action in criminal situations.
- *Safe Houses:* These are homes to which children fearing attack may run for help. Volunteers agree to be available and place prominent "Safe House" signs in their windows where children can observe them.
- *Corridor Monitors:* Volunteers observe conditions in their housing projects and maintain liaison with the police. (See *Vertical Patrol*).
- *Community Education:* The police provide programs or materials that help residents avoid becoming victims of crime
- *Operation Identification:* Citizens prominently and indelibly mark prominent targets of theft (such as cameras and stereos) and label their homes as "Operation ID" participants.
- *Security Surveys of Premises:* Police officers help residents "harden" or make their homes and business less vulnerable to burglary.

Community-Oriented Policing—COP (Radelet, 1973; Hoover, 1992; Trojanowicz, 1994; Trojanowicz, et al., 1982–1994; Carter and Sapp, 1992; Kratcoski, 1995)

COP is at once the most popular current theme in American policing and the most ambiguous. It is difficult to imagine a more politically attractive concept of policing than one embedded in the will and fabric of the community. Mayors, city managers, governors and national officials are beguiled by this imagery. So are many police administrators, who observe that errors of social judgment in ethnically diverse communities put them at greater professional risk than do technical management errors.

Despite its popularity, COP is an illusive concept. The following excerpts from well-known authors illustrate the problem of succinctly defining COP.

In a paper prepared for the Texas Law Enforcement Management Institute, David Carter and Allen Sapp (1992) offer this definition:

> Community policing is a philosophy, not a tactic. It is a proactive, decentralized approach to policing, designed to reduce crime, disorder, and fear of crime while also responding to explicit needs and demands of the community. Community policing views police responsibilities in the aggregate, examining consistent problems, determining underlying causes of the problems, and developing solutions to those problems. (Amended from Trojanowicz and Carter, 1988 and Spelman and Eck, 1987).

In the same paper, which presents a program evaluation model for community policing, Carter and Sapp go on to say:

> Among the fundamentally synonymous terms for community policing are: Problem-Oriented Policing (POP), Community Problem-Oriented Policing (CPOP), Neighborhood-Oriented Policing (NOP), Police Area Representatives (PAR), Citizen-Oriented Patrol Experiment (COPE), Experimental Policing (EP), Neighborhood Foot Patrol, and Community Foot Patrol. Where there are some variations in the proffered definitions of these concepts, for the purpose of this model all these labels are defined the same as *community policing* is above.

Their position, declaring all of these approaches to be the same, is at one end of a spectrum of judgment. Kratcoski (1995) challenges this view as follows:

> Problem-Oriented Policing (POP) has been viewed by some as an alternative to Community-Oriented Policing (COP) (Eck and Spelman, 1987; Goldstein, 1987) and by others as a component of COP (Rosen, 1992; Trojanowicz and Bucqueroux, 1989). Moore (1992) views POP and COP as overlapping concepts with a distinctive thrust differentiating them. He describes POP as a situational approach and COP as fostering a working partnership between the police and the community.

Larry Hoover's introductory chapter to *Police Management Issues and Perspectives* (1992) contains an analytic framework which clearly differentiates community-oriented policing, problem-oriented policing, and the precursor "professional model" of policing. At the core of this piece, Hoover employs the criteria of *scope* and *temporal dimension* to analyze these approaches to policing. The "professional" policing model is said to focus on crime-specific interventions and order maintenance in the short term. Its main strategy is the dispatch of patrol cars in response to single calls for police service, with little attention to the eventual solutions of community problems which prompt these calls. Hence, the focus is short-term community order maintenance.

Problem-oriented policing (POP) is said to address *sustained community order maintenance*, rather than serial patrol responses oriented to the immediate present. Hence, the focus is on long-term order maintenance specifically with a view to underlying community problems.

Community-oriented policing (COP), the most demanding model, is said to require a commitment to comprehensive neighborhood management over the long term. COP places the police at the center of a community network, with primary responsibility for identifying community problems and energizing community resources toward the eventual solution of these problems. Hoover (1992) states:

> Assigning two officers out of a force of two hundred to a housing project for a six-month period to develop an array of approaches to help curb crime and disorder in that project, then proudly announcing to the world that this municipality engages in community policing is absurd. Abandoning rotating shifts or beats for semi-permanent assignments, then announcing community policing has been implemented is absurd. When the chief of a five-person police department (in) a community of 5,000 proudly announces that her or his department has been doing community policing all along but just didn't call it that, it is absurd. Community policing is a dramatically altered deployment scheme that creates some opportunities but precludes others. (p. 21)

He lists some of the functions suggested for COP by Trojanowicz and Bucqueroux (1990):

- Coordinating family assistance
- Helping youngsters manage their lives and build self-esteem
- Taking kids to the zoo, organizing softball teams, organizing fishing derbies
- Controlling gangs
- Helping solve the problem of the homeless
- Organizing neighborhood cleanup campaigns
- Initiating action to demolish abandoned structures
- Easing racial tensions and addressing minority crime concerns

- Assisting undocumented aliens
- Assisting students, tourists, transients, the elderly
- Disseminating information on AIDS

Hoover concludes, "Make no mistake about it, the advocates of community policing foresee the police permanently placed within, in charge of, and managing neighborhoods" (pp. 21–22).

The foregoing citations illustrate the confusing variety of COP definitions and the problem of differentiating it from alternative policing models. The following findings of a recent survey of community policing activities in American law enforcement agencies provide an overview of what many departments report they are doing. Robert Trojanowicz's 1994 report, *Community Policing: A Survey of Police Departments in the United States*, will be quoted and paraphrased in some detail.

> It takes five groups to make community policing work: the police, the community (and all of the subgroups, like businesses and the clergy), the social agencies, the political leaders, and the media. All five groups need to make substantial contributions. (p.5)

The Definition of Community Policing (Nine Ps)

Community policing is a philosophy of full-service, personalized policing where the same officer patrols and works in the same area on a permanent basis, from a decentralized place, working in a proactive partnership with citizens to identify and solve problems.

Philosophy. The community policing philosophy rests on the belief that contemporary challenges require the police to provide full-service policing, proactive and reactive, by involving the community directly as partners in the process of nominating, prioritizing, and solving problems including crime, fear of crime, illicit drugs, social and physical disorder, and neighborhood decay. A department-wide commitment implies change in policies and procedures.

Personalized. By providing the community its own community police officers (CPOs), community policing breaks down the anonymity on both sides—CPOs and community residents know each other on a first-name basis.

Policing. Community policing maintains a strong law enforcement focus; CPOs answer calls and make arrests like any other officer, but they also focus on proactive problem solving.

Patrols. CPOs work and patrol in defined beat areas in their communities. The goal is to free them from the isolation of the patrol car, often by having them walk the beat or rely on other modes of transportation, such as bicycles, scooters, or horses.

Permanent. Community policing requires assigning CPOs permanently (at least 18 months) to defined beats so that they have the time, opportunity, and continuity to develop the new partnership. Permanency means that CPOs should not be rotated in and out of their beats, and they should not be used as "fill-ins" for special assignments and absences of other personnel.

Place. All jurisdictions, no matter how large, ultimately break down into distinct neighborhoods. Community policing decentralizes police officers, often including investigators, so that CPOs can benefit from "owning" their neighborhood beats, in which they act as a "mini-chief," tailoring the response to the needs and resources of the beat area. Moreover, community policing decentralizes decision making, not only by allowing community policing officers the autonomy and freedom to act, but also by empowering all officers to participate in community-based problem solving.

Proactive. As part of providing full-service policing, community policing balances reactive responses to crime incidents and emergencies with a proactive focus on preventing problems before they occur or escalate.

Partnership. Community policing encourages a new partnership between people and their police that rests on mutual respect, civility, and support.

Problem Solving. Community policing redefines the mission of the police to focus on solving problems, so that success or failure depends on qualitative outcomes (problems solved) rather than just on quantitative results (arrests madc, citations issued—so-called "numbers policing"). Both quantitative and qualitative measures are necessary. (Trojanowicz, 1994, pp. 6–7)

The Survey

The National Center for Community Policing at Michigan State University and the FBI's Behavioral Science Services Unit collaborated in designing the questionnaire for Trojanowicz's report. It was sent to all 686 law enforcement jurisdictions having 100+ sworn officers or 50,000+ population (called "large" departments). Of these, 80 percent returned usable questionnaires. The 245 "small" departments surveyed were those which contacted the National Center at MSU between March, 1992 and August, 1993. Of these, 60 percent returned completed questionnaires.

Survey Findings

Large Agency Responses (546 out of 686 surveyed):

- 42 percent (229) said they had community policing
  - 84 percent of these (192) were municipal departments
  - 15 percent of these (35) were sheriff's departments
  - 1 percent of these (2) were state police agencies

Small Agency Responses (148 out of 245 surveyed):

- 66 percent (98) said they had community policing
  - 89 percent of these (87) were municipal departments
  - 11 percent of these (11) were sheriff's departments

Note: The report called attention to the probable skewing of the small agency data, since the entire surveyed sample had voluntarily contacted the National Center and shown interest prior to the survey (eliminating one of the prime conditions of research—random samples to prevent skewing the research in a predetermined direction).

Responding Departments' Reports on Elements of COP Philosophy:

- 54 percent have made department-wide commitment to COP
- 19 percent have not
- 26 percent plan such a commitment

Full Service:

- 94 percent consider CPOs full-service officers
- 88 percent always or sometimes answer calls for service
- 50 percent make *as many arrests as "regular" patrol officers*

Personalized:

- 20 percent of CPOs know more than 40 percent of people on beat
- 21 percent of CPOs know less than 10 percent of people on beat
- 92 percent of CPOs spend much time organizing juvenile activities

Defined Beats:

- 78 percent of departments assign CPOs to defined beats

Permanency:

- 52 percent of CPOs are assigned to beats for two years or more
- 25 percent more are assigned for at least one to two years

Decentralization:

- 66 percent of CPOs have decentralized offices in their beats

Proactive:

- 94 percent report increase in proactivity

Partnership:

- 94 percent report CPOs interact better with citizens
- 93 percent of CPOs involve citizens in nominating problems
- 96 percent report improved police-community relations
- 87 percent report improved police-minority relations
- 66 percent report threat of civil unrest decreased
- 66 percent report CPOs job satisfaction increased by partnership
- 27 percent report CPOs job safety improved by partnership

Problem Solving:

- 95 percent report improved problem-solving ability in the department
- 37 percent report successful problem solving regarding the homeless

Amount of Community Policing:

- 74 percent say their commitment to COP is limited
- 38 percent say entire jurisdiction covered by COP
- 48 percent say limited resources constrain COP coverage
- 79 percent prefer to concentrate COP in a few areas

Support for COP:

	Great Extent	**Moderate Extent**	**Somewhat**
Line officers	12 %	41 %	39 %
Citizens	45 %	32 %	14 %
Political leaders	46 %	36 %	12 %
Media	31 %	40 %	12 %

Operationalizing Community Policing:

Most agencies experiment with COP before making it department-wide. Many keep it limited. Beat areas are selected for many reasons, including crime and drug problems. Of respondents who have implemented COP programs:

- 68 percent say they have changed their mission statement
- 52 percent say their CPOs have a job description (often not much different than "regular" patrol officer job description) 55 percent say officers volunteer for CPO assignment

- ° 15 percent say officers select their beats
- ° 47 percent more say officers have input to beat selection
- ° 62 percent say CPOs wear uniforms all of the time
- ° 36 percent say CPOs wear uniforms most of the time
- ° 75 percent say CPOs' mode of transport is "parking and walking"
- ° 14 percent say CPOs are primarily on foot
- ° 62 percent report using both quantitative and qualitative measures of performance
- ° 58 percent say CPOs attend roll call with "regular" officers
- ° 28 percent say CPOs work with "regular" officers as part of a structured community-based team all of the time, 18 percent most of the time, 41 percent some of the time
- ° 69 percent encourage "regular" officers to park and walk
- ° 12 percent require "regular" officers to park and walk
- ° 23 percent have instituted a recognition/award program for CPOs

Community Policing's Effect on Generating Information:

In CPOs' beat areas, crime reporting has increased by 33 percent since the implementation of community policing.

- ° 93 percent say CPOs solicit information face-to-face
- ° 93 percent say CPOs solicit information in neighborhood meetings
- ° 53 percent say CPOs solicit information in surveys
- ° 24 percent say CPOs solicit information in citywide meetings
- ° 85 percent say CPOs get better information than "regular" officers
- ° 6 percent say CPOs get better intelligence than undercover officers to a great degree, and 39 percent say to some degree
- ° 39 percent say CPOs gather drug intelligence to a great degree
- ° 59 percent say CPOs gather drug intelligence to some degree

Community Policing's Effect on Crime, Disorder, and Fear of Crime in the Neighborhoods Served by CPOs (COP agency responses):

- ° 90 percent say people feel safer with CPOs on the beat
- ° 83 percent say the quality of life in those neighborhoods has improved
- ° 37 percent say that crime has been displaced by COP

- 48 percent say COP has helped reduce serious crime
- 60 percent say COP has helped reduce less serious crime
- 61 percent say COP has helped reduce the climate of violence
- 80 percent say COP has helped reduce fear of crime
- 39 percent say COP has helped reduce high-level drug dealing
- 77 percent say COP has helped reduce street-level drug dealing
- 83 percent say COP has helped reduce the visibility of drug abuse and drug dealing
- 83 percent say COP has helped reduce social disorder
- 82 percent say COP has helped reduce physical disorder

Crime Analysis (Bieck, 1995)

Crime analysis provides data to assist in managing patrol operations and criminal investigations. It includes identifying the temporal and geographic patterns of crime, and patterned methods of criminals which identify them and/or their multiple offenses. Tactical crime analysis, the most common type, identifies crime patterns, trends and information about persons suspected of committing crimes. Crime patterns are used to focus patrol and investigative operations. The FBI's National Center for the Analysis of Violent Crime receives data from local police departments across the country to determine if a number of crimes were committed by the same serial killer, such as Ted Bundy or Henry Lee Lucas. "Taxanomic analysis" is employed to find links among unsolved homicides, assaults and sex offenses. Crime analysis originated in the work of August Vollmer, who first used police records for planning, and established pin maps to identify trouble spots in Berkeley, California. "As for the future, crime analysis will incorporate increased use of automation. . . . Experimentation in developing neural networks and artificial intelligence to identify crime patterns is already underway . . . " (Bieck, 1995, p. 137)

Crime Reporting Audit in St. Louis

This program was tested in the early 1960s; its purpose was to assure the accuracy of crime reporting. Certain dispatches were thought to be downgraded (for example, burglary to larceny, aggravated to simple assault) by reporting officers under pressure from district commanders to keep crime rates low. Each quarter, one weekend was randomly selected for follow-ups on dispatch classifications for forty-eight hours (Friday–Sunday). An analyst from the Governmental Research Institute of St. Louis, accompanied by officers from the inspector's office and field operations command, pulled the radio tickets for calls received and re-interviewed the complainants. Initially it was found that numerous calls were, in fact, being downgraded—in some cases improperly classified as "unfounded" reports. These inspection findings were given to field operations command for correction after each audit. In time it found that the proportion of calls being downgraded was equalled by those being upgraded (both now small numbers) to the disadvantage of the reporting unit. After this audit, it was thought the limits of accurate reporting had been reached. It was thought, however, that continued audits were necessary to assure the accuracy of crime reporting, given the pressures upon district commanders to keep crime rates low.

Criminal Investigation Process: Rand Study (Greenwood and Petersilia, 1975)

The findings and proposed reforms of this comprehensive study created a furor among investigative managers.

Major Findings:

1. On investigative effectiveness: Differences in investigative training, staffing, workload, and procedures appear to have no appreciable effect on crime, arrest, or clearance rates.
2. The method by which police investigators are organized (team policing, specialists vs. generalists, patrolmen investigators) cannot be related to variations in crime, arrest, and clearance rates.
3. On the use of investigators' time: Substantially more than half of all serious reported crimes receive no more than superficial attention from investigators.
4. [A]n investigator's time is largely consumed in reviewing reports, documenting files, and attempting to locate and interview victims on cases that experience shows will not be solved. For cases that are solved . . . an investigator spends

more time in post-clearance processing than he does in identifying the perpetrator.

5. On how cases are solved: The single most important determinant of whether or not a case will be solved is the information the victim supplies to the immediately responding patrol officer. If information that uniquely identifies the perpetrator is not presented at the time the crime is reported, the perpetrator, by and large, will not be subsequently identified.
6. On how cases are solved: Of those cases that are ultimately cleared but in which the perpetrator is not identifiable at the time of the initial police incident report, almost all are cleared as a result of routine police procedures (that is, additional information obtained while investigating other cases, or fortuitous results of traffic stops and field interviews, such as Timothy McVeigh being stopped for a traffic violation).
7. On collecting physical evidence: Most police departments collect more physical evidence than can be productively processed. . . . [A]llocating more resources to increasing the processing capabilities of the department can lead to more identifications than some other investigative actions.
8. On the use of physical evidence: Latent fingerprints rarely provide the only basis for identifying a suspect.
9. On investigative thoroughness: In relatively few departments do investigators consistently and thoroughly document the key evidentiary facts that reasonably assure that the prosecutor can obtain a conviction on the most serious applicable charges.
10. On investigative thoroughness: Police failure to document a case investigation thoroughly may have contributed to a higher case dismissal rate and a weakening of the prosecutor's plea bargaining position.
11. On relations between victims and police: Crime victims in general strongly desire to be notified officially as to whether or not the police have "solved" their case, and what progress has been made toward convicting the suspect after his arrest.
12. On investigative organization and procedure: Investigative strike forces have a significant potential to increase arrest rates for a few difficult target offenses, provided they remain concentrated on activities for which they are uniquely qualified; in practice, however, they are frequently diverted elsewhere.

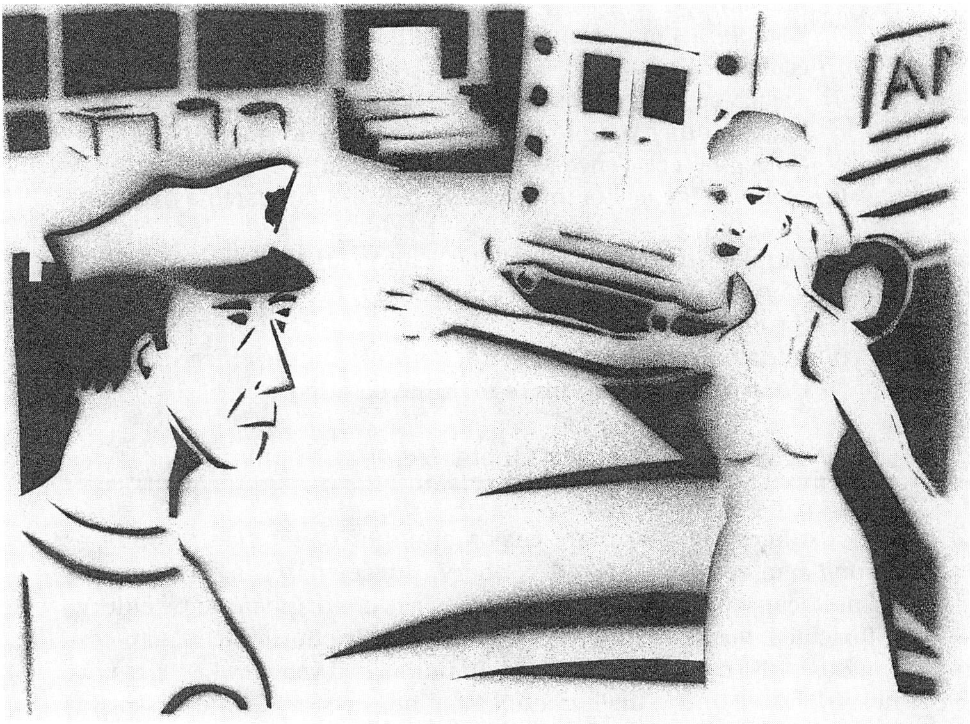

Emergency entrance at City Hospital.

Proposed Reforms:

1. Reduce follow-up investigation on all cases except those involving the most serious offenses.
2. Assign generalist-investigators (who would handle the obvious leads in routine cases) to the local operations commander.
3. Establish a major offenders unit to investigate serious crimes.
4. Assign serious-offense investigations to closely supervised teams, rather than to individual investigators.
5. Strengthen evidence-processing capabilities.
6. Increase the use of information processing systems in lieu of investigators.
7. Employ strike forces selectively and judiciously.
8. Place post-arrest (suspect in custody) investigations under the authority of the prosecutor.
9. Initiate programs designed to impress on the citizen the crucial role he [or she] plays in crime solution.

Decoy or Victim Substitution Operations

Police officers impersonate easy victims of street crimes such as strong-arm robbery, armed robbery, purse-snatching, rape, gang assault, car-jacking and abduction. Decoys often appear to be elderly, intoxicated, very young or defenseless. The "victim" officer is in continuous radio contact with officers in unmarked vehicles keeping pace nearby, who come to his/her aid if an attack occurs. Crime analysis is essential to deploying such operations.

Detoxification Center Project of St. Louis (Laski, 1970; Weber, 1968)

This effort to move "revolving door drunk arrestees" into a treatment program was initiated in 1966 as a cooperative program of the St. Louis Metropolitan Police Department, Washington University's Social Science Institute, St. Mary's Infirmary, Missouri Division of Mental Diseases, and the Governmental Research Institute of St. Louis. It was the first detoxification program sponsored by a police department in the Western Hemisphere. In three police districts (accounting for nearly 82 percent of the drunkenness arrests in 1966, but only 37 percent of the population) public inebriates who had not committed other offenses were admitted to the detox center rather than checked at a City Hospital and booked into the prisoner processing division. The Sisters of Saint Mary, who had administered the Infirmary in an area undergoing urban renewal, admitted and treated the inebriates under the direction of a doctor long experienced in treating alcoholics. The inebriates were withdrawn from alcohol and treated for malnutrition and other associated conditions for seven days. Social workers, counselors and church organizations assisted in the aftercare of patients (finding work, lodging and other supports).

Findings (Comparing 1966 and 1967)

Police Time: The average time expended by an arresting officer was reduced from 96 minutes (including checkup at City Hospital and booking) to 48 minutes for detox center admittance (including preparing the summons and checking wanted records for each inebriate), a reduction of 50.2 percent.

City Courts: Drop in number of drunk-on-street cases from 409 to 268, 34.5 percent.

Medium Security Workhouse: Reduction from 204 persons committed in 1966 to 125 in 1967, a decrease of 38.7 percent. Total inmate days reduced from 3,325 to 1,941 for drunk-on-street, a 41.6 percent reduction.

Treatment: During 1967, 1,120 patients were admitted. Only 100 (9 percent) left against medical advice, an option. The 1,120 admissions represented 674 individuals, of whom 464 were hospitalized one time, while 210 (31 percent) were hospitalized two or more times.

A follow-up study of 200 patients four months after discharge produced the following information:

	Markedly Improved	**Remained Same**	**Deteriorated**
Drinking	47 %	50 %	3 %
Employment	18 %	76 %	6 %
Income	16 %	71 %	13 %
Health	49 %	42 %	9 %
Housing	15 %	82 %	3 %

The patients had an average of 1.0 arrests for intoxication in the three months prior to treatment, but only 0.3 arrests in the three months following treatment (including arrests plus readmissions). In the three months prior to first detox admission 46 percent had been arrested one other time, while only 13 percent were arrested in the three months after discharge.

Anecdotal information from arresting officers indicated that resisting arrest by public inebriates declined dramatically, reportedly because alcoholics viewed the detox experience as less painful than the drunk tank at central holdover. According to the Final Evaluation Report (Weber, 1968) on the detoxification center by a St. Louis police officer, ". . . the impact on the patrol officers has been truly remarkable. Many who were at first openly skeptical . . . have expressed unqualified enthusiasm as a result of some of the Center's success cases whom they have known. Some have even gone so far as to volunteer their services both on and off duty . . ." The author then reported that officers were informally shuttling inebriates across district boundaries into those being served by the center. A case of this kind was reported in the St. Louis *Globe-Democrat*, May 25, 1967, as a "very pretty bit of professional police work."

Differential Police Response Field Test Program: Garden Grove, CA; Greensboro, NC; Toledo, OH (McEwen, Connors, and Cohen 1986)

Pioneered in the Birmingham, Alabama Police Department, DPR was evaluated in three cities between September 1981 and July 1983. The problem addressed by DPR was the need to maintain or improve service quality, reduce response times to urgent calls, and recover patrol time and develop new strategies for crime prevention, all in a time of increasing imbalance between resources and work demands.

DPR Test Objectives: (1) reduce the number of non-emergency calls for service (CFS) handled by immediate mobile response; (2) increase the number of non-emergency CFS handled by a telephone report unit (TRU), by delayed mobile responses or by other alternative responses; (3) decrease the amount of time patrol units spent answering CFS and increase amount of time available for crime prevention or other activities; and (4) increase the availability of patrol units to respond rapidly to emergency calls. A subset of objectives was to: (a) provide satisfactory explanations to citizens at call intake on the nature of the police response to their calls; and (b) provide satisfactory responses to citizens for resolving their calls for service.

Evaluation Objectives: (1) assess the impact of the DPR system on police practices; (2) assess the impact of the DPR system on citizens; and (3) assess the transferability of DPR to other police agencies.

There were major differences among the three departments: one communication center was staffed entirely by sworn personnel, the other two by civilians. One department had a manual CFS processing system, two had CAD (computer-assisted dispatch) systems. Annual CFS workloads ranged from 280 to 503 per officer.

Major Conclusions of the Test:

- The DPR test sites successfully developed a generic model for call classification systems which can be modified by any police department to meet local needs.
- The three sites successfully tested and implemented new call classification systems which resulted from this generic model.
- The new call classification systems and intake procedures (1) increased the amount of information obtained from callers; (2) provided callers with more accurate information on what to expect in terms of the response to their calls; and (3) provided patrol officers with more detailed information on calls prior to arrival at the scene.
- The time required to develop the new call classification systems was underestimated.
- Input for the new systems was needed from telecommunicators as well as from field operations personnel.

Implementation of Alternative Responses: Each of the following alternative responses was implemented to some degree, with variations, at the three test sites:

- Telephone report unit (TRU) for taking reports over the telephone;
- Procedures for delayed mobile response (holding calls for 30 to 60 minutes);
- Procedures for referring calls to other agencies;
- At least one other alternative response from the following possibilities: scheduled appointment, walk-in, mail-in.

True emergency calls for service were not part of the experiment, but were dispatched in the normal expeditious manner, generally to mobile units in the field.

Major Conclusions for Police Practices:

- In all three sites there was a sizable reduction in the number of non-emergency calls handled by immediate dispatch of mobile units. Up to 46.4 percent of all calls could have received alternative responses.
- The objective to increase the amount of time available for patrol units to devote to crime prevention, directed patrol, and other activities was achieved at all three sites. As much

as 50 to 60 percent of all officers' time can be devoted to directed patrol.

- Crime analysis is a key component in support of directed patrol operations.
- Crime scene investigations by patrol officers will need more time, requiring allowances in the allocation plan.
- Proper call screening under the new call classification systems allowed call takers and patrol officers to respond quickly when needed. However, travel time to emergency calls was not significantly reduced at all three sites.
- Particular attention needs to be given to the impact of the DPR system on telecommunicators. The conclusions from an analysis of their role in the DPR project are as follows:
  - The use of civilian call takers and dispatchers had many more advantages than disadvantages. Civilian call takers were better educated, had higher retention rates, and were hired at lower costs, than sworn personnel.
  - Patrol officer satisfaction with telecommunicators at all three sites improved as a result of the DPR project.
  - DPR imposes standards, uniformity and consistency on telecommunicators which may initially be resisted. Such resistance should be anticipated and telecommunicators should be included in the planning and design of the program and in developing and delivering DPR training.
  - Monitoring was useful for communications center managers to assess call takers. This procedure called for frequent sampling of the calls and a formal assessment of how well the call takers handled them.
  - Telecommunicators at all three sites lacked a career development plan. Call taker and dispatcher positions need to be upgraded; the promotional picture needs to be improved; after that, selection standards need to be upgraded.
- Legal implications of DPR need to be considered. With regard to police negligence, case law indicates that, in general, the police are not negligent for not responding to citizens. Thus, diverting calls to alternatives is permissible; in addition, DPR diverts only non-emergency calls. However, if a dispatcher promises a unit and one does not respond, this situation could result in a negligence finding—and in some circumstances, vicarious liability to the department and the city. The DPR model advocates informing all callers of any potential delay whether by a patrol unit or an alternative.
- The findings show that the alternatives are less costly than the traditional response of sending a mobile unit to all calls

for service. Moreover, the productivity levels are much higher for personnel using the alternatives, such as telephone report unit, in comparison to traditional mobile patrol responses.

- The use of evidence technicians in Greensboro was highly successful. These nonsworn technicians were dispatched (as an alternative to using a sworn police unit) to handle the initial calls, write the crime reports, and gather evidence. They handled over 18 percent of nonmobile responses—primarily for burglary, vandalism, and larceny calls.
- Mail-in reports were not found to be successful. (Author's note: Recently, several departments have reported a more successful experience with mail-in reports, after they simplified the report forms.)
- Elimination of service was one additional successful alternative. In Greensboro, prior to the test phase, escort services averaged 100 per week. The department decided to eliminate these services as much as possible, and reduced them to 20 per week during the DPR test phase.

Citizen Satisfaction—Pre-Implementation Surveys:

- The most significant findings were that citizens expressed a willingness to accept alternatives other than the immediate dispatch of a patrol unit to non-emergency calls. Citizens were asked whether they would be willing to accept the alternatives of telephone reports, an appointment, mailing in a report, or coming to the department to file a report in person.
- At all sites, the most acceptable alternative was setting an appointment; the least acceptable was mailing in a report.
- Many citizens stated they would have been willing to wait longer for a response in a number of situations. Nearly half the respondents in Garden Grove were willing to wait more than an hour or longer.
- Citizens were more willing to accept an alternative on a property-related call (burglary, larceny) rather than a call involving a personal incident or potential threat (assault, domestic disturbance).

Citizen Satisfaction—Survey During Test Period:

- Citizen satisfaction with the alternatives remained high. Satisfaction exceeded 90 percent for all options except for the walk-in response in Garden Grove, which had an 88 percent satisfaction level.
- Satisfaction levels are directly related to informing the caller that a delay might occur.

- Communicator style was an important factor in citizen satisfaction with the TRU alternative. A special study in Greensboro showed that the most important attributes were being precise, friendly, nonargumentative, and attentive.
- There was a high citizen satisfaction level with mobile responses by (paraprofessional) cadets in Garden Grove.

Directed Patrol Experiment: New Haven, CT (Cawley et al., 1977)

Three events preceded this pilot project: The Kansas City experiment cast doubt on the utility of random preventive patrol; police departments were finding large amounts (40–60 percent) of patrol time unaccounted for (some called it "preventive patrol time," but skeptics called it "uncommitted time"); and the New Haven PD administration, after comparing patrol car movements with crime analysis data, concluded officers were not positioned well to prevent crime during their uncommitted time. The project had the following elements, some of which were truly innovative:

- An objective of the program was to recover uncommitted time and to reallocate it to a high-priority function, such as deterrence of street drug sales, without reorganizing the department or its resource distribution. It was thought that the time might be reallocated in small batches, which is often how it occurs between dispatches.
- The goal of the program was *crime deterrence* only, and did not seek to apprehend offenders as well as deter crime.
- Crime analysis defined and sorted "suppressible" and "nonsuppressible" crime to avoid allocating deterrence resources to types of crime that could not be prevented by patrols.
- Only suppressible crimes were targeted for reduction efforts by patrol units. Those selected for deterrence included auto theft, purse snatching, commercial burglaries and residential burglaries.
- On the basis of crime analysis data, 50 "D-runs" or directed patrol pattern sheets, were initially prepared, with 5–10 percent of them replaced each month. Thirty to thirty-five D-runs were distributed to patrol officers each shift (about 100 per day). The patrols were given no schedule for the D-runs, but were advised by the dispatcher when to begin one. About 38 percent of patrol time was used for D-runs, which averaged 40 to 45 minutes, and ranged from 10 to 60 minutes' duration.

° A major innovation was that a D-run was given the same status as a serious call-for-service. That is, it was to be completed before the patrol unit was considered available for dispatch. It was reported that 83 percent of the runs were completed. (A sample D-run follows.)

Illustration

Directed Patrol Pattern Sheet
Run Number: 821
Sector: Edward

Problem: Commercial Burglary

Step 1: Location: Grand and Quinnipiac
Tactic: Park Car. Check fronts and backs by walking to bridge and back to car.

Step 2: Location: Grand and Clinton
Tactic Park car at Firestone. Check fronts and backs by walking one side of street to front and back to other side of street.

Step 3: Location: Grand between Clinton and Ferry
Tactic: Park at Ferry and Grand and walk to the church between Atwater and Bright and back to car: check fronts and backs of buildings.

Step 4: Location: Grand between Quinnipiac and James
Tactic: Ride entire length at 5 mph., checking fronts and backs as appropriate. One swing in each direction.

Step 5: Location:
Tactic:

Special Notes:

Estimated Time Required for Run: 45–50 minutes
Green lights (emergency top lights) will be used by the officer while assigned to a deterrent run.

Instruction Sheet Originated By:

Approved By:
Date:

Findings: New Haven reported the following reductions in targeted crimes for 1976, compared with 1975:

Residential burglaries	16 %
Commercial burglaries	8 %
Auto thefts	6 %
Purse snatchings	9 %

There were also reported incidental reductions in thefts from autos and vandalism, although these offenses were not targeted.

Directed Patrol National Survey (Fennessy, 1982)

A national survey of all urban police agencies servicing more than 100,000 people, and a sample of cities below that size. Of 247 surveys mailed, 153 were returned (62 percent response).

Findings:

1. 38 percent of agencies said they had formal directed patrol, and 27 percent informal, and 16 percent said they planned a DP program.
2. 70 percent reported full-time crime analysis units.
3. 69 percent reported call screening policies, and 71 percent formal call prioritization and tele-serve units.
4. 80 percent reported computerized management information for CFS and crime analysis.
5. 79 percent reported a majority of swing shift patrol forces relied on one-officer units, and 73 percent used proportional patrol allocation to match staffing to workload.
6. 80 percent of DP programs were implemented between 1977 and date of study.
7. Of 69 agencies with DP programs: 28 percent reported their patrols spend less than 30 minutes per shift on DP; 43 percent reported 31–60 minutes per shift; 15 percent reported 61–119 minutes; and 15 percent spend over 120 minutes per shift on DP.
8. 56 percent of agencies with formal DP also have specialized crime suppression units (i.e., split force) and 62 percent of the informal DP agencies also employ such units.
9. Benefits of DP reported as follows: (1) increased ability to define and resolve short-term crime problems (69 percent reported major or moderate benefits); (2) increased ability to define patrol performance objectives (37 percent); (3) improved utilization of patrol resources (71 percent); (4) increased ability to evaluate patrol performance (43 percent);

(5) improved morale and job satisfaction in patrol (30 percent); (6) improved supervision of uncommitted patrol time (48 percent); (7) increased arrests and clearances by patrol for Index crimes.

10. Problems reported by 72 agencies with DP programs: (1) inability to consistently free up blocks of patrol time for DP (64 percent); (2) Opposition or lack of interest by middle management (31 percent); (3) opposition or lack of interest by patrol sergeants (36 percent); (4) opposition or lack of interest by line patrol officers (26 percent); (5) inadequate level of crime analysis support (26 percent); and, (6) inadequate directed patrol training.

Foot Patrol: Flint, MI; Newark, NJ (Trojanowicz, 1982; Trojanowicz and Banas, 1985; Police Foundation, 1981)

Findings: Foot patrol has not been shown to reduce crime, but it is thought to reduce fear of crime and to improve relations between citizens and police. It is closely identified with COP, and sometimes confused with it. Many POP schemes make use of it. Foot patrol officers in Flint felt, more than motor patrol officers, that they were doing an important job, keeping up with problems in their patrol area, improving the police/community relationship, doing the job the department considers important, and working as part of a police team. Flint citizens approved two tax increases to retain foot patrol, but balked at a third. Newark Police Director Humbert Williams (*Foot Patrol*, 1985) stated that foot patrol encourages citizens to "use the streets" by reducing disorderly, threatening conditions. The presence of more citizens on the street, in turn, tends to reduce the conditions under which crime occurs, in his opinion. He thus implies a chain of police activities and community conditions which alter crime thresholds.

Significance: Foot patrol, like random car patrol, should not be considered a crime deterrent strategy by itself. Refinements or elaborations of the technique are part of many COP, POP, LOP and other current approaches. It is thought possible to target specific street problems and crimes with foot patrol.

Noisy Audience

Integrated Criminal Apprehension Program (ICAP) (Paraphrased from Gay, 1995)

"ICAP sought to increase the efficiency and effectiveness of all police services by basing patrol deployment and related field activities on systematic data collection, crime analysis and structured planning" (Gay, 1995). Closer collaboration between field operations and investigations was a key aspect of ICAP that differentiated it from other crime analysis applications. It was not found that extensive proactive strategies or tactical decisions resulted from crime analysis or that CA information was used to support suspect-oriented apprehension strategies. It appears that routine patrol and investigative workloads impeded a focus on career criminal apprehensions.

Kansas City Preventive Patrol Study (Kelling, et al., 1974)

Conducted in 1972–73, this study was the first police operational experiment which met the traditional standards of the sciences. It established experimental and control sectors, methods of observation, and quantified its findings. Five patrol beats maintained normal levels of patrol, five ("proactive") were assigned double or triple normal levels, and five ("reactive") were assigned no preventive patrol resources. The research question and criteria were clear: Does a randomly moving, marked police car reduce crime, victimization, fear of crime, traffic accidents, increase arrests, or increase citizen satisfaction?

Findings: The answer was, "No, it does not."

Significance: A limited but provocative finding, incorrectly interpreted by many as an indictment of all patrol methods. It was used improperly by some political officials as a wedge to reduce police manpower during austere times. The research was also unfairly and reflexively criticized by police administrators who feared the implications of the distorted interpretations. The entire episode highlighted our inexperience and lack of sophistication in dealing with research findings. But the long-term results have been positive. Numerous other experiments with patrol followed, such as the Wilmington Split Force, New Haven Directed Patrol, Foot Patrol in Flint and Newark, Differential Police Response in Birmingham, Managing Patrol Operations, Improving Police Management, Integrated Criminal Apprehension Program, and others which are discussed following. When Kelling undertook this important research in the early 1970s, many observant police managers were already questioning the utility of random patrol.

Kansas City: Three Approaches to Criminal Apprehension (Kelling et al., 1976)

Conducted in 1972–73, and 1972–74. There were three elements to this experimentation:

1. The Criminal Information Center (CIC)
2. Location-oriented patrol (LOP)
3. Perpetrator-oriented patrol (POP)

(*Note:* The acronym, POP, is now used to refer to Problem-Oriented Policing. Perpetrator-Oriented Policing is now known as Repeat Offender Program.)

The CIC regularly prepared and distributed information about known, serious offenders to all patrol units of the department, such as mug shots, addresses, auto license numbers, and names of associates. This activity "clearly produced increased arrests among those offenders." The surveillance of areas with high crime rates (LOP) and surveillance of "selected groups of potential criminal perpetrators" (POP) did not show a substantial improvement over usual tactical patrol activities. LOP seemed somewhat more effective than POP.

Kansas City Directed Interactive Patrol (Miron, Bieck and Strecher, 1987)

Developed by KCPD Operations Task Force in 1974. Focused on robbery and residential burglary. Identified 15 patrol activities that impacted crime:

1. Community education
   - Crime information
   - Community meetings
   - Crime prevention displays
   - Community newspaper activities
2. Community organization programs
   - Operation identification
   - Security surveys of premises
   - Block watchers
3. Tactical deployment
   - Safe walkways (heavily patrolled pedestrian routes)
   - Decoy operations
   - Garage and swap sale stings
   - Tac II alarms (patrol cars received alarms directly)
4. Case processing
   - Investigative solvability factors
   - Concealed cameras in premises

- Identification kits
- Height strips (rulers mounted on door jambs to help a robbery victim estimate the robber's height) and description pads (on which a victim jots down main descriptors of the robber) in premises

Kansas City Response Time Study (Bieck, 1978–80)

Conducted March 1, 1975 through January 2, 1976, this experiment analyzed the effect of rapid response on the likelihood of arrest, witness availability, citizen satisfaction with response time and the incidence of citizen injuries received during the commission of a crime. Most previous concern with response time concentrated on dispatch time and travel time to incidents, and for decades enormous amounts of public funding had been invested in reducing both (such as patrol plans, sirens and lights, radio communications systems, coordinated traffic signals, automatic vehicle locators, computer assisted dispatching). This was the first systematic study of time elapsed between the offense and the call to police, and also between an officer's arrival in the general vicinity of the call (for example, apartment complex) and his actual contact with the incident. The study was targeted to the 56 shift/beats having the highest rates of robbery and aggravated assault in 1974 (out of 207 shift/beats). Observers riding with patrols collected data on travel time, radio tapes were analyzed, and citizens were interviewed. The crimes consisted of 949 calls, including 10 rapes, 127 robberies, 84 aggravated assaults, 352 burglaries, 297 larceny-thefts and 79 auto thefts. There were 352 "involvement" crimes (caller was a victim or witness), and 597 "discovery" crimes (caller found the crime after it occurred).

Findings: Of the 352 involvement crimes, 221 were violent and 131 nonviolent. Of 45 arrests for the 221 cases, 12 were response related (5.4 percent of crimes; 26.6 percent of arrests). Of 55 arrests for the 131 cases, 15 were response related (11.5 percent of crimes; 27 percent of arrests). For all violent crime rapid-response dispatches, 7.7 percent resulted in response-related arrests.

Of the 597 discovery crimes, 582 were discovered by citizens and 15 by alarms. Of 6 arrests for the 582 cases, only 1 was response related (0.3 percent of crimes; 16.6 percent of arrests). Of 7 for the 15 alarm cases, all 7 were response related (46.7 percent of cases; 100 percent of arrests).

The largest block on the response-time continuum was the category for citizens delaying (for many reasons) their calls to the police. This delay often exceeded dispatch and travel time.

Significance: Because of the time citizens take to report crimes, the application of technological innovations and human resources to reduce police response time will have negligible impact on crime outcomes. Despite this pessimistic conclusion, there are important planning implications in the findings:

- A major effort must be undertaken to educate the public to notify the police quickly of crimes in progress and just completed.
- Citizen crime-reporting technology beyond 911 might have potential for improving the results of rapid response.
- Finer degrees of crime analysis and systematic debriefing of officers might identify types of crimes and circumstances in which rapid response will yield optimal results.
- Further costly attempts to reduce call-processing and travel time should be held in abeyance until the citizen reporting delays have been improved or until some unanticipated technology is brought into view. The police side of the response continuum can be improved only marginally and at great expense.

Note: In the appendix under General Policy Analysis Reference Information will be found a number of the tables from the Kansas City Response Time Study, which show the correlation between travel time and likelihood of arrest.

Mini-Stations

Also known as storefront stations, these facilities provide telephone and radio communications for a small number of officers assigned to high-crime neighborhoods. One or more officers may remain at the facility at all times, while others engage in foot patrol and remain in contact with the mini-station by radio. Cell phones have been used. Vacant stores or homes are often used for this purpose. A version called the *portable command station* employs a motorized recreational vehicle (RV), which can be moved among high-crime locations. The RV contains a communications center for contact with foot patrol and vertical patrol officers in the area. Officers in mini-stations are expected to work with community crime prevention groups to interdict or respond quickly to crime problems.

Neighborhood-Oriented Policing (NOP)

Most observers consider NOP and COP synonymous; however, there are those who claim a distinction. For instance, some Houston Police officers who were involved in that department's NOP program say it differed from COP. They were not able, however, to articulate clearly the distinctions.

One definition asserts that NOP consists of policing each ethnic/racial pocket of a jurisdiction in a way uniquely suited to that population, especially if the values and behavior of the residents were at odds with those of adjoining neighborhoods. The implication of this definition is that standards of neighborhood order should be tailored to the preferences of local residents, rather than adopted across the entire jurisdiction. In sharp contrast to this, however, was the selection of a tri-ethnic "neighborhood" for one of Houston's NOP operations. The meaning of NOP may be clearly distinguishable from COP to some police officers, but certainly not to all.

Neighborhood Watch (see Community Crime Prevention)

Police-Community Relations Programs (Radelet, 1965, 1973)

This concept originated in 1955, at the first National Institute on Police-Community Relations, convened at the School of Police Administration and Public Safety, Michigan State University. Douglas Gourley's 1950 study of police public relations contained no mention of police-community relations, although 76 of the 196 titles contained in his exhaustive bibliography contained the phrases *human relations*, *public relations*, or *press relations*. Between 1955 and 1967, more than 1,100 police officials representing 180 police agencies participated in conferences sponsored by the National Center on Police and Community Relations at Michigan State University. By 1967, the I.A.C.P. reported that 38 percent of all cities over 50,000 population had established police-community relations programs (ICMA, 1967).

Core Concepts: "Properly understood, the principle is one for total *orientation* of a police organization. . . . not merely for a specialized unit of the department. It is a way for a police officer to view his [or her] work in dealing with citizens. For citizens, it is a way of viewing the police officer: what he [or she] does and how he [or she] does it. . . . Every problem in police work today . . . depends in some sense on police and community cooperation, indeed *partnership*. . . . the police-and-community relation has a *preventive* character. Its thrust is in working together in the community to anticipate and to *prevent* problems. . . . the best way to control a crime is to prevent it.

"Community relations may be . . . viewed as a kind of tripod, based on three equal components: public relations, community service, and community participation. . . . For a police department an example of *community service* would be a youth program . . . *community participation* stresses interprofessional or teamwork approaches to solving community problems . . . the police . . . the courts and other criminal justice institutions . . . schools, religious bodies, social work agencies, various community organizations, labor unions and business management, the mass media . . . No single community force, not even the police, have the total answer. . . . The art of devising programs, therefore, is that of bringing together all these forces in some sort of cooperative, coordinated venture, to cope with problems too complex for any single force to solve alone. It is in this sense that the police-community relations activity takes on a problem-solving function." (Radelet, 1973, pp. 24–25)

These core concepts led to hundreds of community-oriented and problem-solving innovations in policing in the two decades following 1955 and provided the foundation of subsequent movements toward community-oriented and problem-oriented policing.

Policewomen on Patrol: Washington, DC (Bloch, Anderson and Gervais, 1974); St. Louis County (Sherman, 1975); Denver (Bartlett, and Rosenblum, 1977); New York City (Sichel et al., 1978); and Texas and Oklahoma (David, 1978)

The Washington, DC, study began in 1972, after the chief decided to hire 100 women and assign them to patrol duty. An elaborate evaluation project was built around this decision, and eventually more than 80 male and female officers from the same academy class were matched in the research. Policewomen were to be treated identically with policemen; that is, assigned to uniformed patrol before being considered for any other assignment. The orders were followed in general, but it was found that women performed station duties 10 percent of the time, compared to 5 percent for the men. Some police managers stated later that they gave women more station time than men in an effort to spare them from the most dangerous patrol areas. Measurement instruments included personnel records, performance statistics, performance ratings from supervisors, ratings by trained observers, citizen satisfaction (survey), and attitude data obtained from supervisors (survey).

Findings: Officers were rated on a 0–8 scale. Criteria included: Dealing with the Public (M–4.9, W–4.7), Handling a Disorderly Male (M–5.1, W–4.0), Handling a Public Fight (M–5.2, W–3.9), Handling an

Injury Auto Accident (M–5.1, W–4.7), Making a Crime Report (M–4.9, W–5.3), Handling a Disorderly Female (M–4.9, W–4.7), Protecting a Partner from Violence (M–6.1, W–4.5), Performing Street Patrol in General, (M–5.4, W–4.4). Average ratings were M–5.2, W–4.5).

The report states the performance of male and female officers was "similar." However, there were large, significant differences in productivity of men and women while on patrol: (January–June, 1973): Women made only 37.5 percent as many felony arrests as men (M–4.8, W–1.8); only 45.6 percent as many misdemeanor arrests (M–11.4, W–5.2); and wrote only 42.6 percent as many moving traffic citations (M–53.0, W–22.6). On the other hand, policewomen were considered more skilled in diminishing latent violence and presented fewer disciplinary problems. A careful interpretation of these research findings might have challenged the report's contention that male and female officers had performed similarly.

Performance ratings of 66 female and 68 male officers at the end of the probationary year showed no statistical difference, and averaged M–5.5, F–5.3. An interesting finding, probably a carryover of traditional gender roles, was that a majority of both male and female officers expressed a preference for a male partner in a two-officer patrol unit.

Sherman (1975) reported women and men performed equally well on patrol in St. Louis County, Missouri. Quantitative differences between the 16 new female and 16 male officers included more arrests and car stops for male officers; qualitative differences in favor of female officers included greater awareness of citizens' needs during service calls. Bartlett and Rosenblum (1977), Sichel, et al (1978), and David (1978) reported comparable results in evaluations of female officers on patrol.

Earlier research tended to show discomforts of both female and male patrol officers and their supervisors in the unfamiliar working relationship. More recent results seem to indicate that women have settled into patrol work, are more accepted by male colleagues, supervisors and citizens, perform as productively as men, and continue to be less likely to be involved in violent confrontations. It is apparent, as increasing numbers of women enter patrol work, that the police culture is changing along with the larger American culture.

Polygraph Screening of Police Applicants

Systematically adopted by the St. Louis and Chicago police departments during the early 1960s as part of concerted efforts to reform those agencies. The polygraph examination, administered last in the screening process (after thorough aptitude testing, medical examination, background investigation, and other comprehensive selection methods), was found to screen out an astonishing 49 percent of applicants who would formerly have been admitted to the academy. Findings included concealed medical problems (heart problems, epilepsy, history of psychosis), criminal histories, criminal careers which had never resulted in arrest, dangerous driving histories, systematic stealing from employers, and pathological motives for seeking police work. One applicant, following the polygraph exam, admitted wanting to join the department so he could kill somebody. Although controversial and sometimes used to explore inappropriate areas of applicants' lives, the polygraph examination was found to weed out those whose previous behavior had been dangerously antisocial. Police authority would have been a license to harm citizens for those applicants. Polygraph examinations have become a common screening device for police applicants.

Portable Command Stations (See Mini-Stations)

Problem-Oriented Policing (POP) (Goldstein, 1979, 1990; Eck and Spelman, 1987; Kratcoski, 1995)

Herman Goldstein, during his years as Executive Assistant to O. W. Wilson, Superintendent of the Chicago Police Department, observed that patrol units responded repeatedly to calls for service at the same locations. The calls might have been for domestic disturbance, noisy parties, purse-snatching, panhandling, or drag-racing, but the pattern of repeated dispatches to the same locations struck him as significant for police policy. He developed the idea of problem-oriented policing over a period of years.

Kratcoski (1995) lists five basic principles drawn from resources of the National Institute of Justice:

1. Officers of all ranks and from all units should be able to use the system as part of their daily routine.
2. The system must encourage the use of a broad range of information, including but not limited to conventional police data.
3. The system should encourage a broad range of solutions, including but not limited to the criminal justice process.
4. The system should require no additional resources and no special units.
5. Any large police agency must be able to apply it.

Newport News, Virginia, one of the major sites in which POP was developed in its earliest days, identified four stages in the problem-solving process (Eck and Spelman, 1987):

1. Scanning—identifying an issue and determining if it is a problem.
2. Analysis—collecting information on the problem from all available sources.
3. Response—using the information to develop and implement solutions to the problem.
4. Assessment—determining if the response to the problem was effective.

The originator of the concept visualized the following elements in adapting present police methods to problem solving (paraphrased from Goldstein, 1990):

1. Steering the focus of policing *away* from:
   - treating the *incident* as the primary work unit
   - regarding the speediest handling of incidents as the most successful kind of police work
   - dealing with only the most superficial indications of deeper problems, instead of the problems themselves
   - responding to the immediately disturbing and annoying aspects of problems in a way that defers or precludes actual solutions to problems
   - handling incidents as isolated events.
2. Steering the focus of policing *toward*:
   - recognizing patterns of incidents in terms of similar
     - behaviors of offenders
     - behaviors of victims
     - locations or types of environments of incidents
     - persons involved

   This way of thinking requires crime analysis, but other forms of analysis as well.

3. Redefining "problems" of policing away from matters of internal management of the agency and toward community problems.
4. Redefining "success" away from the smooth functioning of the agency in its response to service demands and toward *effectiveness* in dealing with community problems. (In this connection, Goldstein cautions against equating "effectiveness" with the actual solving of community problems which are by nature "intractable" and almost never eliminated (p. 36). He considers it more realistic to use criteria such as reduction of the number of incidents and their seriousness. He says this part of the police role might best be defined as "managing deviance."

5. Goldstein considers "effectiveness" a useful measure of problem solving and states that Eck and Spelman's levels of effectiveness increase the utility of this measure:
   - eliminate the problem
   - reduce number of incidents caused by the problem
   - reduce seriousness of the incidents caused by problem
   - design better methods for handling incidents
   - determine if the problem should be handled by the police
6. Although the police know a tremendous amount about their work demands (calls relating to crime, disorder, and general services) POP calls for a more systematic and rigorous analysis of those service demands, leading to a validation of their reasoning about community problems. This has not been done in most jurisdictions. Goldstein considers the Integrated Criminal Apprehension Program (see listing above) to be a precursor to this kind of analysis and operational planning.
7. Changing the labels of police problems is essential to POP. Terms such as "crime," "street crime," and "violence" are so broad that it's impossible to know what is being discussed when they are used in police policy planning. In an insightful analysis he identifies the very limited utility of definitions based on criminal law (robbery, which might refer to a bank hold-up or a street mugging) and forms of behavior (sexual assault, which can refer to incest, date rape or homosexual abuse of a child). Goldstein calls this process the disaggregating and accurate labeling of problems. To these might be added the dispatch classifications used by police agencies, which tend to conceal significant differences among community problems (for example, "arson," which may be vandalism or insurance fraud, "noise," which may be neighborhood parties, racing autos or industrial operations) (Goldstein, 1990, pp. 39–40).
8. Multiple interests in problems might suggest competing approaches to solving them. Street prostitution, for instance, is shown to have thirteen different community interests, including offensiveness to moral standards of some citizens, a nuisance to passers-by, involvement of juveniles, robbery of patrons, exploitation of prostitutes, involvement of organized crime, drug involvement, and sexually transmitted diseases. Other problems will be found to have other multiple interests, but require analysis to discover them and to make use of them in solutions.

9. Other basic elements of POP include the following:
   - capturing and critiquing the current response: a detailed analysis of what is *actually* being done by the agency
   - an uninhibited search for a tailor-made response: looking beyond the legal definitions and serial dispatches to get at the problem itself
   - adopting a proactive stance: deal with the problem rather than endlessly dispatching cars to symptomatic incidents
   - strengthening the decision-making processes and increasing accountability
   - evaluating results of newly implemented responses

A careful reading of the literature concerning POP and COP establishes that the two approaches overlap but differ in numerous ways. The distinctions between POP and COP given by Hoover under the COP listing are essential to a clear understanding of these policy concepts.

(*Note:* Problem-oriented policing is not to be confused with perpetrator-oriented policing, which is now referred to as repeat offender program.)

Professional Model of Policing (see Traditional Policing)

Repeat Offender, Career Criminal Programs (paraphrased from Gay, 1995)

The most active 10 percent of offenders commit over 50 percent of all reported crimes (Blumstein et al., 1986; Wolfgang, Figlio and Sellin, 1972). But these "career criminals" are only 15 percent of those sentenced to prison annually (Gay and Bowers, 1985). Case-oriented responses and investigations tend to allocate time based on seriousness of the offense, rather than characteristics of the suspect. Targeting scarce resources on the most active and dangerous repeat offenders and collaborating with prosecutors should result in more successful incapacitation of career criminals. This is considered a proactive alternative to traditional police reliance on random patrol and case-oriented investigation policies.

Early police/prosecutor career criminal programs (CCPs) of the 1970s were evaluated and found to be disappointing (Chelimsky and Dahmann, 1981; Springer, Phillips and Connady, 1985).

Police agencies began experimenting with a variety of repeat offender programs (ROPs) in the late 1970s and early 1980s. These were smaller, narrower efforts than the CCPs. A survey in 1984 found 33 law enforcement agencies running ROPs (Gay and Bowers, 1985).

Program elements included: pre-arrest targeting, surveillance, informants; felony warrant services; and post-arrest case enhancement to increase convictions and sentences. Arrests can be made on the basis of "probable cause to believe" the arrestee committed the offense, while conviction requires proof "beyond a reasonable doubt." Case enhancement refers to the gathering of additional evidence after an arrest has been made, so that the conviction standard of proof can be met.

The most researched early ROP operation began in the Metropolitan Police Department of the District of Columbia in 1982. An evaluation (Martin and Sherman, 1986) found the program increased the likelihood of arrest, prosecution on a felony, felony conviction, and length of term for those sentenced to prison. For ROP initiated targets, 47 percent in the experimental group were arrested, while only 6 percent of offenders assigned to the control group were arrested. A lack of management control over target selection criteria resulted in three types of ROP squads: "hunters" (focusing on warrant service), "trappers" (specializing in surveillance, decoys, other covert proactive operations), and "fishers" (who brought back whatever they could find). Despite some criticisms, the Washington ROP was much more successful than prior pre-arrest programs, and paved the way for subsequent ROPs with more formalized candidate selection criteria.

Recent analysis of a post-arrest ROP in the Phoenix PD (Abrahamse et al., 1991) found no increase in conviction rates for ROP cases, but did find significant increases in the likelihood of commitment to prison and length of sentence.

The Police Executive Research Forum (PERF), after reviewing existing ROPs, designed a model ROP that addressed weaknesses and criticisms, and then tested the model in Kansas City, Missouri; Rochester, New York; and Eugene, Oregon (Spelman, 1990). Although a detailed assessment of the model is not yet available, early findings indicate a successful ROP can be established with some specialization and centralization.

The most recent analysis of ROPs involved a statewide analysis of programs in the state of Texas, including a process and impact assessment of the Houston PD's Targeted Offender Program (Gay, 1993).

Robbery-In-Progress Interdiction—St. Louis Hundred-Code

Created in the early 1960s, the hundred-code was designed to reduce the number of patrol units responding to robbery call scenes and to improve coverage of probable getaway routes. After the idea was hatched, timing experiments were held in the field to determine travel time from potential robbery sites. From the timing data, a circular plexiglass template was prepared, with concentric circles representing the number of minutes elapsed since the actual completion of the robbery.

When a robbery was reported by phone or radio, dispatch would announce a hundred-code including the number of the police district in which it was occurring (Second District, 200-code, Ninth District, 900-code, and so on). Response and backup cars were immediately dispatched, and the center of the template placed over the robbery location. The first task was to obtain by radio or phone the time (in progress or minutes since departure) of the robbery. With that information dispatch would begin assigning intercept cars to the most probable escape routes using the concentric elapsed-time circles on the template. Response time of the intercept cars had been calculated into the template design.

For several months the results were astonishing, with field apprehension rates of more than 50 percent for robberies in progress. Then crime analysis reported a fall-off curve. Detailed investigations reported that armed robbers were aware of the hundred-code and adapting to it, some obviously having monitored the department's dispatch frequencies. Some offenders hid in a prepared place within the innermost circle of intercept assignments. Others changed vehicles or clothing before getting to the intercept points. A few caught cabs or buses a block or two from the robbery site. Culmination of this adaptation was found in the wallet of an arrested robbery suspect: a paper copy of the intercept template used by dispatch.

Despite the clever adaptations by professional criminals, the hundred-code continues to be of distinct merit as a police response design. It is as adaptable as the methods employed by criminals to circumvent it.

Safe Houses (see Community Crime Prevention)

Safe Walkways (see Kansas City Directed Interactive Patrol)

San Diego Field Interrogation Study (Boydstun, 1975)

From the earliest days of policing, officers have stopped citizens on the street and asked them to account for their activities. Done subtly, this technique has been acquiesced to by most citizens; done crudely, it has provoked constitutional challenges and charges of police interference in the lives of citizens. When cars were involved, additional issues arose. In time, formal field interrogation reports (FIR) evolved, and were claimed to help in linking FIR'd subjects to crimes later found to have been committed at matching times and places. The legal challenges to FIRs caused some police administrators to eliminate the technique. Others denied its utility. The San Diego PD became the test site for the Police Foundation's study of the issue.

The conclusions of the study were as follows:

1. Some level of field interrogation activity provides a deterrent effect on suppressible crimes in localized areas.
2. The analysis was inconclusive in identifying specific types of suppressible crime most influenced by field interrogation activity. But burglary, petty theft, malicious mischief and disturbances may be the types most affected.
3. Field interrogation activities contributed to 15 percent or more of total arrests made by patrol officers, and supported criminal investigations. *Frequency* of arrests was not shown to be affected by field interrogation activities.
4. Police-community relations appeared not to be adversely affected by field interrogation activities. However, there were indications that a significant increase in field interrogation activity could result in negative public reactions.

San Diego One- and Two-officer Car Study (Boydstun, Sherry and Moelter, 1977)

The first systematic analysis of the relative effectiveness of one- and two-officer patrol cars, an issue of intense debate since motorized patrol began. Criteria included patrol unit performance (officer initiated activities, arrest and dispositions, citizens' complaints), patrol unit efficiency (use of backup support; response time; out-of-service, sick and injury leave; cost per unit), patrol officer safety (assaults on officers, resisting arrest, injuries, patrol vehicle accidents), and officer attitude/perceptions (relevance of staffing issue, personal preferences, opinions regarding unit performance, unit efficiency, officer safety).

Data sources included officers' journals, dispatch records, arrest reports and related documents, personnel records, crime and arrest reports, injury reports, critical incident reports, and several surveys of officers' opinions.

In essence, the findings were of two kinds: First, one-officer cars are as productive, efficient and safe as two-officer cars. At that time it cost only two dollars an hour more to run two one-officer cars than it cost to run one two-officer car ($30 vs. $28). There were fewer injuries to officers patrolling alone. Two officer cars were more productive only in the writing of traffic tickets. Only when backup is required for a majority of calls is it more productive to field two officer cars. Second, most officers prefer to patrol with partners. This subjective preference was found to become more pronounced as the experiment progressed and more opinion surveys were performed.

Thus, the economic and safety issues are squared off against the personal preferences of officers on patrol.

Selective Traffic Enforcement Program (STEP)

The foundation of STEP is crash analysis. Personal injury and fatal vehicle collisions are analyzed so that the driving practices which caused them are identified. These dangerous driving behaviors are then targeted for intensive enforcement. Speeding is most often targeted for enforcement because of the ease with which violations are detected and documented (for example, radar and similar devices); there are, however, other, more dangerous driving behaviors. These include driving while intoxicated, improper lane changes, inattentive driving, running through red lights and stop signs, passing on hills and curves, ignoring dangerous road conditions (such as wet, snowy, icy, or uneven), following too closely, and many others. An "enforcement index" relates the number of hazardous driving citations issued in relation to the number of injury and fatal accidents, and thus evaluates a department's traffic enforcement policies and programs.

Split Force Patrol Experiment: Wilmington, DE (Cawley et al., 1977)

The focus was on criminal apprehension, rather than crime suppression, as in the New Haven Directed Patrol experiment.

Studies in the early 1970s indicated that much patrol time (40 percent or more) was uncommitted to any identifiable activity (Cawley et al., 1977). The Vollmer doctrine was that randomly moving patrols suppressed crime; however, many chiefs had rejected that idea by the 1960s, and believed so-called crime-prevention time was largely wasted. A commonsense business perspective suggested that this uncommitted time should be recovered and re-allocated to high priority objectives. Two approaches emerged: The New Haven Directed Patrol experiment (See listing above, under directed patrol experiment), which assigned patrol units to brief directed activities (30–90 minutes), and the Wilmington Split Force experiment, which required the reorganization of the patrol force and new missions for the reorganized units.

In effect, Wilmington PD divided its patrol function into (1) exclusively answering calls for service (basic patrol), and (2) crime control (structured patrol). About two-thirds of the original patrol force was allocated to calls, and one-third to crime control. The structured units would always respond to dispatches for serious crimes, thus supporting the basic units dispatched to take the report. The redesign of patrol included many sophisticated aspects which challenged the capacity of police officers to adapt. One of them was a so-called push-pull scheduling method, which could order officers to report several hours earlier or later, on two weeks notice, to match patrol resources to anticipated work demands. This feature did not survive long into the experiment, when officers registered dismay with an additional challenge to their family responsibilities.

Other problems for the basic (call-response) patrol officers were having to maintain a stationary position between calls (while writing reports, and optimally located for dispatches), and the demeaning sense of dealing only with mundane calls.

Arrests made by the structured (crime control) patrol units increased dramatically (virtually doubled); however, this increase was offset by decreases in arrests by detectives. A result was increasing strain between patrol and investigative units and their managers.

Careful analysis of these findings concluded that the structured patrol force had, in effect, become a uniformed investigative force, which was nearly always first on the scene of a serious crime. The structured patrol then had first access to the kind of patrol information which had formerly enabled detectives to clear crimes, and also had unlimited investigative time, because they were not "on the radio."

There is much to suggest that this approach to patrol has merit. The original model tended to insult the older basic patrol officers (who perhaps should have been structured officers, because of their longer experience), and confer undue status on the younger, "aggressive" officers of the structured patrol, who had insufficient experience to capitalize on their freedom from dispatch control to make serious inroads on felony crime.

Sting Operations (see also Decoy or Victim Substitution Operations)

Sting operations offer crime opportunities to those who are motivated to commit them, or false invitations to those wanted by the police. The narcotics "buy-bust" consists of officers posing as buyers of illegal drugs and then arresting the drug sellers. Police women pose as prostitutes and arrest men who solicit their services. Persons for whom arrest warrants have been issued are invited to pick up contest prizes, unclaimed insurance benefits, or unexpected tax rebates at an office building where they are arrested. Suspected fences are offered obviously stolen property at ridiculously low prices.

Storefront Stations (see Mini-Stations)

Tactical Patrol Force (TPF) (see also Directed Patrol and Split Force Patrol)

Traditional patrol operations require that all police cars be available for dispatch: "under radio control." This restricts patrol officers to their defined beats to enable them to respond quickly to calls in their own sectors. A TPF is formed by removing a number of cars from radio service and assigning them to interdict specific crimes, such as street robberies, business burglaries, thefts from autos, and other suppressible crimes.

Team Policing (Sherman, Milton and Kelly, 1973; Schwartz and Clarren, 1977)

The main elements of virtually all team policing models are:

- geographic stability of patrol
- maximum interaction among team members
- maximum communication among team members and the community

Some models went further and included the following elements:

- unity of supervision over all shifts
- lower-level flexibility in policy making
- unified delivery of all police services
- combined investigative and patrol functions

In essence a police "team" was virtually a small police agency within a large department, with full responsibility for policing within a defined area. One striking model required every patrol officer to be a generalist and each officer to practice one kind of specialty (such as juvenile, family violence, sex crimes, or emergency medical response).

Traditional Policing

This refers also to the "professional policing model," and "calls for service policing." All patrol officers are placed in motor vehicles, assigned to patrol beats and expected to concentrate on responding promptly to radio dispatches. They are expected to suppress criminals' opportunities by surveillance of their beats between radio calls.

Truancy Squad

Officers are assigned to seek school-age children who are in places other than schools. Under special city ordinances, the children are taken into custody and transported to their schools or homes to determine their reasons for being absent from school. This is a delinquency prevention program, particularly in areas that have high rates of shoplifting and malicious mischief.

Vertical Patrol

In some cities, subsidized housing projects are given the same level of policing as privately-owned apartment complexes: officers answer calls for service, but patrol in vehicles only on the perimeter of the housing units. Vertical patrol involves placing patrol officers inside housing units, walking the corridors and stairwells, and riding the elevators. Some housing projects furnish vacant apartments as "mini-stations" for vertical patrol officers. Others identify corridor monitors among the residents with whom officers maintain contact. Some municipal housing authorities, such as New York, maintain their own police agencies, operating independently of the jurisdiction in which the housing project resides.

Victim Substitution Operations
(see Decoy or Victim Substitution Operations)

References

Abrahamse, A., P. Ebener, P. Greenwood, N. Fitzgerald, and T. Kosin (1991). "An Experimental Evaluation of the Phoenix Repeat Offender Program." *Justice Quarterly*, 8: 141–68.

Banas, D. W. and R. C. Trojanowicz (1985). *Uniform Crime Reporting and Community Policing: An Historical Perspective*. Community Policing Series No. 5. East Lansing: National Center for Community Policing, Michigan State University.

Bartlett, H. W. and A. Rosenblum (1977). *Policewomen Effectiveness*. Denver: Civil Service Commission of Denver.

Belknap, J., M. Morash, and R. Trojanowicz (1986). *Implementing a Community Policing Model for Work with Juveniles*. Community Policing Series No. 8. East Lansing: National Center for Community Policing, Michigan State University.

Bieck, W. H. (1995). "Crime Analysis." In *Encyclopedia of Police Science*, W. G. Bailey (ed.). New York: Garland Publishing.

_____ (Principal Analyst) (1980). *Response Time Analysis*, Volumes I–IV. Unpublished research report. Kansas City, Missouri Police Department.

Bloch, P. B., D. Anderson and P. Gervais (1974). *Policewomen on Patrol: Final Report*. Washington, DC: The Police Foundation.

Bloch, P. B. and J. Bell (1976). *Managing Criminal Investigations: The Rochester System*. Washington, DC: The Police Foundation.

Blumstein, A., J. Cohen, J. Roth, and C. Visher, (eds.) (1986). *Criminal Careers and Career Criminals*, Vol. 1. Washington, DC: National Academy Press.

Boydstun, J. E. (1975). *San Diego Field Interrogation: Final Report*. Washington, DC: The Police Foundation.

Boydstun, J. E. and M. E. Sherry (1975). *San Diego Community Profile: Final Report*. Washington, DC: Police Foundation.

Boydstun, J. E., M. E. Sherry, and N. P. Moelter (1977). *Patrol Staffing in San Diego: One- or Two-Officer Units*. Washington, DC: Police Foundation.

Brandstatter, A. F. and L. A. Radelet (eds.) (1968). *Police and Community Relations: A Sourcebook*. Beverly Hills: Glencoe Press.

Bufe, N. C. (1955). "Traffic Services," in *Encyclopedia of Police Science*, 2nd ed., W. G. Bailey (ed.). New York: Garland Publishing.

Cardarelli, A. P. and J. McDevitte (1995). "Toward a Conceptual Framework for Evaluating Community Policing." In *Issues in Community Policing*, P.C. Kratcoski and Duane Dukes (eds.). Cincinnati: Anderson Publishing.

Carter, D. L. (1992). "Community Alliance." In *Police Management Issues and Perspectives*, L. T. Hoover (ed.), pp. 61–86. Washington, DC: Police Executive Research Forum.

Carter, D. L. and A. D. Sapp (1992). *Program Evaluation Model for Community Policing*. Huntsville: Texas Law Enforcement Management Institute.

Cawley, D., J. Miron, J. Kelly, and V. Strecher (1977). *Improving Police Management: Participant's Manual*. Washington, DC: U.S. Department of Justice, National Institute of Justice.

Chaiken, J. and M. Chaiken (1982). *Varieties of Criminal Behavior*. Santa Monica: The RAND Corp.

Chelimsky, E. and J. Dahmann (1981). *Career Criminal Program National Evaluation: Final Report*. U.S. Department of Justice, National Institute of Justice. Washington, DC: U.S. Government Printing Office.

Cordner, G. W. and R. C. Trojanowicz (1992). "Patrol." In *What Works in Policing*, G. W. Cordner, and D. C. Hale (eds.). Cincinnati: Anderson Publishing Co.

Cordner, G. W. and D. C. Hale (eds.) (1992). *What Works in Policing: Operations and Administration Examined.* Cincinnati, OH: Anderson Publishing Co.

Couper, D. L. (1991). *Quality Policing: The Madison Experience*. Washington, DC: Police Executive Research Forum.

David, J. (1978). "Perspectives of Policewomen in Texas and Oklahoma." *Journal of Police Science and Administration* 12: 395–403.

Eck, J. E. (1992). "Criminal Investigations." In *What Works in Policing*, G. W. Cordner and D. C. Hale (eds.). Cincinnati: Anderson Publishing Co.

_____ (1979). *Managing Case Assignments: The Burglary Investigation Decision Model Replication*. Washington, DC: Police Executive Research Forum.

Eck, J. E. and W. Spelman (1987). *Problem-Solving: Problem-Oriented Policing in Newport News*. Washington, DC: Police Executive Research Forum.

Fennessy, E. F. (1982). *Police Directed Patrol Programs: An Initial Assessment*. Unpublished report. Washington, DC: National Institute of Justice, U.S. Department of Justice.

Gay, B. W. (1995). "Repeat Offender Programs." In *The Encyclopedia of Police Science*, 2nd ed., W. G. Bailey (ed.). New York: Garland Publishing: 687–91.

_____ (1993). "Policing Hard Core Offenders: An Analysis of Targeted Offender Programs in Texas that Use Pre-arrest targeting and Post-arrest Case Enhancement Strategies to Selectively Incapacitate Career Criminals." Ph.D. diss. Sam Houston State University, Huntsville, TX.

Gay, W. and R. Bowers (1985). *Targeting Law Enforcement Resources: The Career Criminal Focus*. Washington, DC: U.S. Department of Justice, National Institute of Justice.

Goldstein, H. (1990). *Problem-Oriented Policing*. New York: McGraw-Hill.

_____ (1987). "Toward Community-Oriented Policing: Potential, Basic Requirements, and Threshold Questions." *Crime and Delinquency* 33(1): 6–30.

_____ (1979). "Improving Policing: A Problem-Oriented Approach," *Crime and Delinquency*, 25:236–58.

Greene, J. R. and R. B. Taylor (1988). "Community-Based Policing and Foot Patrol: Issues of Theory and Evaluation." In *Community Policing: Rhetoric or Reality*, J. R. Greene and S. D. Mastrofski (eds.). New York: Praeger.

Greenwood, P. and J. Petersilia (1975). *The Criminal Investigation Process—Volume I: Summary and Policy Implications*. Santa Monica: RAND Corporation.

Grennan, S. (1988)."Findings on the Role of Officer Gender in Violent Encounters with Citizens." *Journal of Police Science and Administration*. 15: 78–85.

Hartman, F. X., L.P. Brown, and D. W. Stephens (1988). *Community Policing: Would You Know It If You Saw It?* East Lansing, MI: Neighborhood Foot Patrol Center.

Hoover, L. T. (1992). "Police Mission: An Era of Debate." In *Police Management Issues and Perspectives*, L. T. Hoover (ed.), pp. 1–30. Washington, DC: Police Executive Research Forum.

International City Management Association (1967). *Yearbook*. Washington, DC: ICMA.

Kelling, G. L. and M. H. Moore (1988). *The Evolving Strategy of Policing*. Washington, DC: National Institute of Justice.

Kelling, G. L., T. Pate, R. A. Bowers, and R. Parks (1976). *Three Approaches to Criminal Apprehension in Kansas City*. Washington, DC: Police Foundation.

Kelling, G. L., T. Pate, D. Dieckman, and C. E. Brown (1974). *The Kansas City Preventive Patrol Experiment: A Summary Report*. Washington, DC: Police Foundation.

Kratcoski, P.C. (1995). "Community-Oriented Policing: COP and POP." In *The Encyclopedia of Police Science*, 2nd ed., W. G. Bailey (ed.), pp. 95–98. New York: Garland Publishing.

Laski, M. (1970). *LEAA Project Report: The St. Louis Detoxification and Diagnostic Evaluation Center*. Washington, DC: Law Enforcement Assistance Administration, U.S. Department of Justice. (U.S. GPO: 1970 O-373-790)

Martin, S. and L. Sherman (1986). *Catching Career Criminals: The Washington, DC Repeat Offender Project*. (Report No. 3) Washington, DC: Police Foundation.

McElroy, J., C. A. Cosgrove, and S. Sadd (1990). *CPOP: The Research*. New York: Vera Institute of Justice.

McEwen, J. T., E. F. Connors III, and M. I. Cohen (1986). *Evaluation of the Differential Police Response Field Test*. Washington, DC: NIJ, U.S. Department of Justice. (Reprints (238 pp.) available from the Police Foundation)

Miron, H. J., W. H. Bieck, and V. G. Strecher (1987). *Improving Police Management: Participant Handbook,* pp. 82–83. Washington, DC: Police Management Association.

Moore, H. M. (1992) "Problem-solving and Community Policing." In *Modern Policing*. M. Tonry and N. Morris (eds.). Chicago: University of Chicago Press.

Oettmeier, T. N. (1992). "Matching Structure to Objectives." In *Police Management Issues and Perspectives*, L. T. Hoover (ed.), pp. 31–60. Washington, DC: Police Executive Research Forum.

O'Leary, L. R. (1995). "Assessment Centers" In *The Encyclopedia of Police Science*, 2nd ed., W. G. Bailey (ed.), pp. 37–39. New York: Garland Publishing.

Pate, A. M., M. A. Wycoff, W. G. Skogan, and L. W. Sherman (1986). *Reducing Fear of Crime in Houston and Newark: A Summary Report*. Washington, DC: Police Foundation.

Payne, D. M. and R. C. Trojanowicz (1985). *Performance Profiles of Foot Versus Motor Officers*. Community Policing Series No. 6. East Lansing: National Center for Community Policing, Michigan State University.

Petersilia, J., P. Greenwood, and M. Lavin (1978). *Criminal Careers of Habitual Felons*. Santa Monica: The RAND Corp.

Pindur, W. (1983). *The Story of ICAP in the Portsmouth Police Department*. Norfolk, VA: Old Dominion University.

Police Foundation (1981). *The Newark Foot Patrol Experiment*. Washington, DC: Police Foundation.

_____ (1977). *Domestic Violence and the Police: Studies in Detroit and Kansas City*. Washington, DC: Police Foundation.

Pontell, H. (1984). *A Capacity to Punish: The Ecology of Crime and Punishment*. Bloomington, IN: Indiana University Press.

Radelet, L. A. (1973). *The Police and the Community*. Beverly Hills: Glencoe Press.

_____ (1965). "Police Community Programs: Nature and Purpose." *The Police Chief*. (March).

Rosen, M. (1992). "An Interview with Commissioner Lee P. Brown of New York." *Law Enforcement News* 18 (May 15), no. 358:11.

Schwartz, A. I. and S. N. Clarren (1977). *The Cincinnati Team Policing Experiment*. Washington, DC: The Police Foundation.

Sherman, L. J. (1975). "Evaluation of Policewomen on Patrol in a Suburban Police Department." *Journal of Police Science and Administration*. 3: 434–38.

Sherman, L. J., C. H. Milton, and T. V. Kelly (1973). *Team Policing: Seven Case Studies*. Washington, DC: The Police Foundation.

Sichel, J. L., L. N. Friedman, J. C. Quint, and M. E. Smith (1978). *Women on Patrol—A Pilot Study of Police Performance in New York City*. New York: Vera Institute of Justice.

Skolnick, J. H. and D. H. Bayley (1988). *Community Policing: Issues and Practices Around the World*. Washington, DC: National Institute of Justice, U.S. Department of Justice.

_____ (1986). *The New Blue Line: Police Innovation in Six American Cities*. New York: Free Press.

Spelman, W. (1990). *Repeat Offenders*. Washington, DC: Police Executive Research Forum.

Spelman, W. and D. Brown (1984). *Calling the Police: Citizen Reporting of Serious Crime*. Washington, DC: National Institute of Justice.

Spelman, W. and J. E. Eck (1987). *Problem-Oriented Policing: The Newport News Experiment*. Washington, DC: Police Executive Research Forum.

Springer, J., J. Phillips, and L. Cannady (1985). *The Effectiveness of Selective Prosecution by Career Criminal Programs*. Washington, DC: EMT Group.

Strecher, V. G. (1995). "Revising the Histories and Futures of Policing." In *The Police and Society: Touchstone Readings*, V. E. Kappeler (ed.). Prospect Heights, IL: Waveland Press.

_____ (1992). "Current Perspectives on Policing." In *Police Management Issues and Perspectives*, L. T. Hoover (ed.). Washington, DC: Police Executive Research Forum.

Trojanowicz, R. (1994). *Community Policing: A Survey of Police Departments in the United States*. East Lansing: National Center for Community Policing, Michigan State University.

_____ (1990). "Community Policing Is Not Police Community Relations." *FBI Law Enforcement Bulletin*. (October).

_____ (1982). *An Evaluation of the Neighborhood Foot Patrol Program in Flint, Michigan*. East Lansing: National Center for Community Policing, Michigan State University.

Trojanowicz, R. and D. W. Banas (1985a). *Perceptions of Safety: A Comparison of Foot Patrol Versus Motor Patrol Officers*. East Lansing: National Center for Community Policing, Michigan State University.

——— (1985b). *Job Satisfaction: A Comparison of Foot Patrol Versus Motor Patrol Officers*. Community Policing Series No. 2. East Lansing: National Center for Community Policing, Michigan State University.

——— (1985c) *The Impact of Foot Patrol on Black and White Perceptions of Policing*. Community Policing Series No. 4. East Lansing: National Center for Community Policing, Michigan State University.

Trojanowicz, R. and J. Belknap (1986). *Community Policing: Training Issues*. Community Policing Series No. 9. East Lansing: National Center for Community Policing, Michigan State University.

Trojanowicz, R. and B. Bucqueroux (1990). *Community Policing: How to Get Started*. Cincinnati, OH: Anderson Publishing.

Trojanowicz, R. and H. A. Harden (1985). *The Status of Contemporary Community Policing Programs*. Community Policing Series No. 3. East Lansing: National Center for Community Policing, Michigan State University.

Trojanowicz, R. and B. Pollard (1986). *Community Policing: The Line Officer's Perspective*. Community Policing Series No. 11. East Lansing: National Center for Community Policing, Michigan State University.

Trojanowicz, R., B. Pollard, F. Colgan, and H. Harden (1986). *Community Policing Programs: A Twenty-Year View*. Community Policing Series No. 10. East Lansing: National Center for Community Policing, Michigan State University.

Trojanowicz, R., M. Steele, and S. Trojanowicz (1986). *Community Policing: A Taxpayer's Perspective*. Community Policing Series No. 7. East Lansing: National Center for Community Policing, Michigan State University.

Weber, J. M. (1968). *Final Evaluation Report: The St. Louis Detoxification and Diagnostic Evaluation Center*. St. Louis: Social Science Institute, Washington University.

Wilson, J. Q. and G. L. Kelling (1982). "Broken Windows: The Police and Neighborhood Safety." *Atlantic Monthly* 249 (March 1982).

Wolfgang, M., R. Figlio, and T. Sellin (1972). *Delinquency in a Birth Cohort*. Chicago: University of Chicago Press.

Chapter **4**

Cases and Exercises

The purpose of these cases and exercises is to apply the methods and principles of the previous chapters. Some of the exercises are simple economic analyses of problems, programs and resources. Others raise the social and political values dimension alone. Still others probe economic and social value issues which intersect or conflict.

Policy analysis covers an enormous number of issues and behaviors. To simulate some of them, you will participate in group discussion by role-playing various personalities outlined in the appendix. Alternatively, you will be asked to imagine a council meeting considering various proposals—for example, a truancy program or a weapons sweep of a housing project. You'll be asked to assess probable voting behavior based on the thumbnail personality sketches in the appendix. The purpose of such exercises is to give you an idea of what planners must consider when confronting an issue: physical constraints, economic factors, political possibility of a plan receiving city council approval given the personalities on the council.

Some of the exercises introduce types of situations which must be addressed by planners. For example, the appendix describes a subsidized high-rise housing project, Hi-Lo. An option for providing police service is vertical patrol—the environmental factors of a high-rise (building structure, density of population) defining this type of patrol.

Conventional conceptions of patrol assign a street-surface area. The density of population in a high rise suggests that in this instance vertical layers should be considered. If standard practice assigns a four square block area for an officer on foot, then the special circumstances here would suggest what equivalent?

While vertical patrol is a choice based on fairly quantifiable economic and service demands, measuring the success of vertical patrol brings us into the area of social value issues. Victimization of one person highlights an associated problem—the climate of fear caused by an environment in which so many friends and relatives are victimized. Programs to reduce the fear of crime have been found effective in cities, such as Newark and Houston. Fear reduction has been credited with changing peoples' daily living patterns, and reducing the threat of crime.

You may be appointed by the instructor to a "task force" that is assigned to solve one of the exercises. Task forces are commonly appointed by police managers to study the kinds of problems presented in this book. They may consist of officers and planning specialists of various ranks (as suggested for policy planning groups in chapter 2). Conversely, task forces may consist of members of a single rank, or may include citizens having special expertise to analyze the problem.

Some of the cases and exercises require special forms for response or peer evaluation. Tear-out sheets are at the end of the chapter. The instructor may choose to direct your attention to specific data in the appendix when assigning exercises, or it may be your responsibility to find the appropriate data sources.

In some exercises there are numerically correct answers; in others, the quantified results will be approximate. In most of the cases there are no "correct" outcomes—only agreement or consensus that the outcome is acceptable. This mirrors the reality of the world of public policy planning.

Economics and Resource Allocation in Policy Planning

LEARNING OBJECTIVES:
- Quantification of problems
- Workload analysis
- Quantification of planned operations
- Costs of operations
- Resource allocation and recovery

1. ILLUSTRATION OF PATROL RESOURCE REQUIREMENTS

Compute how many one-officer cars can be staffed around the clock every day of the year. Assume equal staffing of three shifts.

Oceana PD:	Number of patrol cars ________
Americus County SD:	Number of patrol cars ________
Exurbia PD:	Number of patrol cars ________

Your analysis should assume that a car will be on the street 24 hours a day, 365 days a year.

Note: In the appendix, a table called the Calculation of Relief Factor is provided for your use in analyzing the staffing requirements for all assignments that cover twenty-four hours every day of the year. It illustrates:

- the number of working shifts in a year
- the number of days an officer is not available for duty and conversely available for duty.

It is based on three different models of personnel policies and fringe benefits in police and local detention facilities. It presents an actuarial basis of time available for duty rather than the assumption that an officer will be on duty whenever she/he is not on vacation or scheduled days off.

2. ILLUSTRATION OF COST OF OFFICER'S WORKING TIME

Compute the cost of one hour of a patrol officer's time for Oceana PD, the cost for an Americus County deputy and for an Exurbia patrol officer. Include fringe benefit costs.

3. ILLUSTRATION OF COST ANALYSIS OF PATROL RESOURCE ALLOCATION

Determine the officer salary cost (including fringe benefits) of staffing a patrol car for one year:

Oceana PD:	One-officer car cost $ _______
	Two-officer car cost $ _______
Americus County SD:	One-deputy car cost$ _______
	Two-deputy car cost$ _______
Exurbia PD:	One-office car cost $ _______
	Two-officer car cost $ _______

4. ILLUSTRATION OF COST ANALYSIS OF INVESTIGATIONS

Determine investigative salary costs as follows:

	Per Hour	**Per Day**	**Per Week**
Oceana PD:			
Detective working alone	$ ____	$ ____	$ ____
Det. Sgt./Detective team	$ ____	$ ____	$ ____
Americus County SD:			
Detective working alone	$ ____	$ ____	$ ____

Det. Sgt./Detective team $ ____ $ ____ $ ____
Exurbia detective $ ____ $ ____ $ ____

5. ILLUSTRATION OF WORKLOAD ANALYSIS: CALLS FOR SERVICE RESPONSE

   Compute the average number of calls for service (CFS) each patrol unit will have to respond to each 8-hour shift.

   Oceana PD: Average CFS per car per shift ____

   Americus County SD: Average CFS per car per shift ____

   Exurbia PD: Average CFS per car per shift ____

6. ILLUSTRATION OF WORKLOAD ANALYSIS: PART I CRIMES RESPONSES

   Compute the average number of Part I crimes each patrol unit will have to respond to each five-day week.

   OPD: Average index crimes per car per week ____

   ACSD: Average index crimes per car per week ____

   EPD: Average index crimes per car per week ____

7. ILLUSTRATION OF RESOURCE RECOVERY: DISCONTINUED FUNCTION

   Americus county only: If code 4 dispatches (medical problems) are transferred to the fire department's EMS (those not requiring police services), and code 4 calls average 48 minutes:

   Compute the amount of patrol time recovered for the police department and the dollar value of that time.

   ACSD: Hours recovered __________ $ __________

8. ILLUSTRATION OF NEEDLESS PATROL RESPONSE COSTS

   Ninety-one percent of alarm calls are false alarms. Using elapsed time figures for alarm calls, compute the amount of patrol time being wasted and the cost of that patrol time.

   OPD: Hours wasted per year ______ Cost ______

   EPD*: Hours wasted per year ______ Cost ______

   ACSD: Hours wasted per year ______ Cost ______

   *Same average man-hours per call as Oceana PD

9. ILLUSTRATION OF POLICY RESOURCE ANALYSIS: VERTICAL PATROL DISTRICT FOR HI-LO HOUSING PROJECT

   Estimate the personnel and equipment requirements for a vertical patrol district to serve the Hi-Lo housing project. The unit would patrol the interiors of the 36 square-block housing units of Hi-Lo, serving 122,400 residents.

10. Illustration of POP Problem-Analysis Based on Incidents

During the past year the following incidents have occurred:

- ACSD Code 3 in Southport Village—Disturbance involving long-time Southport shrimpers and Vietnamese shrimpers. Assault charges dropped.
- ACSD Code 2 on Southport dock—Vandalism: nets damaged on shrimp boat owned by Vietnamese refugee.
- ACSD Code 3 on Southport dock—Disturbance. Vietnamese shrimper is selling shrimp off the dock. Southport shrimpers push his catch and coolers off the dock, into the harbor. Southport shrimpers claim Vietnamese are violating the law and the established wholesale system for selling shrimp catches. They also accuse Vietnamese of "overfishing" harbor waters. Vietnamese accuse Southporters of theft of their catch and assault.
- OPD Code 10 in Ward 105—Tires slashed on van delivering shrimp from Vietnamese boat to Cong An Restaurant in Little Saigon. No witnesses.
- ACSD Code 1 on Southport dock—Arson. Vietnamese boat set afire and afloat in harbor.
- ACSD Code 2 on Southport dock—Southport shrimper reports diesel fuel contaminated; damage to engine.
- OPD Code 20 in Ward 105. Suspected arson at Cong An Restaurant.
- ACSD Code 1 in Precinct 4—Aggravated assault on Southport shrimper, who left waterfront tavern intoxicated. He never saw his attackers, who hooded his head, bound him, took him to a secluded beach and clubbed him thoroughly.
- ACSD Code 3 in Southport Village—Disturbance. Southport shrimpers occupy tables at Saigon Cafe, intimidate Vietnamese shrimpers.

Examine these incidents in the context of POP. Propose a nondispatched, proactive intervention to cope with the problem.

11. Illustration of COP problem-analysis based on multiple inputs

Consider how the analysis of your POP problem might be reoriented to make it a COP problem.

Roscoe Beach spots Trinh selling shrimp off the dock.

Social and Political Values Exercises

LEARNING OBJECTIVES: ✏ Social-political value impacts on police policy, operations, and planning

12. ETHNIC GANG PROFILING EXERCISE: A QUESTION OF POLICE POLICY AND CITY POLITICS

SITUATION:

Detective Dave Chu, who has worked vice, robbery and extortion cases citywide, has noticed MO patterns for some multiple-offender crimes that he thinks are specific to gangs of identifiable ethnic and racial membership. For instance, he believes there are MOs for extortion crimes in the Asian community that he quickly ties to either Koreans, Vietnamese or Taiwanese Chinese gangs; still others can be differentiated between Latino gangs of Mexican, Caribbean and Central American cultural backgrounds.

Detective Dave Chu has mentioned his observations to Federal Agent John Haver, who is a liaison agent for interstate extortion cases. Agent Haver has observed similar patterns in other cities. He and Detective Chu have prepared a proposal to study ethnic gang crime patterns systematically. Haver's agency can provide the modest funding for the data coding and analysis. All they want is the Oceana PD's approval to do the research. They promise not to compromise identities or interfere with the department's work.

Both Chu and Haver believe this research will improve the department's crime analysis efforts, case-linking (identifying crimes committed by the same offender or gang), case enhancement, and result in more prosecutions and convictions.

According to city policy, a proposal of this kind must be submitted through the mayor's office to the city council.

TASK FORCE ASSIGNMENT:

1. Take a task-force position on whether the department should recommend this research to the mayor and city council.
2. Make judgments and report them on the following points:
   a. Will the chief support the research proposal?
   b. Will the mayor support the research proposal?
   c. How will *each member* of the city council vote on the research proposal? (Mark *yes* or *no* on form provided.)
   d. What benefits and harms may befall the police department if the research is conducted?

Each task force will be asked to report its findings. (Tear out and use Oceana, Exurbia and Americus County voting summary forms found at the end of the chapter.)

13. ILLUSTRATION OF CITY/TOWN/COUNTY POLITICS: TRUANCY, SHOPLIFTING

Oceana Crime Analysis reports that most daytime shoplifting in both the city and county is being committed by truants. A Metro law-enforcement task force suggests that an inter-agency truancy squad be created and that the following policies be adopted:

- School-age children found in public places will be taken into custody and transported to either their homes, to their parents, or to school officials.
- Juvenile citations for truancy will be issued in all cases, with copies to truants' schools.

Analyze the vote of city council members, town council members and county commissioners and report their votes on the voting summary forms provided.

(Tear out and use Oceana, Exurbia and Americus County voting summary forms found at the end of the chapter.)

14. REPEAT OFFENDER PROGRAM AND POLITICS (ROP)

Analyze the city council vote on a proposal to establish a repeat offender program (*aka* known offender or career-criminal program). This program will be structured along the lines of the ROP Unit of the Washington, DC, PD as depicted in the NIJ video, *Repeat Offender Project.* (Tear out and use an Oceana voting summary form found at the end of the chapter)

15. ILLUSTRATION OF CITY POLITICS: SEARCHING HI-LO FOR WEAPONS

It has been proposed by the Housing Authority that searches of Hi-Lo apartments be conducted by Oceana PD/Housing Authority staff teams to locate and confiscate firearms, pursuant to the Housing Authority's policy prohibiting firearms in the Hi-Lo project. Residents found to be in possession of firearms will then be evicted. The city attorney is of the opinion that the Chicago case decision is not binding in Oceana, because there is a "prohibited contraband" provision in Hi-Lo's contracts with residents. Analyze the city council vote on this proposal and report it on the voting summary form.

(Tear out and use an Oceana voting summary form found at the end of the chapter.)

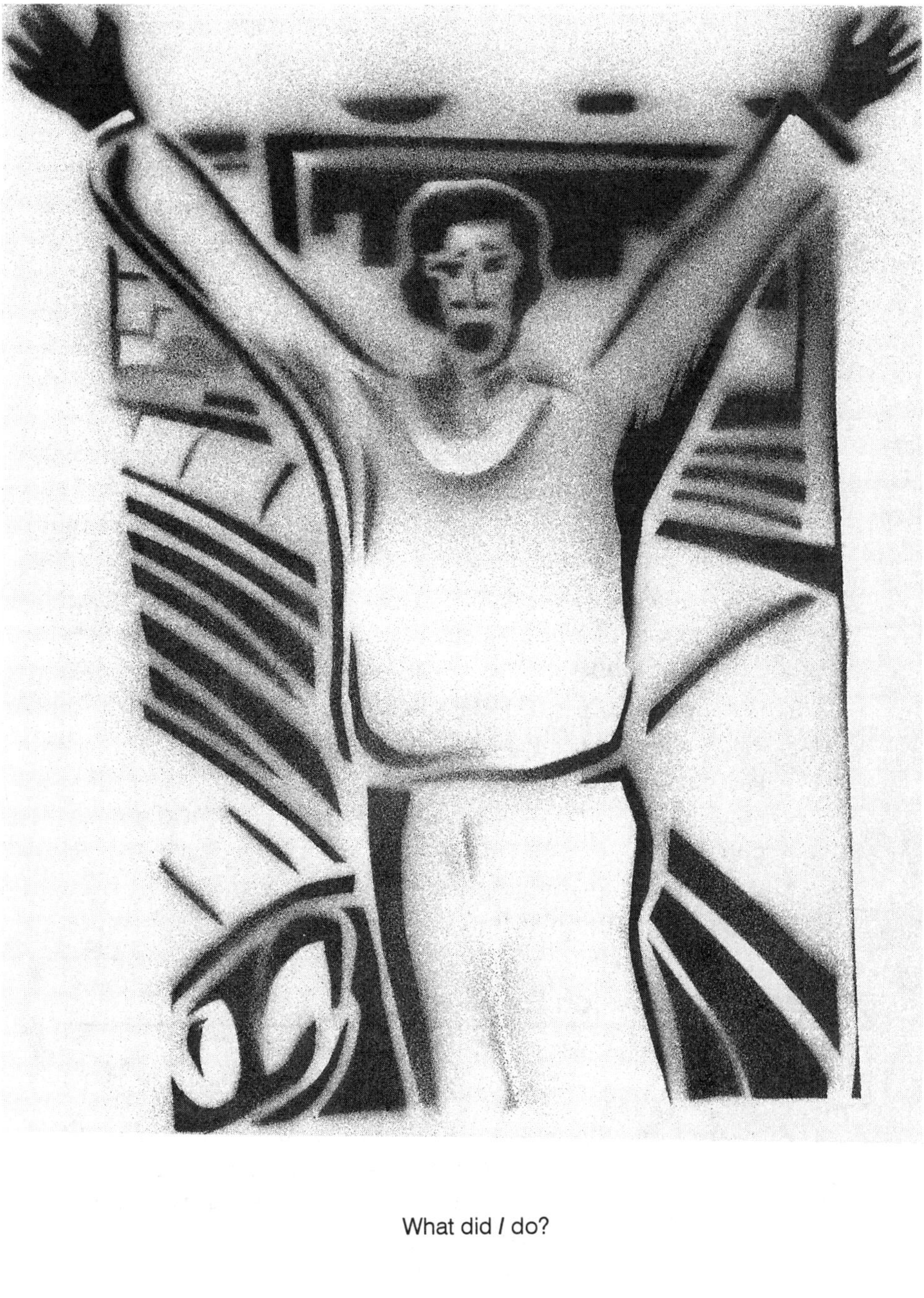

What did *I* do?

Values and Costs Exercises

LEARNING OBJECTIVES: ✏ Interactions of social-political values and economic factors in police policy and operational planning.

16. DECOY SQUAD: RESOURCES AND POLITICS—OCEANA AND EXURBIA

 A victim substitution program, often referred to as a decoy squad, has been proposed to deal with purse snatching, mugging of tourists and public inebriates, car-jackings, late-night mall abduction-rapes, and other street offenses.

 - Clearly state the goal of such a unit.
 - Decide on the size and composition of such a unit.
 - Decide how often the unit should be deployed.
 - Decide on alternative activities of the unit.
 - Analyze the vote of Oceana's city council and Exurbia's town council on the creation of such a unit.

 (Tear out and use Oceana and Exurbia voting summary forms found at the end of the chapter.)

17. Using the Uniform Crime Reports, look up your own home town or city or county of employment. Compute the following figures to compare with those of Oceana, Exurbia and Americus County:

 - Part I offenses per 1,000 population
 - Part I offenses per PD or SD employee
 - Percent index crimes cleared by arrest
 - Police or sheriff's department employees per 1,000 population
 - Ratio of civilian employees to sworn officers

 (No forms required. Submit in your format.)

Classroom Discussion Exercises

18. OCEANA DETECTIVES PETITION FOR NEW PAY GRADE

 The Oceana Professional Police Officers' Union has petitioned the chief for a new pay grade. Presently detectives earn patrol officer salary because they are considered patrol officers on investigative assignments. In effect, there is no "rank" of detective in Oceana. The union claims most police departments have a rank, or at least a higher pay grade, for detectives. The chief claims his flexibility in assigning officers will be lost if the new rank or pay grade is created.

PPOU is demanding the same percentile pay differential paid Exurbia PD detectives over patrol officer salaries.

Calculate the pay of Oceana PD detectives if this differential is adopted. Calculate the annual budget increase this would cause.

19. HANDGUNS AND VICTIMIZATION

A study published in 1996 reported that 1,570 murders and 4,177 rapes could have been prevented in 1992 if people had been permitted to carry concealed weapons. The study also claimed 60,000 aggravated assaults could have been avoided.

The authors of the study asserted:

> By the very nature of these guns being concealed, criminals are unable to tell whether the victim is armed before they strike, thus raising criminals' expected costs for committing many types of crimes.

They believe criminals tend to turn to property crimes in states which allow concealed weapons. Currently twenty-four states have such laws. Gun control advocates believe the decline in crime rates in such states is a result of the waiting period imposed on handgun purchases by federal law.

A 1995 study by the University of Maryland found that murders committed with guns increased when concealed weapons were permitted. Such laws make criminals more likely to arm themselves with deadly weapons and use them more quickly, according to Douglas Weil, Research Director at the Center to Prevent Handgun Violence.

The city council is debating the issue of passing a law to allow concealed weapons. All the members are aware of the two studies. A similar debate was tabled last year, but proponents have reintroduced it in part because of the new study. A sticking point is that the study was funded by the Olin Foundation, which is headed by members of the family that established Olin Corporation. The foundation family members are no longer connected with the corporation. Winchester, which manufactures bullets, is a division of Olin Corporation.

What position will the police department take on this issue?

Chicago Tribune Aug. 10, 1996, Section 1, p. 17

20. DOMESTIC VIOLENCE POLICY

Summarized below is a real-life example of how an intractable problem can be addressed through planning. The population of San Diego is 1.3 million. The police receive about 15,000 domestic-violence calls annually. National profiles of domestic violence indicate the seriousness of the problem:

- One woman is battered every 18 seconds.
- Twenty-five percent of victims are pregnant.
- The major cause of injury for women is battering.
- Thirty-three percent of female murder victims are killed by partners.
- Sixty-two percent of boys aged 11–20 arrested for homicide have killed their mothers' assailants.
- Children from domestic-violence environments are 1,000 times more likely to become abusive as adults than are those from stable environments.

One of the most important hurdles which a successful plan must address is status-quo thinking. The San Diego police department employed rethinking and retraining techniques to set up a domestic-violence unit in 1992 that became a national and international model.

A female detective who helped set up the unit, Anne O'Dell, described the reconceptualization that was necessary before the unit could be effective:

> All police and sheriff's departments start out with the same problem. They believe domestic violence is not fixable. Worse, police are actually obstructing public safety by not dealing with their attitude about domestic violence. . . . Around the world it's the same issue: how to change law enforcement culture and antiquated perspectives of those who think things were always like this and always will be. That means confronting officers' own biases and assumptions about male entitlement that negatively impact the application of the law. . . Admonitions to "sleep it off" or "quiet down or I'll charge you with disturbing the peace" from officers responding to all calls do not deal with the reality of subsequent homicides. . . .
>
> The administration must show police a different approach will work. It also helps to show they are liable if they went out on a series of calls and did nothing.

Domestic-violence homicides accounted for 40 percent of the total homicides in San Diego in the 1980s. The national average at the time was 30 percent. In 1986 California passed legislation which required police officers to report every domestic-violence call. Also in 1986, the city attorney instituted a new domestic-violence policy which provided for the continuation of prosecutions even when witnesses became uncooperative (which happens frequently because of fear of retaliation from the abuser). Officer O'Dell researched the files and discovered that in recent years domestic issues accounted for 40 percent of calls for service. She also checked the addresses of homicides to determine how many calls had been made before the killing. She found that the average was five previous calls for police officers. As she stated, "It was clear police attitudes and lack of specialized training were part of the problem." Those responsible for studying the issue of domestic violence realized that victims' rights, police response, and judicial action all needed to be addressed. A task force was established in 1989 to determine how the police, courts, and social service agencies could support each other rather than working at cross-purposes.

Denise Frey, YWCA Domestic Violence Institute Director, pointed to re-education and community cooperation in working toward prevention and treatment. Police and prosecutors cooperated to design procedures to establish consistent approaches to domestic abuse. Training and an emphasis on cooperation was implemented for police officers, workers in shelters, medical personnel, and staff from the prosecutor's office. The San Diego Domestic Violence Council devised 12 committees to focus on particular aspects of intervention in domestic violence. Services included advocacy, therapy, transportation, and legal advice. The Department of Social Services and the San Diego County Probation Department worked to coordinate efforts with other departments. Links were established between agencies who deal with child abuse and the agencies addressing domestic violence. As council member Sandra Miller of the Family Violence Project at Children's Hospital stated, "Children who witness battering, whether they are violated or not, are being abused, and will have problems." The council helped with referrals to parenting classes, drug and alcohol treatment programs, and domestic-violence treatment programs.

For two years prior to establishing the domestic-violence unit, police officers were trained. The unit was staffed with 18 officers and these goals: "Stop the violence, make the victim safe(r), and hold the batterer accountable." The unit was nicknamed "the homicide prevention unit." The first supervisor of the unit, Ratelle Armstead, recalled, "Pulling 18 front-line people off robbery and homicide to work on what was still identified as a family matter created a lot of department tensions." No new monies were allocated to the domestic-violence unit. Officers were initially skeptical; they expected more work and fewer results regarding "real crime." After the new unit was established, domestic-violence reports doubled, and fatalities decreased by 59 percent.

As mentioned earlier, police are required to make a report on every 911 call. In about 35 percent of the cases, no violence is involved and the report is given to volunteers who make visits to help prevent future problems. The remaining 65 percent of the cases go to prosecutors. The protocol established and the training received by officers in reporting crimes of domestic violence has given prosecutors the means to resolve 95 percent of the cases successfully (conviction or a guilty plea).

The problems are not solved, but a better system has been established to address the issue. Domestic-violence calls recorded by law enforcement agencies across the United States vary widely—not because of regional differences in violence but because of lack of reporting, training, support, and minimal sources for referrals. Joan Kuriansky, Director of the Justice Department's Stop Violence Against Women Grants Technical Assistance Project, states that when training is given, reports go up, and homicides go down. Her project sets up training at the request of state and local agencies. San Diego is one of four national training locations. The planning and cooperation between the police, prosecutors, and the community have succeeded in reformulating an approach to a serious problem and making progress toward achieving safer homes and communities.

Now that you have had a chance to read about a successful planned venture, take some time to reflect on some "what if" scenarios. "What if" a political convention comes to town and 85 percent of the domestic-violence unit is reassigned to security for two weeks? If the trained officers are unable to respond to domestic-violence calls, what will happen? How should management plan for such an occurrence?

Preparation for Role-Playing Cases

The three cases presented later in this chapter require a great deal of preparatory work. In order to participate in scenario role-plays, you must be familiar with the Metro database in the appendix and alternative strategies of policing. Following are the general directions to follow for each of the three cases.

Officials Involved in Oceana, Exurbia and Americus County

Mayor Tara Warfield	Curtis Quick, Ex. City Manager
101 Miles Gorton	Ex. 1 Lyman Tortes
102 Aaron Haenosch	Ex. 2 Loretta Lindquist
103 Lucretia Pope	Ex. 3 Jocko Lightfoot
104 Genevieve Jacobi-Davis	Ex. 4 Jason Probus
105 Meng Tzu Lin	Ex. 5 Errol S. Falconer
106 LaToya Kateshia Jones	
107 Dr. Jacob Steinmeier	Roughneck Hogan, County Adm
108 Sierra Nevada Greenpeace	1a Winston Chesterfield
109 Charlie Marx, Ph.D.	1b Schmooze Rosengarten
110 Lorton Simmons	2a Rev. J. Shackelford
111 Pete Cjakowski	2b Hugs Honey
112 Malcolm Brothers Santoro	3a Bobby Cratchett
113 Rosario Magdato Flynn	3b Rooney Toones
114 Lupe Reyes	4a Jimmy Jimenez
115 Sandor Lucas	4b Miles Atwood
116 Jody Harris	5a Dozer Jackson
117 Bull Dog Bodine	5b Bull Mix
	6a Limey Groves
Oceana Chief Mike Duro	6b Picker Pizarro
Exurbia Chief Jack Tracy	7a Toby Maddox
Sheriff Randall Scott	7b Joe Canoe-To-Catch-Rice
Jail Adm. Sam the Slamm	8a Roscoe Beach
Paul Plumber, State CJ Agency	8b Gen. Tran Van Dong

Planning Commission Directions

1. Read the strategic policy case study, its mission and data.
2. Read the pertinent sections of the Oceana/Exurbia/Americus County database. These include, at minimum, the police and sheriff's departments data plus the profiles of government officials.

- Examine demographic breakdowns of city, town, and county, crime analysis and calls-for-service levels of the city, town, and county. Areas to be patrolled, population densities and numbers of residences are important characteristics of city and county locales.
- Give particular attention to Ward 112 and the surrounding wards to become familiar with crime and service demands in those areas.
- Study the groups of city council members and county commissioners who have joined forces to advocate certain modes of law enforcement—which they may only dimly understand.

3. Examine the *roles* (descriptions follow "Rules of Engagement") which will be represented in the cases. Although the voting power of each role is listed, it can be challenged and modified in plenary sessions. Invest yourself in your role according to the vizualization you have constructed for council members. You may assume the identity of a single member of the role as best representing the entire membership. This allows you to refer to other members and their differences of judgment about the issues that arise.
4. *Remember*—you are an *advocate* of your position and do *not* necessarily speak *reasonably* about the issues. Try to be a consensus-builder, but:
   - Represent *your* assigned role.
   - Ask the questions from *the council member's* point of view.
   - Define the issues from *the council member's* point of view.
   - Be civil, but not necessarily nice.

Rules of Engagement

1. At the outset, each role may assume the members listed in its group will vote as a unit. *However*, as the situation unfolds you may split the votes of your role as appropriate to each of its members.
2. *Plenary Sessions:* Discussions of the case problems at which all roles are represented.
3. *Caucuses:* Any role may ask to caucus (have private discussion) with one or more other roles during plenary sessions.
4. *Recess:* Any role may ask for a recess during any plenary session. The commission chair (instructor) will decide whether requests for recesses are reasonable or excessive.
5. *Rule of Order:* Issues of procedure or weight of evidence will

be decided by the commission chair.

6. Amendments to the definitions of program elements can be presented by any role.

Initial Beliefs and Positions of Factions for Case 1

ROLE 1—COMMUNITY-ORIENTED POLICING

BASIC POSITIONS:

1. Mayor Warfield wants COP and so do we. COP is state-of-the-art policing, and the city should have it, being prosperous and modern.
2. This new chief of police should be willing to modernize the department and follow the mayor's cutting-edge policies.
3. Putting all the officers on routine patrol is wasteful, and it isolates them from the public. Put most of them on foot patrol or in neighborhood mini-stations or something.
4. All of the current theory about COP is our platform. We're talking *neighborhood problem management*, here, for the long haul.

ROLE 2—RAPID RESPONSE CALLS-FOR-SERVICE PATROL

BASIC POSITIONS:

1. Preventive patrol and rapid response are the only police policies that have stood the test of time. Anything else is an experiment with the safety of citizens and their property.
2. There is no agreement about what COP really is. It seems to be different everywhere they claim to have adopted it.
3. COP only reduces *fear of crime*, not crime itself. Even its advocates admit that. We need to reduce crime, not just fear.
4. We need *every* available car on preventive patrol, so that we deter crime and have enough cars available for the most immediate response to calls for service from residents, business and industry. We know this works.

ROLE 3—CRIME SUPPRESSION BY SPLIT FORCE PATROL

BASIC POSITIONS:

1. For *crime suppression*, have only enough cars on routine patrol to handle the calls. Assign the rest to beef up the tactical patrol force and deploy it in and around the 112th ward, to contain the crime problem in that "war zone." Keep crime from spreading outward to the city's and county's "good" neighborhoods.
2. Roughneck Hogan says, "The city needs to quit those welfare

calls: carryin' people to the hospital, and all that. Let private charities do that stuff; it's not police work."

3. Bull Mix says, "As for COP, it's only an illusion of more police protection. Hell, even those fellas at Harvard say it doesn't actually reduce crime, only fear of crime. Like putting folks out in the bull pasture and telling 'em not to worry. Ordinarily I stay out of the city's business, but when they talk about putting their officers out just to walk around and jawbone, it looks to me like an invitation for the troublemakers in the center of town to get out of their corral."
4. Council member Lucas strongly opposes vertical patrol or any other expansion of police service in Ward 112. He states, "Hi-Lo residents themselves are the problem. The only added police in the 112th and its immediate vicinity should be a big truancy squad that rounds up the young hoodlums and gives them a choice of school or jail. They talk about a 'thin blue line.' Dammit, let's put a *thick* blue line around those people."

ROLE 4—VERTICAL PATROL FOR HI-LO

BASIC POSITIONS:

1. We have 122,400 people in the Hi-Lo housing project, packed into one-third of a square mile. That's a density of 360,000 people per square mile, compared to 16,580 per square mile for the rest of the city. Think about that.
2. Once we step inside one of those fifty buildings we leave law and order behind. We have no protection from the predators. Look at the crime analysis reports and you'll see what a jungle the Feds created when they built Hi-Lo.
3. There are 400 apartments in every building. Any other 400 homes in Oceana would get a hundred times—a *thousand* times—the attention from patrols. The only time we see a cop is when there has been a crime inside one of the buildings, and then they get in and out as fast as they can. They act scared to come inside. They could be. *We* are.
4. Newark, New Jersey, has had vertical patrol in its housing projects for a long time, since the 1980s. It's time to give equal protection to people who happen to be poor.
5. We want officers in the corridors, the stairwells, the elevators. We will cooperate by volunteering as corridor watchers, like block watchers in single-family neighborhoods.
6. Also we want *crime alarm buttons* in the corridors, elevators and stairwells so victims can set off a loud bell to call the police to where the crimes are happening.

ROLE 5—PROTECT UNIVERSITY VILLAGE

BASIC POSITIONS:

1. We want a special policing district in what is informally called "University Village." This sprawling district of old homes, museums, quaint boutiques, cinemas and specialty restaurants is clustered around the University campus, Medical Center, Stadium, Arena, the refurbished railroad depot, through part of Wards 109 and 110 into Old Chinatown in Ward 105, to the Zoo in Ward 108, and Parkview Heights, on the boundary of 107–108. This resolution calls for neighborhood-oriented policing and foot patrol, but also a continuation of rapid response to calls for service.
2. Lucretia Pope says, "University Village is Oceana's treasure. If it dies because of fear of crime, the city will die with it and become one huge slum."
3. Councilman Meng Tzu Lin wants foot patrols in Chinatown's restaurant district because of the numerous street robberies and purse snatchings.
4. Sierra Greenpeace says, "Preserve our park."
5. Lorton Simmons says, "I chose to build my computer plant downtown because I believed in Oceana and wanted to keep the jobs here. Protect my hard-working employees, many of whom live in Hi-Lo until they earn their way out of it."
6. We don't really know if COP can help University Village if it spreads scarce police resources all over the city. We don't know if everyone in the city needs an officer to talk with, but we *do know* University Village is in danger and worth spending extra resources to preserve.

ROLE 6—GOAL-ORIENTED LAW ENFORCEMENT

BASIC POSITIONS:

1. There is general agreement that random patrol does not prevent crime. In fact, most authorities believe there is no verified finding that shows *any* single police approach prevents crime.
2. Instead of having nearly a thousand of our officers aimlessly patrolling the city and county streets, and only a few assigned to tactical patrol and investigative duties, let's define our policing goals and set priorities. Answering routine calls for service could be done by about one-third to one-half of the officers now on patrol. The rest could be assigned to *crime control* and *clearance*, and serious *order maintenance* measures. We are certain that new strategies would improve our

index crime clearance rate and reduce both fear of crime, and crime itself.

3. We are *not* saying we know at this moment what to do with the uniformed officers freed from the tyranny of trivial radio dispatches. But Chief Duro has shown us the findings of many successful experiments with concepts such as problem-oriented policing, location-oriented policing, repeat-offender programs, directed patrol, safe walkways, decoys, stings, and team policing.

   These may not be as appealing as that simple COP notion, but we think it will take a combination of goal-oriented strategies to get the job done. The key to all of this is DPR, differential police response—that will let us recover patrol time now spent on trivial calls. Let's not take the simple route to solve a complex problem.

ROLE 7—CORRECTIONS: MORE CELLS OR FEWER INMATES

BASIC POSITIONS:

Jail Adminstrator Samantha Slamm has completed her assessment of jail operations as ordered by Sheriff Scott. Her "urgent priority" problems include the following:

1. Hundreds of sentenced felons, awaiting transfer to the state prison, remain in the Americus County Jail.
2. Recent sweeps by Oceana PD have swelled the jail population with pre-trial arrestees charged with drug street sales and possession, fights, car-stripping, prostitution, vandalism, and a variety of misdemeanors. Many of these arrests result from the city's Campaign Against Fear, a proactive effort by the tactical patrol force to suppress symptoms of disorder.
3. Samantha suggests that summonses be issued in lieu of physical arrest for many of the minor property crimes.
4. It's simple: more cells or fewer misdemeanor prisoners.

ROLE-PLAYING CASE 1: Strategic Planning of City-County Policing

Mayor Tara Warfield returns from the annual meeting of the U.S. Conference of Mayors brimming with enthusiasm for COP—Community-Oriented Policing. A speaker from PERF and a panel of mayors lauded COP, which they hailed as a massive re-orientation of law enforcement away from traditional (read "old fashioned"), isolated and abrasive models of policing based on citywide, standardized calls-for-service (CFS) management.

Confronted by an electorate increasingly fragmented due to the diversity of race, ethnicity, language, socioeconomic status and values, Mayor Warfield wants her new chief of police to adopt "modern" policies that will enhance her administration.

She calls in Chief Miguel Duro, who has been on the job only three months. She asks him to establish a task force to plan the city's new approach to policing—COP. She hands him the COP articles from the mayors' conference, eager for his positive reaction.

Somewhat shaken by the mayor's sudden and direct involvement in basic police administration, Chief Duro tells her that he's been assessing the structure and operations of the department with the intention of modernizing it, but that he is more inclined toward problem-oriented policing (POP), or maybe neighborhood-oriented policing (NOP) or location-oriented policing (LOP), in combination with a repeat offender program (ROP) and differential police response to save time and money.

The mayor stares at him in astonishment. "POP? LOP? NOP? It's your little joke, right?" She laughs shortly. "POP, LOP and NOP! Well, Chief, the rest of the country is talking COP." She points to the articles and says, "Look that stuff over, Chief, and let me know what you think. It sounded pretty good to me." She watches him leave, thinking, "Have I made a mistake?" The chief leaves, thinking, "Have I made a mistake?"

The next day Chief Duro calls a meeting of senior staff and appoints a task force to study the results of his three-month assessment of the department's structure and operations. He directs them to consider COP as a primary mechanism for improving the department—*but also POP, NOP, LOP, DPR and ROP*. Within a week of the chief's meeting things start happening:

- *Oceana Tides*, the local daily, headlines a city hall leak about the mayor's COP proposal. A sidebar story details the chief's task force meeting (another leak) about LOP, NOP, DPR and ROP, with a whiff of the mayor-chief disagreement.
- The Hi-Lo Coalition of Residents petitions the mayor to install "vertical patrol" in the housing project. The African-American members of the city council draft a bill to authorize the implementation of vertical patrol. The department has never patrolled inside the housing units.
- The mayor privately chides the chief for expanding his task force beyond COP. The chief tries to describe POP, LOP, NOP, and so on, but the mayor is miffed. COP is all she wants to hear.

- Sheriff Randy Scott gets Americus County into the fray by answering a reporter's question about the COP ruckus in Oceana. "Well, you know, our county is a nice quiet place, and we don't need law enforcement fads. We use methods that have stood the test of time. Our most serious crime occurs because Oceana PD deploys its tactical patrol force in the 104th and 107th wards. That displaces city street crime out to the county's second precinct. We just don't have the resources to put much patrol there. I've asked Chief Duro to pull his TPF out of there, but he hasn't done it. We just hope the TPF will not be deployed farther south, in the 111th, 113th and 115th wards. That would push crime toward Legend Isle and would threaten the state's finest family recreation and tourism draw."
- The Professional Police Officers Union (PPOU) headlines its weekly newsletter with: "COP and Vertical Patrol—Ideas Whose Time Has *Not* Come." The union asserts that COP is "something that nobody knows how to do." Response time to critical calls for service, the newsletter states, would be seriously degraded throughout the city if officers were sent out to "walk and talk," "chin and grin," as they call COP.

The Situation at this Point

The public argument of law enforcement officials and politicians stimulates the emergence of new factions among the local governments. Most members are ill-informed about law enforcement methods, and have a different take on the nature of the problem. The seven factions are: (1) COP, (2) Rapid Response to All Calls For Service, (3) Crime Suppression by Split Force Patrol, (4) Vertical Patrol for Hi-Lo, (5) Protect University Village, (6) Goal-Oriented Law Enforcement, and (7) Corrections: More Cells or Fewer Inmates. Following are the members of these advocacy groups.

Advocacy Groups

COMMUNITY-ORIENTED POLICING		8 VOTES
Mayor Tara Warfield	3a Bobby Cratchett	
101 Miles Gorton	6a Limey Groves	
113 Rosario Magdato Flynn	6b Picker Pizarro	
1b Schmooze Rosengarten	7b Joe Canoe	
RAPID RESPONSE TO ALL CALLS FOR SERVICE		8 VOTES
County Adm. Roughneck Hogan	Sheriff Randall Scott	
2a Rev. Justin Shackelford	7a Toby Maddox	
2b Hugs Honey	Oceana PD Union	
5a Dozer Jackson	Ex1 Lyman Tortes	
CRIME SUPPRESSION BY SPLIT PATROL FORCE		8 VOTES
107 Dr. Jacob Steinmeier	5b Bull Mix	
115 Sandor Lucas	Ex2 Loretta Lindquist	
8a Roscoe Beach	Ex3 Jocko Lightfoot	
8b Gen. Tran Van Dong	Ex4 Jason Probus	
VERTICAL PATROL FOR HI-LO		6 VOTES
Hi-Lo Residents Coalition	106 LaToya Jones	
112 Brothers Santoro	116 Jody Harris	
4b Miles Atwood	4a Jimmy Jimenez	
PROTECT UNIVERSITY VILLAGE		7 VOTES
103 Lucretia Pope	109 Dr. Charlie Marx	
104 Genevieve Jacobi-Davis	110 Lorton Simmons	
105 Meng Tzu Lin	117 Bull Dog Bodine	
108 Sierra Greenpeace		
GOAL-ORIENTED LAW ENFORCEMENT		8 VOTES
Chief of Police Miguel Duro	Ex Chief Jack Tracy	
102 Aaron Haenosch	Ex City Mgr. Curtis Quick	
111 Pete Cjakowski	1a Winston Chesterfield	
114 Lupe Reyes	3b Rooney Toones	
CORRECTIONS: MORE CELLS OR FEWER INMATES		2 VOTES
Sam the Slamm, Americus County Jail Admin.		
Ex5 Councilman Errol Stanley Falconer		
	TOTAL	47 VOTES

A Second Precipitating Incident

The State CJ Planning Commission informs the city and county that it has obtained a $12,200,000 grant from the National Institute of Justice to develop a showcase law enforcement system, possibly in Metropolitan Oceana and Americus County. To qualify for the grant, the city and county must garner the support of the law enforcement community, policy makers and citizens of the metroplex.

The grant will cover the planning and implementation of the policing model, including start-up costs. Whoever qualifies for the grant will be eligible for follow-up grants to cover as much as 50 percent of law enforcement budget increases attributable to the innovations for the initial five years of operation.

State CJ Commission Field Representative Paul Plumber (instructor's role) has been dispatched to convene a meeting of all officials and community representatives named above. This group of people will be referred to as the Planning Commission. The mission of the Planning Commission is to reach a consensus on the new model of law enforcement.

The proposal should include a workable combination of program elements from the list below, recognizing that overlap and conflict among program elements must be minimized (e.g., an effective program that is too expensive to include, or a combination of program elements that draw excessive human resources from a department, or a program that is too abrasive for the citizens of a neighborhood). In order to decide which program elements to include in a program package, first vote on the feasibility of individual programs, then combine programs that had the most votes into packages. At this point, look for inconsistencies and conflicts among program elements.

The following program elements are described in chapter 3. They may be used as described; however, different definitions are possible; in fact, some of these differences provoke arguments among law enforcement professionals. Therefore, alternative descriptions of program elements can be introduced and defended on their merits. The full commission will decide whether an alternative description is acceptable.

Calls for Service Policing (see Traditional Policing)
Career Criminal Program (see Repeat Offender Program)
Community Crime Prevention
Community-Oriented Policing (COP)
Decoy Operations or Victim Substitution Operations
Differential Police Response (DPR)
Directed Patrol
Foot Patrol
Integrated Criminal Apprehension Program (ICAP)
Location-Oriented Patrol (LOP) (see Kansas City: Three Approaches to Criminal Apprehension)
Mini-Stations

Neighborhood-Oriented Policing (NOP)
Neighborhood Watch (see Community Crime Prevention)
Portable Command Stations (see Mini-Stations)
Problem Oriented Policing (POP)*
Professional Model of Policing (see Traditional Policing)
Repeat Offender Program (ROP)
Safe Houses (see Community Crime Prevention)
Safe Walkways (see Kansas City Directed Interactive Patrol)
Selective Traffic Enforcement Program (STEP)
Split Force Patrol
Sting Operations
Storefront Stations (see Mini-Stations)
Tactical Patrol Force (TPF)
Team Policing
Traditional Policing
Truancy Squad
Vertical Patrol
Victim Substitution Operations (see Decoy Operations)

Field Representative Paul Plumber is prepared to furnish additional details concerning these elements of law enforcement systems. (Tear out and use Signup Sheet for Advocacy Roles, Program Proposals—Voting Tally, and Program Packages—Voting Tally found at the end of the chapter.)

ROLE-PLAYING CASE 2: Proposal to Build New Housing Project in County

Oceana's 112th District is the most crime-ridden in the metropolitan region. In particular, the Hi-Lo (high-rise, low-cost) housing project, has become one of the most dangerous dwelling places in the nation. It was modeled after the infamous Pruitt-Igoe housing development in St. Louis, Missouri, which was eventually demolished because of its miserable living conditions, including uncontrollable crime.

It is not only a matter of the crime that occurs in the 112th itself. Much of the crime in the surrounding districts is said to be fueled by conditions in the 112th, some of it committed by its residents. University students, sports arena patrons and elderly residents in 109

*Kansas City PD also experimented with "Perpetrator-Oriented Patrol," which is now generally known as Repeat Offender Program; their acronym of that time, POP, now refers to Problem-Oriented Policing.

Dealing in the 112th

attribute most of their crime to tough kids from 112; police officials do not disagree, but seem unable to cope with their complaints. The stadium, railroad depot and city hospital require guards at all doors and parking lots, and warn travelers and patients not to wander beyond the lights and guards. Most of the crime at the medical center, university, arena, the park in 108, commercial districts and adjacent residential neighborhoods in 105, 106, 107, 109, 110, 111, 114 and 115 is believed to be an overflow of the "crime culture" of the 112th.

The U.S. Government owns land in Americus County: parcels in Precincts 2, 3 and 6, and one bridging Precincts 4 and 7. The U.S. Department of Housing and Urban Development (HUD) has announced that the least livable, most dangerous upper floors of the Hi-Lo project will be phased out, and that a "low density" housing project will be built on one or more of the U.S.-owned parcels of land in Americus County. More land may be purchased adjacent to parcels already owned.

It is tentatively planned that 10,000 residents of Hi-Lo will be moved out in the first phase of the new project, and eventually many thousands more.

HUD has announced that free enterprise will be encouraged, that every effort will be made to "privatize" the planning, design, construction and administration of what is already being dubbed the Lo-Lo (low density, low cost) housing project. This announcement has engaged the lively interest of developers, architects, construction firms and financiers. The following factors enter into the situation:

1. The planning will require 1–2 years.
2. Support and opposition positions are already shaping up in the city and county.
3. The news media have seized on the issue of *crime* in the 112th and broadened it to *fear of crime* county-wide. Hi-Lo has become the symbol of crime and danger in the region.
4. News of the proposal has intensified ill will toward Hi-Lo throughout the city and county. Even Hi-Lo's residents are more discontented and impatient because of HUD's projection of improved housing for them. The crisis mood brushes aside the fact that any solution to the Hi-Lo crime problem will take a long time.
5. Citizens and politicians are goading the Oceana PD to get the 112th and city crime under control: "We can't wait for new housing to be built."
6. In the disarray triggered by the HUD announcement and the media's intensification of it, local and state governments are beset by a crisis of confidence. It is not clear which unit of government should tackle which problem first.

In this atmosphere the State Criminal Justice Policy Council has dispatched Paul Plumber, Regional Field Representative, to meet with local government officials and citizens. The mission of this intergovernmental planning commission is to unwind the crisis of confidence, and to develop a prospectus and plan for the long term.

Situation Assessment

Consider the HUD proposal and also the immediate sense of crisis which has been unintentionally provoked by it. As a commission of citizens and governmental leaders, analyze the situation and submit an *assessment report* on the following aspects of the HUD proposal:

a. The socioeconomic implications for the city, county and state, positive and negative.
b. The social/political cooperation and conflict likely to emerge among city and county residents, groups and governments.
c. Political positions and coalitions which will emerge and harden among the government officials of the city, county and state. Also identify coalitions among constituent groups and special interest groups.
d. Implications for criminal justice in the city, the county and the state.
e. Alternatives to the HUD proposal.

For each of these, list your assessment points *briefly* in outline fashion. Cover in greater detail those likely to affect criminal justice policies, operations and resources.

As you discuss implications for criminal justice, be specific and detailed about foreseeable changes in service demands, anticipated and desired change in the workforce makeup, effects on philosophy of criminal justice, consequences for citizens, strains on resources and altered applications of resources. Remember the initial guidelines.

Try to be a consensus-builder, but:

- Represent your *assigned* role in the crisis.
- Ask the questions from *the council member's* point of view.
- Define the issues from *the council member's* point of view.
- Be civil, but not necessarily nice.

The *assessment report* should include a *dissent report* which contains unresolvable differences in situation assessment and identifies the proponents of dissenting assessments.

Strategic Policy Planning

Formulate and state a policy position for the city, county and state criminal justice agencies concerning the proposed HUD housing development and the immediate effects of its announcement:

a. *A short-term plan of action* for the next 1–6 months to deal with actual crime, the fear of crime and the crisis of confidence regarding the city and county governments' ability to contain crime.
   - Oceana Police Department's role
   - Exurbia Police Department's role
   - Americus County Sheriff's Department role

b. *A long-term strategic plan* for providing the criminal justice needs of both Hi-Lo and Lo-Lo and their surrounding environments.
   - Oceana Police Department's role
   - Exurbia Police Department's role
   - Americus County Sheriff's Department role

Roles

1. Mayor Tara Warfield, and moderate city council members:

   101 Miles Gorton, refinery manager
   103 Lucretia Pope, president of major brewery
   105 Meng Tzu Lin, president, Asian Merchants Association
   110 Lorton Simmons, computer executive in core of city
   117 B. D. Bodine, Airline Pilots' Association president

2. Conservative city council members:

   102 Aaron Haenosch, property owners' advocate
   107 Dr. Jacob Steinmeier, medical equipment manufacturer
   111 Pete Cjakowski, country-western singer
   115 Sandor Lukas, blue collar, hard-hat welder

3. Liberal city council members:

   104 Genevieve Jacobi-Davis, teachers' union president
   106 LaToya Kateshia Jones, attorney of underdogs
   108 Sierra Nevada Greenpeace, environmentalist
   109 Charlie Marx, Ph.D., radical sociologist
   113 Rosario Magdato Flynn, "melting-pot militant"
   114 Lupe Reyes, realtor, LULAC support base

4. Hi-Lo coalition of residents, multi-ethnic association of one representative for each apartment unit. Executive committee of four, representing major ethnic/racial resident groups:

Non-Hispanic Whites (23 percent)
Non-Hispanic Blacks (47 percent)
Hispanics (27 percent)
Other (3 percent)

5. African-American city council members:

   112 Malcolm "Brothers" Santoro, Black Hispanic
   116 Jody Harris, "Southside Attitude Man"

6. County Administrator Roughneck Hogan and conservative commissioners:

   1a Winston Chesterfield, land developer, mall builder
   2a Reverend Justin Shackelford, survivalist preacher
   3a Bobby Cratchett, working class residents' representative
   3b Rooney Toones, VP, Oceana Legend Isle, *big* employer
   5a Jack "Dozer" Jackson, owns major construction firm
   5b Thomas Bull Mix, rancher
   6a Limerick "Limey" Groves, citrus heiress, growers' representative
   7a Toby Maddox, south county industry representative
   8a Roscoe Beach, old family shrimper

7. Liberal county commissioners:

   1b Schmuel "Schmooze" Rosengarten, northern retirees' representative
   2b Sheila "Hugs" Honey, PR firm (Love Island is a client)
   4a Carlos Jimmy Jimenez, Latino activist, Vietnam veteran
   4b Miles Atwood, civil rights/labor leader
   6b Ernesto "Picker" Pizarro, migrant worker activist
   7b Joe Canoe-to-Catch-Rice, Native American activist
   8b Tran Van Dong, former general, fishing fleet, business

8. Town Manager Curtis Quick and liberal/moderate town council members:

   Ex 2 Loretta Lindquist
   Ex 3 Jocko Lightfoot
   Ex 5 Errol S. Falconer

9. Conservative town council members:

   Ex 1 Lyman Tortes
   Ex 4 Jason Probus

10. Criminal Justice System:

    Oceana Police Chief Miguel Duro
    Exurbia Police Chief Jack Tracy
    Americus County Sheriff Randall Scott
    Jail Administrator Samantha Slamm

11. Regional Field Representative, Paul Plumber, State CJ Policy Council (Moderator of Commission: Instructor's role)

(Tear out and use Sign-up Sheet for Role Asignments, found at the end of the chapter.)

Role-Playing Case 3: Budget Negotiation for City Departments, Pressure Groups

Premise: The Council of Governments has received federal funds in the amount of $8,420,000. These funds can be used for any local government program which enhances the *quality of life*. However, they may not be used to support ongoing governmental programs ordinarily supported by local revenues.

Directive: Each metropolitan government agency is hereby directed to submit a proposal for the use of these funds. The managers of the operating agencies are further directed to give consideration to social issues which are expressed in the community and related to the missions of the agencies they administer.

Any part of the funding may be requested, from approximately $500,000 to the full amount available.

All proposals will be presented to a public joint session of the city council and the mayor's office. The mayor will first evaluate the proposals and forward her evaluations, with a rank-ordering of decision packages, to city council. City council will allocate the funds after open debate and testimony from all interested parties.

Criteria for Evaluating Proposals:

a. Intrinsic potential of the program for improving the quality of life in the metropolitan community.
b. Clarity of the *definition* of the problem and the intended outcomes of the proposal.
c. Reasonableness of the *quantification* of the problem and the expected outcomes of the proposal.
d. Cost-benefit analysis of the proposed program, and a funding request in a systems budgeting format.
e. Criteria and method of evaluating program outcomes.

The mayor, following the public hearings, will retire to prepare her recommendations for funding to the city council. The mayor will present her recommendations, in the form of an executive budget document in systems budget format (described in chapter 2), to the city council.

The city council will then retire to prepare its legislative bill for project funding. This bill will be presented in the public forum.

All roles are free to interact and are encouraged to consider the interests of competing city government units. There is no prohibition against joint proposals.

MADD, DADD, and the Hi-Lo Coalition are free to lobby government units to incorporate their interests in public policies and programs. (Tear out and use Signup Sheet for Role Assignments found at the end of the chapter.)

Each team will present its proposal, complete with budget, to the mayor, with the city council and all other teams observing. The mayor will then decide on an executive budget, containing the decision packages which most impressed her. The mayor's executive budget will be presented to the entire class and then submitted to the city council, which will assemble and pass a legislative budget. The entire class will then evaluate and rate the performances of all role-teams on forms provided. (Tear out and use Systems Budget Request and Criteria for Evaluating Budget Requests found at the end of the chapter.)

Note: The systems budget request form merely presents the elements of a systems budget request, but is not big enough to accommodate all of the information you will need to include in the request. Use the format to prepare your own budget request. Include at least five levels of inputs, costs, and expected impacts. These five levels should not merely contain more and less of the same program inputs, but combinations of approaches. For instance, level +1 for community crime prevention might include business-premise surveys and convenience-store videos, while level +2 would add high-intensity lighting, with its greater cost and expected benefits.

Additional Exercises for Individuals or Task Forces

1. Compute the costs of responding to:
   minor auto accidents
   disturbances
   shoplifting complaints
   traffic-related problems
   abandoned auto complaints
   Compare these costs with those of responding to:
   major accidents
   family violence
   cuttings
   holdup alarms
   rapes
   prowlers
   robberies
   shootings

2. Retrenchment management by resource recovery and redirection:
   Estimate how many calls for service can be eliminated in certain categories.
   Estimate the resource recovery by this reduction.
   Plan the reallocation of resources by purpose.
3. Discuss and contrast the police department's and community's reactions to the following:
   Traditional emphasis on calls for service policing
   COP
   LOP
   DPR
   Vertical patrol
   Foot patrol
   Retrenchment measures (traditional service cutbacks)
   Truancy squad
   Repeat offender surveillance
   Decoy unit
   Sweeps
   Aggressive patrols, stop/interview
   Tactical patrol force: location-oriented
   DWI roadblocks
   Undercover officers in workplace for vice detection
   Case screening, shelving low solvability cases
4. Each of the following has been suggested for implementation by the Oceana PD, Exurbia PD, or Americus County SD. For each program do the following:

   Determine, as far as you are able, the *goal* of the program.
   Evaluate the proposal in terms of:
   - Merton's Ignorance, Error, Habit, Obsessions, and
   - Barnard's prerequisites for authoritative orders

   State what information you would want before developing such a program.
   a. The departments now use written tests based on a set of books to rank-order sworn personnel for promotion at each rank. *Proposal:* Replace this system with an assessment center approach (see chapter 3).
   b. The departments now issue summonses only for traffic cases. *Proposal:* Issue the summons in lieu of arrest for the greatest possible variety of offenses listed for the city, town and county.

c. *Proposal:* Greatly reduce the departments' reliance on radar as a primary means of traffic enforcement and substitute a STEP in place of it.

5. Your task force is charged with converting the field operations bureau of Oceana PD into an MBO-oriented set of goal-directed components. Define the goals (they should be clearly measurable, separable objectives), estimate the service demand level, allocate resources (manpower, budget) to each goal. An example (not necessarily the best) would be: crime control, order maintenance, service delivery.
6. Your task force is assigned to determine the human resource needs of the Americus County Sheriff's Department. The previous sheriff, in office for 28 years, had neglected to analyze the department's workload demands in relation to resources. By the time he lost an election, the department's personnel had given up trying to keep pace with the demands for field services, crime control, or criminal investigation, and had no hope of modernizing the old-fashioned support systems. The new sheriff wants a complete staffing plan based on measurable work demand levels.
7. A task force is recommending team policing operations by geographic sectors in Oceana. The chief of detectives is resisting it, along with some of the field operations command. Develop a team policing layout for Oceana and a scenario for the move to team policing operations with some continuation of specialized investigative services from the bureau of investigation.
8. Develop a job enrichment program which will encourage street police officers and investigators to remain in their assignments rather than seeking supervisory and managerial promotions. Estimate costs and effects.
9. Prepare a plan to institute tele-serve. Measure its costs, savings and other impacts on operations. Detail potential problems in its installation and operation.
10. Prepare a job rotation system for personnel development toward top management. Cover assignments, purposes of them, periods of rotation, and ways of selecting candidates for job rotation.
11. Examine the index crime clearance rates and select a category of crime for which you believe the clearance rate can be improved by a specific measure. You may, on the basis of the crime analysis bulletin, decide on a citywide approach, or select just one or several areas of the city or county on which to focus your apprehension effort. The productivity of the measure(s) should be estimated for each offense and area in which it is deployed.

12. Devise a scheme for CFS prioritization in the communications center of Oceana PD, for its installation in field operations and its acceptance by officers and the community (see DPR, chapter 3).
13. "Civilianize" those functions of the Americus County SD which merit this treatment. Restructure the human resource requirements of the agency. Estimate both recovered costs and additional costs, including potential side effects in the department and the community.
14. Design a pilot-test of NOP, POP or LOP operation in one high-density, high-crime area of the city. Select site, estimate needs (problem assessment), target problems, estimate resources required, estimate impact on (1) problems targeted, (2) existing operations of the department, (3) budget, if new resources are needed.
15. Aside from drug and alcohol cases, physical evidence is being submitted for only about 12 percent of all other offenses. Your task force has been presented with research findings that show: (1) proximity of a forensic lab is the highest correlate of greater utilization of physical evidence, and (2) attitude of police executives, reflected in policy, is the operant variable in greater use of physical evidence. At present, all evidence is being sent to the state laboratory. With these findings in mind:

    Develop a case for/against (1) an Oceana Police Department lab, (2) an Americus County Sheriff's Department lab, or (3) a Metropolitan lab.
    Cost out re-allocations from present resources and additional budgetary requirements.
16. Analyze the costs and benefits of utilizing retired professionals as volunteer specialists as:

    Crime analysts
    Evidence technicians
    Mental health and family crisis responders
    Home security assessors, advisors
    Victim assistance service providers
    Other functions
17. Oceana tactical patrol operations in tracts 104, 111 and 114 are displacing street crime into adjoining Americus County neighborhoods. ACSD does not have the resources to counter this Oceana crime control measure. Prepare a policy to cope with this problem on a short-term basis.
18. Crime analysis in Oceana is pretty well developed, but it is now apparent there are gaps in its database because Americus County is not maintaining any kind of crime data. Major problem: ACSD

is using incident report forms which do not capture enough information to support crime analysis. Set out the requirements for ACSD to initiate a crime analysis program in order to coordinate with OPD.

19. Years ago the Oceana PD had a detail which patrolled for homosexuals in public restrooms around the city. During the sixties, this unit was disbanded and the policy became one of treating the sexual behavior of consenting adults with "benign neglect." Recently complaints about homosexual conduct and propositions in public restrooms have increased. Formulate a departmental policy response.
20. Devise a policy for the purpose of appropriately utilizing college-educated officers in either Oceana PD or Americus County SD.
21. Examine the desirability and feasibility of including citizens in police policy development. How might this be done?
22. Devise a long-term plan to involve supervisors, managers and executives in the training of their immediate subordinate levels to strengthen the climate of authority in the agency (see Barnard in chapter 2).
23. Prepare a phased plan for closely integrating the work of field operations and the bureau of investigations.
24. There is a public clamor for foot patrol in Oceana, and a city council resolution favoring it, because of recent publicity about its use in Boston, Newark, Flint, and other cities. Chief Mike Duro has assigned your task force to devise a demonstration program in "the most feasible impact area" of the city. Please do so, estimating costs, effects and impacts on other units and functions.
25. Plan a way of evaluating the various case-screening models against each other, and with the traditional case-selection methods of detectives. Specify your criteria, types of offenses to be screened, and the scales you would apply to the cases.
26. *Resource allocation by function.* Restructure the Oceana PD field operations bureau and decide how many sworn personnel are to be:

    Retained on radio-dispatched CFS patrol
    Assigned to crime interdiction, which may include:
        Foot patrol
        ROP, LOP, POP
        Any other strategic or tactical operations (see appendix)

27. *Costing tele-serve vs. dispatched patrol reports*

First, estimate the number of calls in each code which might be handled by taking reports over the telephone. Assume there are limited duty police officers available for the "tele-serve" operation.

Second, compute the approximate cost of answering those calls with one-officer patrol responses.

Third, estimate the number of hours required to write tele-serve reports for the total calls diverted from patrol response.

Fourth, estimate the cost of taking these calls in each code by telephone, and the total cost of taking all tele-serve reports.

Fifth, determine the difference in cost between taking these calls by mobile patrol response and by tele-serve.

Voting Summary—Oceana

(Use this tear-out sheet for Exercise 12)

Official	Team 1		Team 2		Team 3		Team 4		Team 5	
Task Force	Y	N	Y	N	Y	N	Y	N	Y	N
Chief Duro	Y	N	Y	N	Y	N	Y	N	Y	N
Mayor Warfield	Y	N	Y	N	Y	N	Y	N	Y	N
101 Gorton	Y	N	Y	N	Y	N	Y	N	Y	N
102 Haenosch	Y	N	Y	N	Y	N	Y	N	Y	N
103 Pope	Y	N	Y	N	Y	N	Y	N	Y	N
104 Jacobi-Davis	Y	N	Y	N	Y	N	Y	N	Y	N
105 Lin	Y	N	Y	N	Y	N	Y	N	Y	N
106 Jones	Y	N	Y	N	Y	N	Y	N	Y	N
107 Steinmeier	Y	N	Y	N	Y	N	Y	N	Y	N
108 Greenpeace	Y	N	Y	N	Y	N	Y	N	Y	N
109 Marx	Y	N	Y	N	Y	N	Y	N	Y	N
110 Simmons	Y	N	Y	N	Y	N	Y	N	Y	N
111 Cjakowski	Y	N	Y	N	Y	N	Y	N	Y	N
112 Santoro	Y	N	Y	N	Y	N	Y	N	Y	N
113 Flynn	Y	N	Y	N	Y	N	Y	N	Y	N
114 Reyes	Y	N	Y	N	Y	N	Y	N	Y	N
115 Lucas	Y	N	Y	N	Y	N	Y	N	Y	N
116 Harris	Y	N	Y	N	Y	N	Y	N	Y	N
117 Bodine	Y	N	Y	N	Y	N	Y	N	Y	N
COUNCIL TOTALS										

Voting Summary—Town of Exurbia

(Use this tear-out sheet for Exercise 12)

Official	Team 1		Team 2		Team 3		Team 4		Team 5	
Task Force	Y	N	Y	N	Y	N	Y	N	Y	N
Chief Tracy	Y	N	Y	N	Y	N	Y	N	Y	N
City Manager Quick	Y	N	Y	N	Y	N	Y	N	Y	N
1 Tortes	Y	N	Y	N	Y	N	Y	N	Y	N
2 Lindquist	Y	N	Y	N	Y	N	Y	N	Y	N
3 Lightfoot	Y	N	Y	N	Y	N	Y	N	Y	N
4 Probus	Y	N	Y	N	Y	N	Y	N	Y	N
5 Falconer	Y	N	Y	N	Y	N	Y	N	Y	N
COUNCIL TOTALS										

Voting Summary—Americus County

(Use this tear-out sheet for Exercise 12)

Official	Team 1		Team 2		Team 3		Team 4		Team 5	
Task Force	Y	N	Y	N	Y	N	Y	N	Y	N
Sheriff Scott	Y	N	Y	N	Y	N	Y	N	Y	N
County Admin. Hogan	Y	N	Y	N	Y	N	Y	N	Y	N
1a Chesterfield	Y	N	Y	N	Y	N	Y	N	Y	N
1b Rosengarten	Y	N	Y	N	Y	N	Y	N	Y	N
2a Shackelford	Y	N	Y	N	Y	N	Y	N	Y	N
2b Honey	Y	N	Y	N	Y	N	Y	N	Y	N
3a Cratchett	Y	N	Y	N	Y	N	Y	N	Y	N
3b Toones	Y	N	Y	N	Y	N	Y	N	Y	N
4a Jimenez	Y	N	Y	N	Y	N	Y	N	Y	N
4b Atwood	Y	N	Y	N	Y	N	Y	N	Y	N
5a Jackson	Y	N	Y	N	Y	N	Y	N	Y	N
5b Mix	Y	N	Y	N	Y	N	Y	N	Y	N
6a Groves	Y	N	Y	N	Y	N	Y	N	Y	N
6b Pizarro	Y	N	Y	N	Y	N	Y	N	Y	N
7a Maddox	Y	N	Y	N	Y	N	Y	N	Y	N
7b Canoe	Y	N	Y	N	Y	N	Y	N	Y	N
8a Beach	Y	N	Y	N	Y	N	Y	N	Y	N
8b Van Dong	Y	N	Y	N	Y	N	Y	N	Y	N
COMMISSION TOTALS										

Voting Summary—Oceana

(Use this tear-out sheet for Exercise 13)

Official	Team 1		Team 2		Team 3		Team 4		Team 5	
Task Force	Y	N	Y	N	Y	N	Y	N	Y	N
Chief	Y	N	Y	N	Y	N	Y	N	Y	N
Mayor	Y	N	Y	N	Y	N	Y	N	Y	N
101 Gorton	Y	N	Y	N	Y	N	Y	N	Y	N
102 Haenosch	Y	N	Y	N	Y	N	Y	N	Y	N
103 Pope	Y	N	Y	N	Y	N	Y	N	Y	N
104 Jacobi-Davis	Y	N	Y	N	Y	N	Y	N	Y	N
105 Lin	Y	N	Y	N	Y	N	Y	N	Y	N
106 Jones	Y	N	Y	N	Y	N	Y	N	Y	N
107 Steinmeier	Y	N	Y	N	Y	N	Y	N	Y	N
108 Greenpeace	Y	N	Y	N	Y	N	Y	N	Y	N
109 Marx	Y	N	Y	N	Y	N	Y	N	Y	N
110 Simmons	Y	N	Y	N	Y	N	Y	N	Y	N
111 Cjakowski	Y	N	Y	N	Y	N	Y	N	Y	N
112 Santoro	Y	N	Y	N	Y	N	Y	N	Y	N
113 Flynn	Y	N	Y	N	Y	N	Y	N	Y	N
114 Reyes	Y	N	Y	N	Y	N	Y	N	Y	N
115 Lucas	Y	N	Y	N	Y	N	Y	N	Y	N
116 Harris	Y	N	Y	N	Y	N	Y	N	Y	N
117 Bodine	Y	N	Y	N	Y	N	Y	N	Y	N
COUNCIL TOTALS										

Voting Summary—Town of Exurbia

(Use this tear-out sheet for Exercise 13)

Official	Team 1		Team 2		Team 3		Team 4		Team 5	
Task Force	Y	N	Y	N	Y	N	Y	N	Y	N
Chief Tracy	Y	N	Y	N	Y	N	Y	N	Y	N
City Manager Quick	Y	N	Y	N	Y	N	Y	N	Y	N
1 Tortes	Y	N	Y	N	Y	N	Y	N	Y	N
2 Lindquist	Y	N	Y	N	Y	N	Y	N	Y	N
3 Lightfoot	Y	N	Y	N	Y	N	Y	N	Y	N
4 Probus	Y	N	Y	N	Y	N	Y	N	Y	N
5 Falconer	Y	N	Y	N	Y	N	Y	N	Y	N
COUNCIL TOTALS										

Voting Summary—Americus County

(Use this tear-out sheet for Exercise 13)

Official	Team 1		Team 2		Team 3		Team 4		Team 5	
Task Force	Y	N	Y	N	Y	N	Y	N	Y	N
Sheriff Scott	Y	N	Y	N	Y	N	Y	N	Y	N
County Admin. Hogan	Y	N	Y	N	Y	N	Y	N	Y	N
1a Chesterfield	Y	N	Y	N	Y	N	Y	N	Y	N
1b Rosengarten	Y	N	Y	N	Y	N	Y	N	Y	N
2a Shackelford	Y	N	Y	N	Y	N	Y	N	Y	N
2b Honey	Y	N	Y	N	Y	N	Y	N	Y	N
3a Cratchett	Y	N	Y	N	Y	N	Y	N	Y	N
3b Toones	Y	N	Y	N	Y	N	Y	N	Y	N
4a Jimenez	Y	N	Y	N	Y	N	Y	N	Y	N
4b Atwood	Y	N	Y	N	Y	N	Y	N	Y	N
5a Jackson	Y	N	Y	N	Y	N	Y	N	Y	N
5b Mix	Y	N	Y	N	Y	N	Y	N	Y	N
6a Groves	Y	N	Y	N	Y	N	Y	N	Y	N
6b Pizarro	Y	N	Y	N	Y	N	Y	N	Y	N
7a Maddox	Y	N	Y	N	Y	N	Y	N	Y	N
7b Canoe	Y	N	Y	N	Y	N	Y	N	Y	N
8a Beach	Y	N	Y	N	Y	N	Y	N	Y	N
8b Van Dong	Y	N	Y	N	Y	N	Y	N	Y	N
COMMISSION TOTALS										

Voting Summary—Oceana

(Use this tear-out sheet for Exercise 14)

Official	Team 1		Team 2		Team 3		Team 4		Team 5	
Task Force	Y	N	Y	N	Y	N	Y	N	Y	N
Chief	Y	N	Y	N	Y	N	Y	N	Y	N
Mayor	Y	N	Y	N	Y	N	Y	N	Y	N
101 Gorton	Y	N	Y	N	Y	N	Y	N	Y	N
102 Haenosch	Y	N	Y	N	Y	N	Y	N	Y	N
103 Pope	Y	N	Y	N	Y	N	Y	N	Y	N
104 Jacobi-Davis	Y	N	Y	N	Y	N	Y	N	Y	N
105 Lin	Y	N	Y	N	Y	N	Y	N	Y	N
106 Jones	Y	N	Y	N	Y	N	Y	N	Y	N
107 Steinmeier	Y	N	Y	N	Y	N	Y	N	Y	N
108 Greenpeace	Y	N	Y	N	Y	N	Y	N	Y	N
109 Marx	Y	N	Y	N	Y	N	Y	N	Y	N
110 Simmons	Y	N	Y	N	Y	N	Y	N	Y	N
111 Cjakowski	Y	N	Y	N	Y	N	Y	N	Y	N
112 Santoro	Y	N	Y	N	Y	N	Y	N	Y	N
113 Flynn	Y	N	Y	N	Y	N	Y	N	Y	N
114 Reyes	Y	N	Y	N	Y	N	Y	N	Y	N
115 Lucas	Y	N	Y	N	Y	N	Y	N	Y	N
116 Harris	Y	N	Y	N	Y	N	Y	N	Y	N
117 Bodine	Y	N	Y	N	Y	N	Y	N	Y	N
COUNCIL TOTALS										

Voting Summary—Oceana

(Use this tear-out sheet for Exercise 15)

Official	Team 1		Team 2		Team 3		Team 4		Team 5	
Task Force	Y	N	Y	N	Y	N	Y	N	Y	N
Chief	Y	N	Y	N	Y	N	Y	N	Y	N
Mayor	Y	N	Y	N	Y	N	Y	N	Y	N
101 Gorton	Y	N	Y	N	Y	N	Y	N	Y	N
102 Haenosch	Y	N	Y	N	Y	N	Y	N	Y	N
103 Pope	Y	N	Y	N	Y	N	Y	N	Y	N
104 Jacobi-Davis	Y	N	Y	N	Y	N	Y	N	Y	N
105 Lin	Y	N	Y	N	Y	N	Y	N	Y	N
106 Jones	Y	N	Y	N	Y	N	Y	N	Y	N
107 Steinmeier	Y	N	Y	N	Y	N	Y	N	Y	N
108 Greenpeace	Y	N	Y	N	Y	N	Y	N	Y	N
109 Marx	Y	N	Y	N	Y	N	Y	N	Y	N
110 Simmons	Y	N	Y	N	Y	N	Y	N	Y	N
111 Cjakowski	Y	N	Y	N	Y	N	Y	N	Y	N
112 Santoro	Y	N	Y	N	Y	N	Y	N	Y	N
113 Flynn	Y	N	Y	N	Y	N	Y	N	Y	N
114 Reyes	Y	N	Y	N	Y	N	Y	N	Y	N
115 Lucas	Y	N	Y	N	Y	N	Y	N	Y	N
116 Harris	Y	N	Y	N	Y	N	Y	N	Y	N
117 Bodine	Y	N	Y	N	Y	N	Y	N	Y	N
COUNCIL TOTALS										

Voting Summary—Oceana

(Use this tear-out sheet for Exercise 16)

Official	Team 1		Team 2		Team 3		Team 4		Team 5	
Task Force	Y	N	Y	N	Y	N	Y	N	Y	N
Chief	Y	N	Y	N	Y	N	Y	N	Y	N
Mayor	Y	N	Y	N	Y	N	Y	N	Y	N
101 Gorton	Y	N	Y	N	Y	N	Y	N	Y	N
102 Haenosch	Y	N	Y	N	Y	N	Y	N	Y	N
103 Pope	Y	N	Y	N	Y	N	Y	N	Y	N
104 Jacobi-Davis	Y	N	Y	N	Y	N	Y	N	Y	N
105 Lin	Y	N	Y	N	Y	N	Y	N	Y	N
106 Jones	Y	N	Y	N	Y	N	Y	N	Y	N
107 Steinmeier	Y	N	Y	N	Y	N	Y	N	Y	N
108 Greenpeace	Y	N	Y	N	Y	N	Y	N	Y	N
109 Marx	Y	N	Y	N	Y	N	Y	N	Y	N
110 Simmons	Y	N	Y	N	Y	N	Y	N	Y	N
111 Cjakowski	Y	N	Y	N	Y	N	Y	N	Y	N
112 Santoro	Y	N	Y	N	Y	N	Y	N	Y	N
113 Flynn	Y	N	Y	N	Y	N	Y	N	Y	N
114 Reyes	Y	N	Y	N	Y	N	Y	N	Y	N
115 Lucas	Y	N	Y	N	Y	N	Y	N	Y	N
116 Harris	Y	N	Y	N	Y	N	Y	N	Y	N
117 Bodine	Y	N	Y	N	Y	N	Y	N	Y	N
COUNCIL TOTALS										

Voting Summary—Town of Exurbia

(Use this tear-out sheet for Exercise 16)

Official	Team 1		Team 2		Team 3		Team 4		Team 5	
Task Force	Y	N	Y	N	Y	N	Y	N	Y	N
Chief Tracy	Y	N	Y	N	Y	N	Y	N	Y	N
City Manager Quick	Y	N	Y	N	Y	N	Y	N	Y	N
1 Tortes	Y	N	Y	N	Y	N	Y	N	Y	N
2 Lindquist	Y	N	Y	N	Y	N	Y	N	Y	N
3 Lightfoot	Y	N	Y	N	Y	N	Y	N	Y	N
4 Probus	Y	N	Y	N	Y	N	Y	N	Y	N
5 Falconer	Y	N	Y	N	Y	N	Y	N	Y	N
COUNCIL TOTALS										

Sign-up Sheet for Advocacy Roles

(Use this tear-out sheet for Role-Playing Case 1)

Indicate your first, second and third preferences.

Community-Oriented Policing		8 Votes
Rapid Response to All Calls for Service		8 Votes
Crime Suppression by Split Patrol Force		8 Votes
Vertical Patrol for Hi-Lo		6 Votes
Protect University Village		7 Votes
Goal-Oriented Law Enforcement		8 Votes
Corrections: More Cells or Fewer Inmates		2 Votes
	Total	47 Votes

Program Proposals—Voting Tally

Strategic Approaches and Concerns

(Use this tear-out sheet for Role-Playing Case 1)

	COP	Rapid Response	Crime Suppress	Vertical Patrol	Protect U-Village	Goal Oriented	Corrections
Role 1: 8 Votes COP	___	___	___	___	___	___	___
Role 2: 8 Votes Rapid Response	___	___	___	___	___	___	___
Role 3: 8 Votes Suppress Crime	___	___	___	___	___	___	___
Role 4: 6 Votes Vertical Patrol for Hi-Lo	___	___	___	___	___	___	___
Role 5: 7 Votes Protect University Village	___	___	___	___	___	___	___
Role 6: 8 Votes Goal-Oriented Law Enforcement	___	___	___	___	___	___	___
Role 7: 2 Votes Corrections	___	___	___	___	___	___	___
Totals (47)	___	___	___	___	___	___	___

Program Packages—Voting Tally

(Use this tear-out sheet for Role-Playing Case 1)
To be used when combinations of program elements are considered by commission.

	Package One		Package Two		Package Three	
Elements:	____	____	____	____	____	____
	____	____	____	____	____	____
	____	____	____	____	____	____
	Yes	No	Yes	No	Yes	No
Role 1: 8 Votes COP Advocates	__	__	__	__	__	__
Role 2: 8 Votes Rapid Response	__	__	__	__	__	__
Role 3: 8 Votes Suppress Crime	__	__	__	__	__	__
Role 4: 6 Votes Vertical Patrol for Hi-Lo	__	__	__	__	__	__
Role 5: 7 Votes Protect University Village	__	__	__	__	__	__
Role 6: 8 Votes Goal-Oriented Law Enforcement	__	__	__	__	__	__
Role 7: 2 Votes Corrections	__	__	__	__	__	__
Totals (47)	__	__	__	__	__	__

Sign-up Sheet for Role Assignments

(Use this tear-out sheet for Role-Playing Case 2)

Indicate your first, second and third preferences.

1. Mayor and moderate city council members:
2. Conservative city council members:
3. Liberal city council members:
4. Hi-Lo coalition of residents:
5. Roughneck Hogan and conservative county commissioners:
6. Liberal county commissioners:
7. African-American city council caucus:
8. Town manager and liberal/moderate town council members:
9. Conservative town council members:
10. Criminal justice system:
11. Regional CJ field representative: (Instructor's role)

Sign-up Sheet for Role Assignments

(Use this tear-out sheet for Role-Playing Case 3)

Indicate your first, second and third preferences.

Mayor	________
City Council Liberals	________
City Council Moderates	________
City Council Conservatives	________
Health Department	________
Parks and Recreation Department	________
Americus County Jail	________
Oceana Police Department	________
Hi-Lo Coalition	________
DADD (Dads Against Dangerous Drugs)	________
MADD (Mothers Against Drunk Driving)	________

Systems Budget Request

(Use this tear-out sheet for Role-Playing Case 3)

Title of major departmental unit ______________________

Title of decision unit ______________________

Problem to be targeted ______________________

Service goal of decision unit ______________________

	$Costs	Quantified Inputs of Action Program	Resource Levels Personnel, Equip., Supplies, Contracts	Expected Impacts Quantified Outputs
Level +3				
Level +2				
Level +1				
Level −1				
Level −2				
Level −3				

Note: The ways of increasing (+) and decreasing (−) resource and program levels are discussed in chapter 2.

Criteria for Evaluating Budget Requests

(Use this tear-out sheet for Role-Playing Case 3)

	Intrinsic Potential[1]	Clarity[2]	Reasonableness[3]	Cost-Benefit Analysis[4]
Health Dept.	1 2 3 4 5	1 2 3 4 5	1 2 3 4 5	1 2 3 4 5
Parks & Rec.	1 2 3 4 5	1 2 3 4 5	1 2 3 4 5	1 2 3 4 5
County Jail	1 2 3 4 5	1 2 3 4 5	1 2 3 4 5	1 2 3 4 5
Oceana PD	1 2 3 4 5	1 2 3 4 5	1 2 3 4 5	1 2 3 4 5
Hi-Lo Coalition	1 2 3 4 5	1 2 3 4 5	1 2 3 4 5	1 2 3 4 5
DADD	1 2 3 4 5	1 2 3 4 5	1 2 3 4 5	1 2 3 4 5
MADD	1 2 3 4 5	1 2 3 4 5	1 2 3 4 5	1 2 3 4 5

1 = poor 3 = average 5 = excellent

[1] Intrinsic potential of the program for improving quality of life in the city

[2] Clarity of definition of problem and intended impacts of the program

[3] Reasonableness of the quantification of the problem and expected impacts of the program

[4] Cost-benefit analysis of the proposed program and proposed funding level

Peer Ratings of Budget Negotiation Scenario Performance

(Use this tear-out sheet for Role-Playing Case 3)

		Fair			Good			Excellent		
Mayor	1	2	3	4	5	6	7	8	9	10
Council Liberals	1	2	3	4	5	6	7	8	9	10
Council Moderates	1	2	3	4	5	6	7	8	9	10
Council Conservatives	1	2	3	4	5	6	7	8	9	10
Health Department	1	2	3	4	5	6	7	8	9	10
Parks & Recreation	1	2	3	4	5	6	7	8	9	10
County Jail	1	2	3	4	5	6	7	8	9	10
Oceana Police Dept.	1	2	3	4	5	6	7	8	9	10
Hi-Lo Coalition	1	2	3	4	5	6	7	8	9	10
DADD	1	2	3	4	5	6	7	8	9	10
MADD	1	2	3	4	5	6	7	8	9	10

Appendix

Database for Policy Analysis, Planning

CITY OF OCEANA

TOWN OF EXURBIA

AMERICUS COUNTY

Composite Information about the Metropolitan Area

The Oceana-Americus County Metro Area is a composite of the entire United States of America. Among its characteristics which approximate the averages of our nation, according to the U.S. Census Bureau (1990), are the following:

- Population distribution between central city and suburban and rural county
- Population density:
  —Oceana approximates the central cities of the United States

—Exurbia represents the towns.
—Precincts 1–4 represent the suburban counties.
—Precincts 5–8 represent the rural counties.

- Racial distributions are those of the United States.
- Racial designations are those of the U.S. Census Reports.

The governments of this city, town and county are representative of those found across the nation. Of course, it was impossible to present an example of every governmental model because of the extraordinary diversity found in the United States. Those chosen are among the most common. The politicians portrayed here mirror the representation in local politics. Each example presented could be found in cities, towns and counties of the United States.

Crime and service demands on policing are based on the Uniform Crime Reports and actual data regarding calls for police service from several police agencies. They are broadly representative of workloads found in local policing. Police and local corrections resources are based on data from police agencies and the Uniform Crime Reports. General policy analysis information is drawn from a variety of sources, each identified.

Oceana, Exurbia and Americus County Explained

These three communities comprise the Oceana-Americus County Metropolitan Area. The entire metro area is contained within the boundaries of Americus County.

The political subdivisions of Oceana are called wards, while those of Americus County are called precincts, by longstanding political tradition. Exurbia is too small to have political subdivisions. Luxore Towne and Southport Village are unincorporated, and thus within the jurisdiction of Americus County. Luxore is the most affluent community in the metro area, and employs a private security firm for policing needs. Southport Village relies on the Americus County Sheriff's Department, as do all other unincorporated areas outside of Oceana and Exurbia and Luxore Towne.

Oceana is a port city, sharing characteristics with New Haven, Norfolk, Savannah, Mobile, Corpus Christi, Long Beach, San Diego, Seattle, Duluth, Milwaukee and Toledo. It is one of the old settlements along the coast, an object of early explorations because of its magnificent natural harbor and high ground north and west above the harbor. Being many generations old, Oceana has undergone several complete cycles of building, deterioration and rebuilding with all the population movements implied by those historical processes. As happens with attractive urban sites, the city grew from a coastal trading village into a large industrial, commercial center with a high-density core population by the mid-1900s. Machine tools, farm machinery and automobiles are manufactured here. Where submarines were once built in the port area, ocean-going vessels are now dry-docked and refitted. Following World War II, the city experienced the classic demographic in-migration common to growing cities, with the resulting outward movement of city-center residents. For some years the in-migrants were rural African Americans; in recent years Latinos and Asians have predominated. One thing is clear: the traditional white political dominance and black/white population ratios and social dynamics are no longer the focus of cultural changes in the city. There are still elderly residents who talk about a "nice" city that has now become somehow rough and disturbingly alien to its earlier culture. Or maybe they merely remember what their parents told them about those "good old days in the nice city."

Exurbia is a typical bedroom suburb, built and incorporated by whites fleeing the city ahead of the surge of new, nonwhite residents. It has no industrial base and only small neighborhood service businesses, such as pharmacies and groceries. Its eastern boundary is hard against the west side commercial district of Oceana's 107th Ward. Exurbia's tax base is barely sufficient to eke out minimal police, fire and educational services.

Americus County, more than Oceana, is first seen when approached from the shipping lanes. The high ground on the northern boundary between city and county has become the preserve of the old money in the area. Estates dot the green hillsides and overlook the yacht basin. Precinct 1 of north county is a white-populated suburban region; its leisure-class enclave, Luxore Towne, is one of the ten richest communities in the nation. Precinct 5, to the north, is rural, with ranches, citrus groves, farms and some producing oil wells. Precincts 2, 3 and 4 are suburban, with populations spilling into them from Oceana as new in-migrants concentrate in the core-city living space. Precincts 6, 7 and 8 contain the great dynastic citrus holdings of old families and growing agribusinesses and the productive phosphate mining, processing and shipping interests. Throughout the county, the traditionally rural land-uses are seen to be threatened by urban encroachment, economic development, steeply escalating land costs, and what long-time rural residents consider "exploitation."

Both Oceana and Americus County have become the homes of modern, high-tech producers of computers, aircraft, bio-medical equipment, electronic systems and publications. They also accommodate home offices for airlines, news media, frozen seafood giants, sugar producers and pharmaceutical chains.

Maps of Oceana and Metro Area

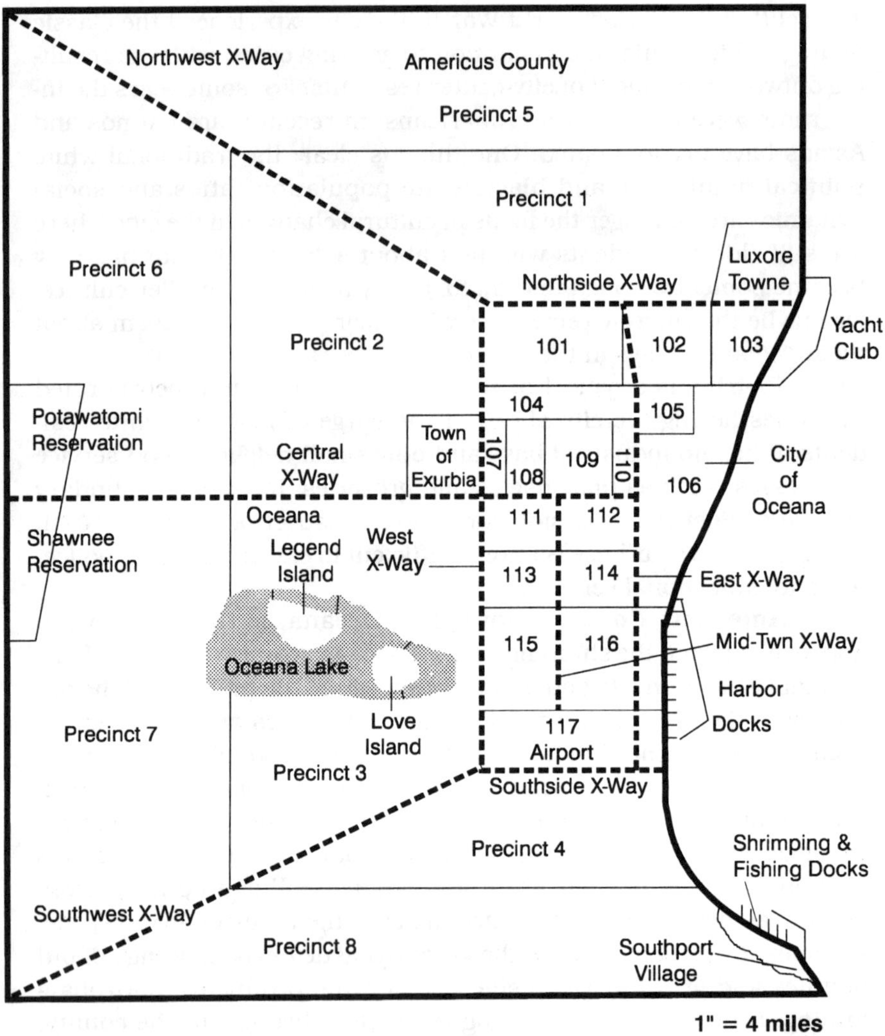

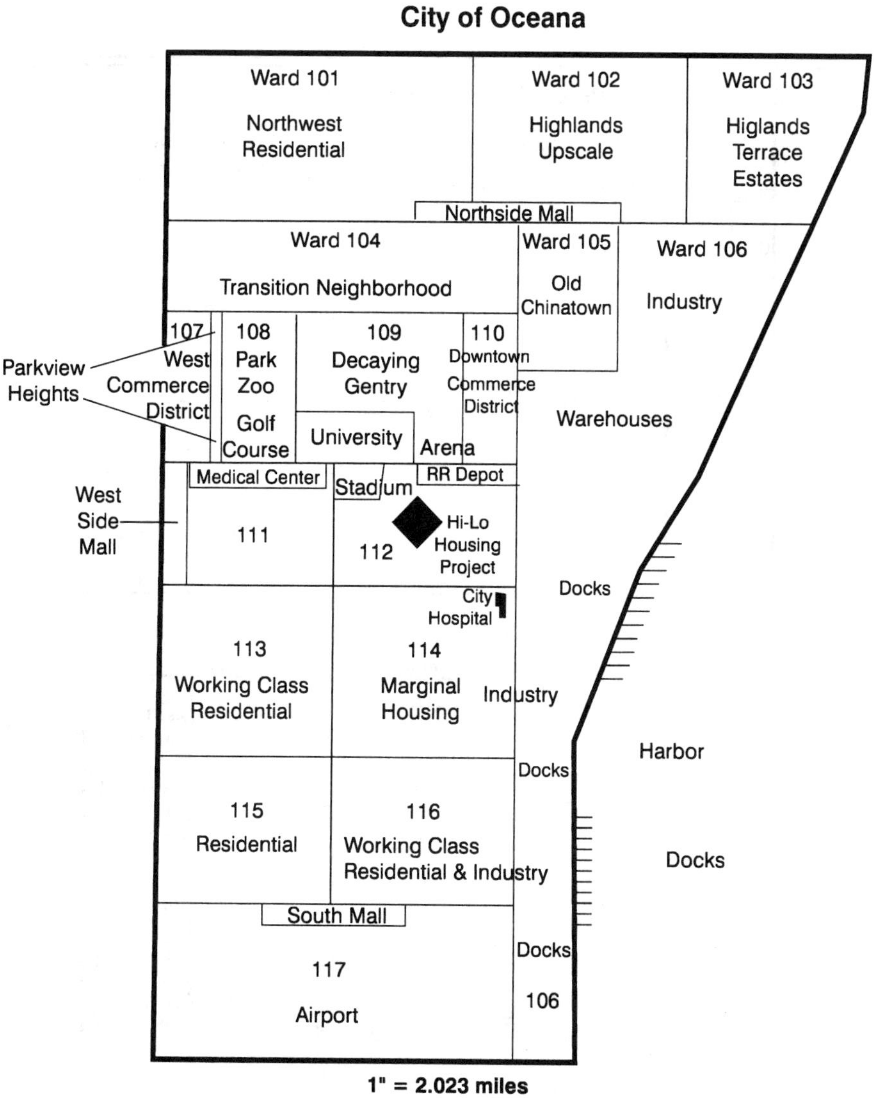
City of Oceana
Ward 101
Northwest Residential
Ward 102
Highlands Upscale
Ward 103
Higlands Terrace Estates
Northside Mall
Ward 104
Transition Neighborhood
Ward 105
Old Chinatown
Ward 106
Industry
107
West Commerce District
108
Park Zoo
Golf Course
109
Decaying Gentry
University
110
Downtown Commerce District
Arena
Parkview Heights
Warehouses
Medical Center
Stadium
RR Depot
West Side Mall
111
112
Hi-Lo Housing Project
Docks
City Hospital
113
Working Class Residential
114
Marginal Housing
Industry
Harbor
Docks
115
Residential
116
Working Class Residential & Industry
Docks
South Mall
117
Airport
Docks
106
1" = 2.023 miles

Staff Allocations and Annual Budgets of Oceana, Exurbia and Americus County

Table 1: Oceana Police Department Staff

	PD Total	Chief's Office [1]	Bureau of Fld Opns [2]	Bureau of Investig. [3]	Bureau of Admin. [4]	Bureau Aux Serv. [5]
Chief	1	1				
Ass't Chf	2		1	1		
Captain	20	2	17		1	
Det. Capt.	8			8		
Lieutenant	35	7	23		1	4
Det. Lieut.	48	2		43		3
Sergeant	155	5	133		7	10
Det. Sgt.	115			110	5	
Detective	115			115		
Ptrl Officr	1089		1081		8	
Total Swrn	1588	17	1255	277	22	17
Civ Directr	2				1	1
Othr Civiln	531	7	14	27	183	300
Totals	2121	24	1269	304	206	318

No. Staff Black	No. Staff Hispanic	No. Staff Othr Min	No. Staff Female	(Total)	
0	0	0	0	1	**Chief**
0	0	0	0	2	**Ass't Chf**
1	1	0	1	20	**Captain**
1	1	0	0	8	**Det. Capt.**
3	2	0	3	35	**Lieutenant**
4	2	0	5	48	**Det. Lieut.**
15	5	2	23	155	**Sergeant**
13	5	1	21	115	**Det. Sgt.**
13	9	1	25	115	**Detective**
120	100	10	250	1089	**Ptrl Officr**
170	125	12	328	1588	**Total Swrn**
0	0	0	0	2	**Civ Directr**
58	42	16	285	531	**Othr Civiln**
228	167	28	613	2121	**Totals**

[1] The Chief's Office includes: Command Post, Staff Inspection, Internal Affairs, and Legal Affairs

[2] The Bureau of Field Operations includes: Patrol and Special Operations

[3] The Bureau of Investigation includes: Invesitgative Units and Evidence Unit

[4] The Bureau of Administration includes: Personnel, Academy, Planning/Budgeting, Data Systems, Labor Relations and Media Relations

[5] The Bureau of Auxilary Services includes: Rec/ID, Communications, Detention, Forensics Lab, Criminal Analysis, Property, Supply, Automotive and Facility Maintenance

Table 2: Oceana Police Department
Annual Budget

TOTAL BUDGET			$87,760,918
Personnel			
Salaries & Wages*	61,293,340		
Fringe benefits	15,936,268		
Total Personnel		88%	77,229,608
Contractual Services	7,898,483 (9%)		
Equipment	877,609 (1%)		
Supplies/Expendables	1,755,218 (2%)		
Total Non-personnel		12%	10,531,310

***SALARY ACCOUNT DETAIL**

SWORN PERSONNEL				CIVILIAN PERSONNEL			
TITLE	No.	AVERAGE SALARY	SALARY TOTAL	TITLE	No.	SALARY	SALARY TOTAL
Officers	1,321	30,680	40,528,280	Various	389	17,700	6,885,300
Sgt.	166	35,680	5,922,880	Superv.	123	22,700	2,792,100
Lt.	58	40,680	2,359,440	Mgr-2	11	27,700	304,700
Capt.	33	45,680	1,507,440	Mgr-1	6	32,700	196,200
Exec.	11	57,000	627,000	Exec.	2	45,000	90,000
Chief	1	80,000	80,000				
Totals	1,590		51,025,040		531		10,268,300

Total Sworn and Civilian Salaries	61,293,340
26% Fringe Benefits	15,936,268
Total Personnel Costs	77,229,608

Note: Detectives are simply patrol officers assigned to investigative duties; they receive no additional pay. Similarly, detective sergeants, detective lieutenants, and detective captains are paid the same as their uniformed counterparts.

Table 3: Exurbia Police Department Staff

	PD Total	No. Staff Black	No. Staff Hispanic	No. Staff Othr Min	No. Staff White	No. Staff Female
Chief	1	0	0	0	1	0
Lieutenant	2	0	0	0	2	0
Sergeant	5	0	0	0	5	1
Detective	1	0	0	0	1	0
Ptrl Officr	24	1	1	0	22	7
Total Swrn	33	1	1	0	31	8
Civilians	12	2	1	1	8	10
Total	45	3	2	1	39	18

Table 4: Exurbia Police Department
Annual Budget

TOTAL BUDGET		$1,337,150
Personnel		
Salaries & Wages*	1,045,000	
Fringe benefits		
Total Personnel		$1,243,550
Contractual Services		$ 13,370
Equipment		$ 26,000
Supplies/Expendables		$ 54,230
Total Non-personnel		$ 93,600

***SALARY ACCOUNT DETAIL**

SWORN PERSONNEL				CIVILIAN PERSONNEL			
TITLE	No.	AVERAGE SALARY	SALARY TOTAL	TITLE	No.	SALARY	SALARY TOTAL
Officers	24	24,000	576,000	Disp.	5	16,000	80,000
Det.	1	26,000	26,000	Clk.Typ.	2	12,000	24,000
Sgt.	5	30,000	150,000	Recept.	1	13,000	13,000
Lt.	2	35,000	70,000	Rec.Clk.	2	14,000	28,000
Chief	1	40,000	40,000	Sec.	1	16,000	16,000
Totals	33			Ad.Asst.	1	22,000	22,000
Totals	33		862,000		12		183,000
Total Sworn and Civilian Salaries						1,045,000	
19% Fringe Benefits						198,550	
Total Personnel Costs						1,243,550	

Table 5: Americus County Sheriff's Department Staff

	ACSO Total	Shrf Offc	Jail Div.	Field Ops	Inv. Div.	Civil Div.
Sheriff	1	1	0	0	0	0
Undrshriff	1	1	0	0	0	0
Captain	15	0	6	5	3	1
Lieutenant	38	0	19	11	8	0
Sergeant	175	0	87	37	44	7
Corr Offcr	453	0	453	0	0	0
Deputy	425	0	0	288	44	93
Total Swn	1108	0	565	341	99	101
Civilians	71	0	65	2	2	2
Total	1179	2	630	343	101	103

No. Staff Black	No. Staff Hispanic	No. Staff Othr Min	No. Staff Female	
0	0	0	0	Sheriff
0	0	0	0	Undrshriff
1	1	0	1	Captain
1	1	0	0	Lieutenant
6	5	1	34	Sergeant
36	27	5	150	Corr Offcr
21	12	0	7	Deputy
65	46	6	192	Total Swn
12	8	3	38	Civilians
77	56	9	230	Total

Table 6: Americus County Sheriff's Department Annual Budget

TOTAL BUDGET		$47,131,650
Personnel		
Salaries & Wages*	30,906,000	
Fringe benefits	6,799,320	
Total Personnel		37,426,330
Contractual Services		
Equipment	COMBINED	
Supplies/Expendables		

***SALARY ACCOUNT DETAIL**

TITLE	NUMBER	AVERAGE SALARY	TOTAL SALARIES
Sheriff	1	75,000	75,000
Jail Admin. (Capt.)	1	54,200	54,200
Captain	14	45,000	360,000
Lieutenant	38	37,200	1,413,600
Sergeant	176	32,200	5,667,200
Deputy Sheriff	425	27,200	11,560,000
Correctional Officer	453	22,500	10,192,500
Civilian Staff (Medical, counseling, general support)	71	18,500	1,313,500
Totals	1,179		30,906,000

22% Fringe Benefits	6,799,320
Total Personnel Costs	37,705,320

Note: ACSD detectives receive the same salary as uniformed deputies.

Calculation of Relief Factor for 24-Hour Patrol and Correctional Positions

For use in calculating the staffing requirements for all assignments requiring 24-hour service every day of the year. The following table presents:

- the number of days in a year of work
- the number of days an officer is *not available for duty* and conversely *available for duty* during a year

It is based on three different models of benefits and personnel policies in police and local detention facilities. It presents an actuarial basis of time available for duty rather than the assumption that an officer will be on duty whenever she/he is not on vacation or scheduled days off. Oceana follows Model 3, ACSD follows Model 2, and Exurbia Model 1.

Work Demand Days for One Year: 365 X 3 Shifts = 1095 Shift-days
Average Days an Officer Is Not Available for Duty Each Year:

	Model 1	**Model 2**	**Model 3**
Days off	104	104	104
Vacation	5	10	15
Holidays	3	8	12
Sick	5	6	7
Injury	5	2	4
Light duty	0	2	4
Compensatory time	0	4	4
Leave without pay	0	2	2
Administrative leave	0	2	1
Training	0	6	12
Total days *not available*	122	146	165
Days *available* each year	243	219	200

Officers required for each 24-hour assignment for year:

Model 1: $\frac{\text{1,095 shift-days}}{\text{243 available days}} = 4.5$

Model 2: $\frac{\text{1,095 shift-days}}{\text{219 available days}} = 5.0$

Model 3: $\frac{\text{1,095 shift-days}}{\text{200 available days}} = 5.5$

Examples—If department has 100 patrol officers:

Model 1—$\frac{100}{4.5}$ = 22 one-officer patrol cars can be staffed 24 hours per day

Model 2—$\frac{100}{5.0}$ = 20 one-officer patrol cars can be staffed 24 hours per day

Model 3—$\frac{100}{5.5}$ = 18 one-officer patrol cars can be staffed 24 hours per day

Crime and CFS Analysis in Oceana, Exurbia and Americus County

Police departments compile several kinds of data which are similar but not identical. This often leads us to find differences among tables which we believe are errors. For example, Part I Crimes (Index Crimes in FBI Uniform Crime Reports [UCR] terminology) are defined by UCR criteria and often do not correspond to the definitions of police dispatch codes or the prosecutor's state criminal code definitions. Thus the numbers of murders reported in the Uniform Crime Reports and city arrest and prosecution reports are nearly always different. News media are often confused about these differences and accuse local police agencies of publishing erroneous crime figures. For example, the UCR figure for murders cleared by arrest might be 100, while the prosecutor charged only 90 persons, because state law defines ten of the crimes as lesser degrees of homicide (for example, manslaughter).

Dispatch data (calls for service) do not match Uniform Crime Reports or prosecutor's charges because the purpose of dispatch codes is to tell the patrol officer the nature of the problem, rather than its legalistic definition. "Murder" is seldom found in a local dispatch code because the dispatcher knows only that there is an apparent, unexplained death to investigate. It may have been caused by an accident, suicide, negligence, or intentional killing. A "cutting" dispatch may become a murder. A "sex offense" may become a rape or a child sexual assault. The same event may be classified by dispatch code as a "cutting," by the jail booking desk as "assault with a deadly weapon," by the prosecutor as "simple assault," and by the UCR as "aggravated assault." There is no pragmatic way of reconciling data from dispatches, UCR, jail booking charges, and prosecution charges.

Another confusing difference is the seeming discrepancy between dispatch codes. Oceana PD established a detailed dispatch taxonomy of 54 codes that Exurbia PD later adopted. Americus County, conversely, has a very limited dispatch scheme of 12 codes which obscure details. The former sheriff eschewed modernization, and the newly-elected sheriff has not gotten around to changing the dispatch code. His dispatchers tell the patrols any necessary details of the calls and then classify them in these overly-broad categories. The new sheriff may or may not adopt Oceana's dispatch codes when he changes his department's outmoded classifications.

Table 7: Oceana Annual Calls for Service

Disp Code		101	102	103	104	105	106	107	108	109
1	Aban Veh	258	65	52	600	665	736	271	220	749
2	Acc Minr	1033	258	207	2401	2660	2944	1084	878	2995
3	Acc Majr	163	41	33	379	420	464	171	138	474
4	Acc Pvt	231	58	46	537	595	658	243	196	670
5	Assault	421	105	84	980	1085	1200	442	358	1222
6	Asst Pub	245	61	49	568	350	697	257	208	709
7	Burglary	539	135	108	1254	1390	1538	566	458	1565
8	Burg Alrm	1957	489	391	4550	5039	5577	1998	1663	5675
9	Burg Veh	268	67	54	622	689	763	281	228	776
10	Crim Mis	389	97	78	904	1000	1108	408	330	1127
11	Cutting	20	5	4	46	50	57	21	17	57
12	Disturb	2310	577	462	5371	5949	6584	2426	1964	6700
13	Dist-Fam	462	115	92	1074	1190	1317	485	393	1340
14	Dist-Nei	121	30	24	281	311	345	127	103	351
15	DOA	77	19	15	180	200	221	81	66	225
16	Drunk	73	18	15	171	189	209	77	62	213
17	DWI	52	13	10	120	133	147	54	44	150
18	Fam Viol	130	30	25	315	340	250	140	110	400
19	Fight	122	30	24	283	313	347	128	103	353
20	Fire	49	12	10	114	126	139	51	42	142
21	Forgery	12	3	2	27	30	34	12	10	34
22	Hldup Alm	236	34	27	316	350	387	143	115	394
23	Info	367	92	73	853	945	1046	385	312	1064
24	Injrd Per	150	40	30	335	380	550	154	128	412
25	Liqr Viol	20	5	4	47	53	58	21	17	59
26	Misc	625	156	125	1453	1610	1782	656	531	1813
27	Miss Per	37	9	7	85	94	105	38	31	106
28	Miss Chld	33	8	6	76	84	93	34	28	95
29	Narc Law	106	26	21	245	272	300	111	90	306
30	Off in Trbl	14	4	3	33	37	41	15	12	42
31	Ord Viol	69	17	14	161	178	198	73	59	201
32	Patrol By	211	53	42	490	542	600	221	179	611
33	Prop Fnd	41	10	8	95	105	116	43	35	118
34	Prop Lst	17	4	3	39	43	48	18	14	49
35	Prowler	78	19	16	181	201	222	82	66	226
36	Rape	15	4	3	35	39	43	16	13	43
37	Rcov Prop	47	12	9	110	122	136	50	40	138
38	Robbery	5	3	2	27	35	44	10	7	34
39	Rob Indv	40	10	8	94	104	115	43	34	117
40	Sex Off	43	11	9	101	112	124	45	37	126
41	Shooting	55	13	11	126	140	155	57	46	158
42	Shoplift	110	27	22	256	283	314	116	94	319
43	Suicide	88	22	18	205	227	252	93	75	256
44	Susp Per	360	90	72	837	927	1026	378	306	1044
45	Susp Veh	217	54	44	505	560	620	228	185	631
46	Theft	435	109	87	1011	1120	1239	457	370	1261
47	Theft Veh	177	44	35	411	455	504	185	150	512
48	Threats	196	49	39	455	504	448	205	166	568
49	Thrt Bmb	6	2	1	14	16	18	7	5	18
50	Trff Relat	220	55	44	512	567	627	231	187	638
51	Trff Viol	150	37	30	348	385	426	157	127	434
52	Vice	6	1	1	14	15	17	6	5	17
53	Want Per	448	112	90	1043	1155	1278	471	381	1300
54	Weapons	158	39	31	367	406	449	165	185	457
Totals		13712	3399	2720	31657	34790	38716	14237	11621	39494

Disp Code		110	111	112	113	114	115	116	117	Totals
1	Aban Veh	542	865	3098	930	1485	748	1058	568	**12910**
2	Acc Minr	2169	3460	12394	3718	5938	2995	4234	2272	**51640**
3	Acc Majr	342	546	1957	587	937	472	668	358	**8150**
4	Acc Pvt	485	774	2772	832	1328	670	947	508	**11550**
5	Assault	885	1411	5055	1517	2422	1221	1727	926	**21061**
6	Asst Pub	514	819	2935	880	1406	709	1002	538	**11947**
7	Burglary	1133	1806	6474	1942	3101	1563	2211	1186	**26969**
8	Burg Alrm	4110	6555	23483	7045	11252	5675	8023	4305	**97787**
9	Burg Veh	562	896	3213	964	1539	776	1097	588	**13383**
10	Crim Mis	816	1302	4664	1400	2234	1127	1593	855	**19432**
11	Cutting	41	66	236	71	112	56	80	42	**981**
12	Disturb	4852	7739	27723	8317	13284	6700	9472	5082	**115512**
13	Dist-Fam	970	1547	5545	1663	2656	1340	1894	1016	**23099**
14	Dist-Nei	254	405	1451	435	695	350	495	266	**6044**
15	DOA	163	259	930	279	445	224	317	170	**3871**
16	Drunk	154	245	880	264	422	212	300	161	**3665**
17	DWI	108	172	620	186	296	150	211	113	**2579**
18	Fam Viol	284	488	1680	554	754	455	553	200	**6708**
19	Fight	255	407	1460	438	700	352	498	267	**6080**
20	Fire	103	163	587	176	281	142	200	107	**2444**
21	Forgery	25	39	142	42	68	33	48	26	**587**
22	Hldup Alm	285	455	1631	489	780	394	557	300	**6893**
23	Info	771	1229	4403	1321	2109	1064	1504	807	**18345**
24	Injrd Per	304	448	1480	454	854	355	593	416	**7083**
25	Liqr Viol	43	68	245	73	117	59	83	44	**1016**
26	Misc	1313	2094	7502	2250	3594	1813	2563	1375	**31255**
27	Miss Per	77	122	440	132	210	106	150	80	**1829**
28	Miss Chld	68	109	390	117	187	94	133	71	**1626**
29	Narc Law	222	353	1267	380	607	306	432	232	**5276**
30	Off in Trbl	30	48	173	52	82	42	59	31	**718**
31	Ord Viol	146	232	832	250	398	200	284	152	**3464**
32	Patrol By	442	705	2528	758	1211	610	863	460	**10526**
33	Prop Fnd	86	136	489	147	234	118	167	89	**2037**
34	Prop Lst	35	56	202	60	96	49	69	37	**839**
35	Prowler	164	261	936	281	448	226	320	171	**3898**
36	Rape	31	50	179	54	85	43	61	32	**746**
37	Rcov Prop	100	159	570	171	273	138	195	104	**2374**
38	Robbery	20	38	140	42	67	34	48	26	**582**
39	Rob Indv	85	135	486	146	232	117	166	89	**2021**
40	Sex Off	91	145	522	156	250	126	178	95	**2171**
41	Shooting	114	181	766	195	311	158	222	119	**2827**
42	Shoplift	231	368	1321	396	632	318	451	242	**5500**
43	Suicide	186	595	1060	318	507	256	362	194	**4714**
44	Susp Per	756	1206	4322	1296	2070	1044	1476	792	**18002**
45	Susp Veh	457	728	2609	783	1250	630	891	478	**10870**
46	Theft	913	1456	5218	1565	2500	1261	1782	956	**21740**
47	Theft Veh	371	591	2120	636	1015	512	724	388	**8830**
48	Threats	411	655	2348	704	1125	567	802	430	**9672**
49	Thrt Bmb	13	20	75	22	35	18	25	14	**309**
50	Trff Relat	462	737	2642	792	1265	638	902	484	**11003**
51	Trff Viol	314	500	1794	538	860	433	612	329	**7474**
52	Vice	13	20	72	21	34	18	24	13	**297**
53	Want Per	942	1502	5382	1614	2578	1300	1838	986	**22420**
54	Weapons	331	528	1892	567	906	457	646	347	**7931**
Totals		28594	45894	163335	49020	78277	39474	55810	29937	**680687**

Table 8: Oceana Analysis of Annual Calls for Service

Disp Code		Ave MHrs per Call	Totals Calls	Tot MHrs All Calls	Av Units per Call	# Calls 2+ Units
1	Aban Veh	:33	12910	7250	1.3	2649
2	Acc Minr	1:06	51640	56130	1.5	15686
3	Acc Majr	2:14	8150	15956	2.8	5470
4	Acc Pvt	:46	11550	8779	1.2	1907
5	Assault	1:04	21061	22810	1.8	11443
6	Asst Pub	:52	11947	10895	1.5	5300
7	Burglary	1:18	26969	13931	2.1	17132
8	Burg Alrm	:19	97787	32573	1.3	25547
9	Burg Veh	:57	13383	12892	1.5	4889
10	Crim Mis	:41	19432	13507	1.4	5387
11	Cutting	3:04	981	2960	3.1	796
12	Disturb	:42	115512	82565	1.9	73212
13	Dist-Fam	1:05	23099	25197	2.1	18747
14	Dist-Nei	:42	6044	4267	1.7	3344
15	DOA	1:27	3871	5661	1.4	858
16	Drunk	:51	3665	3102	1.7	1756
17	DWI	2:03	2579	5341	1.9	1337
18	Fam Viol	1:23	6708	9824	2.1	5696
19	Fight	:57	6080	5821	2.5	5193
20	Fire	:43	2444	1848	1.6	1063
21	Forgery	2:13	587	1310	1.7	260
22	Hldup Alm	:23	6893	2629	1.9	4348
23	Info	:43	18345	13481	1.2	3601
24	Injrd Per	:52	7083	6146	1.8	3812
25	Liqr Viol	:37	1016	654	1.6	436
26	Misc	:49	31255	25857	1.4	9049
27	Miss Per	1:00	1829	1848	1.4	503
28	Miss Chld	1:15	1626	2047	1.8	717
29	Narc Law	1:29	5276	7917	1.9	3115
30	Off in Trbl	2:29	718	1805	5.3	697
31	Ord Viol	:28	3464	1609	1.3	766
32	Patrol By	:03	10526	659	1	468
33	Prop Fnd	:57	2037	1939	1.2	329
34	Prop Lst	:34	839	488	1.1	103
35	Prowler	:35	3898	2283	1.8	2362
36	Rape	3:24	746	2544	3.3	485
37	Rcov Prop	:48	2374	1720	1.4	561
38	Robbery	4:28	582	2671	5.3	541
39	Rob Indv	1:42	2021	3470	2.2	1188
40	Sex Off	1:14	2171	3204	1.6	1089
41	Shooting	3:01	2827	8276	3.5	2137
42	Shoplift	2:03	5500	11337	1.4	1818
43	Suicide	1:11	4714	5252	1.8	2337
44	Susp Per	:38	18002	11459	1.8	10361
45	Susp Veh	:32	10870	5884	1.7	5326
46	Theft	:50	21740	18236	1.3	4823
47	Theft Veh	1:17	8830	11365	1.9	3928
48	Threats	:46	9672	7557	1.3	2348
49	Thrt Bmb	2:24	309	750	3.2	250
50	Trff Relat	:31	11003	5715	1.3	2727
51	Trff Viol	:54	7474	6793	1.4	2120
52	Vice	:34	297	173	1.6	130
53	Want Per	1:20	22420	30396	1.4	7127
54	Weapons	:42	7931	5502	1.3	1688
Totals		:50	680687	554285	1.6	288962

Table 9: Exurbia Annual Calls for Service

Disp Code		Totals
1	Aban Veh	163
2	Acc Minr	654
3	Acc Majr	82
4	Acc Pvt	146
5	Assault	255
6	Asst Pub	400
7	Burglary	341
8	Burg Alrm	354
9	Burg Veh	1580
10	Crim Mis	246
11	Cutting	12
12	Disturb	258
13	Dist-Fam	292
14	Dist-Nei	77
15	DOA	86
16	Drunk	190
17	DWI	113
18	Fam Viol	148
19	Fight	112
20	Fire	57
21	Forgery	22
22	Hldup Alm	36
23	Info	804
24	Injrd Per	310
25	Liqr Viol	45
26	Misc	1370
27	Miss Per	165
28	Miss Chld	71
29	Narc Law	67
30	Off in Trbl	49
31	Ord Viol	152
32	Patrol By	462
33	Prop Fnd	37
34	Prop Lst	180
35	Prowler	170
36	Rape	12
37	Rcov Prop	104
38	Robbery	27
39	Rob Indv	56
40	Sex Off	27
41	Shooting	6
42	Shoplift	219
43	Suicide	52
44	Susp Per	215
45	Susp Veh	288
46	Theft	375
47	Theft Veh	142
48	Threats	246
49	Thrt Bmb	4
50	Trff Relat	482
51	Trff Viol	496
52	Vice	6
53	Want Per	26
54	Weapons	38
Totals		8389

Table 10: Americus County Annual Calls for Service

Precinct	Code 1 Part I Crime	Code 2 Part II Crime	Code 3 Interpers. Conflict	Code 4 Medical Problem	Code 5 Traffic Problem	Code 6 Public Nuisance	Code 7 Suspicius Circum.
1	2723	7235	2979	2180	4256	4682	1490
2	5988	10611	4369	3121	6242	6866	2185
3	7983	11576	4767	3405	6810	7490	2383
4	6896	9164	3774	2695	5391	5930	1887
5	271	1447	596	426	851	936	280
6	485	1929	794	567	1135	1248	397
7	907	2894	1192	851	1702	1873	596
8	1697	3376	1390	993	1986	2185	695
Totals	26,950	48,232	19,861	14,238	28,373	31,210	9,913

Code 8 Dependnt Person	Code 9 Public Morals	Code 10 Assist	Code 11 Alarm	Code 12 Info Req. or Offer	Totals	Precinct
1702	851	6384	1277	5533	41292	1
2497	1249	9363	1873	8115	62479	2
2724	1362	10214	2043	8852	69609	3
2156	1078	8086	1617	7008	55682	4
340	170	1277	255	1107	7956	5
454	227	1702	340	1475	10753	6
681	341	2554	511	2213	16315	7
794	397	2979	596	2582	19670	8
11,348	5675	42559	8512	36885	283,756	Totals

Table 11: CFS Workload Analysis—Americus County

CFS CODE	
1	PART I CRIMES. Detailed in the table: Index Crimes in City, Town, County.
2	PART II CRIMES (48,232). These include all offenses other than Part I crimes. Thirty percent (14,470) involve arrests for this great variety of offenses, many of them minor misdemeanors (petty larceny, shoplifting, drunk in public, disturbance, noise, etc.).
3	INTERPERSONAL CONFLICT (19,861). Forty percent (7,944) involve offense or traffic violation. Nine percent (1,788) involve physical arrests; 830 summonses issued. Incidents range from neighbor disputes to tavern and street fights, labor problems, inter-ethnic confrontations, stadium/arena fights, traffic altercations, pet squabbles, youth-gang shoving matches, abortion confrontations.
4	MEDICAL PROBLEMS (14,186). 1,702 involve offense or traffic violations, and 511 arrests. Incidents include person collapsed on street, industrial accidents, drug overdoses, unconscious inebriates, seizures, heart attacks, pit-bull attacks, bee stings, requests for trip to city hospital.
5	TRAFFIC PROBLEMS (28,373). Seventy percent (19,861) involve offenses, with 993 arrests, 15,483 summonses.
6	PUBLIC NUISANCE (31,210). 8,484 involve offenses, 2,460 arrests, 943 summonses.
7	SUSPICIOUS CIRCUMSTANCES (9,930). 3,515 involve offenses, 273 arrests.
8	DEPENDENT PERSON (11,349). 162 involve offenses, 19 arrests. Subjects are mentally ill, drunk, in hypoglycemic shock, homeless, runaway, etc.
9	PUBLIC MORALS COMPLAINT (5,675). 4,225 involve offenses, 2,434 arrests. Voyeurism, exhibitionism, public restroom sexual activities, topless at beach, prostitution, porn on display, massage parlor billboards/signs, art show at city museum, rap record lyrics, condoms on display, lovers in park, etc.
10	ASSISTANCE (42,559). 850 involve offenses, 460 arrests.
11	ALARMS (8,512). Commercial and private, average 36 minutes, 91 percent false.
12	INFORMATION REQUESTED OR GIVEN (36,885). Not otherwise classified above. Most are referred within or outside department. This category involves phone intake operation, but only 50 percent require dispatch of patrols.

Table 12: Patrol Car Allocations

Oceana Wards	Pop.	Square Miles	Part I Crimes	Total Dispatchs	% of Dispatchs	No. of Ptrl Cars	No. of Officers	Sq. Miles per Car
101	33,500	6.5	970	13,712	2	4	22	2.3
102	4780	5	137	3,399	0.5	1	6	6.8
103	2,580	3.25	54	2,720	0.4	1	5	6.14
104	35,375	3.25	2,000	31,657	4.67	8	44	0.53
105	35,000	2	2,230	34,790	5	9	50	0.44
106	20,000	9	3,078	38,716	5.7	10	55	0.37
107	15,225	0.5	2,100	14,237	2.2	4	22	0.9
108	120	1.25	2,106	11,621	1.73	3	16	1.14
109	9,610	3.25	1,000	39,494	5.8	10	55	0.32
110	12,000	0.75	1,100	28,594	4.2	8	44	0.43
111	26,080	2.50	3,598	45,894	6.7	12	66	0.24
112	170,100	2.75	25,442	163,335	24	43	238	0.06
113	36,130	3	4,000	49,020	7.2	13	71	0.19
114	80000	3.25	9,997	78,277	11.5	21	115	0.08
115	40,000	3.25	4,100	39,474	5.8	10	55	0.12
116	49,000	3.5	6,100	55,810	8.2	15	82	0.06
117	500	7	3,278	29,937	4.4	8	44	0.11
Totals	570,000	60	71,290	680,687	100	180	990	0.33
Exurbia	25,000	5	1,576	12,327	100	5	24	1
County Precincts								
1	90,726	25	2,723	41,292	14.6	7	35	3.6
2	133,063	35	5,988	62,479	22	11	55	3.2
3	145,160	40	7,983	69,609	24.5	12	60	3.3
4	114,918	30	6,896	55,682	19.6	10	50	3
5	18,144	58	271	7,956	2.8	1	5	58
6	24,193	75	485	10,753	3.8	2	10	38
7	36,291	75	907	16,315	5.7	3	15	25
8	42,338	65	1,697	19,670	7	4	20	16
Totals	604,833	403	26,950	283,756	100	50	250	8

Table 13: Index Crimes in City, Town, County

Oceana	Murder	Rape	Robbery	Aggrav. Assault	Burglary	Larceny	Motr Veh Theft	Arson	Totals
101	1	9	91	48	235	462	116	7	970
102	0	1	13	7	33	66	16	1	137
103	0	1	5	3	13	26	6	0	54
104	3	19	188	100	484	952	239	15	2000
105	4	21	209	112	540	1062	266	16	2230
106	5	29	289	154	746	1466	367	22	3078
107	3	20	197	105	509	1000	251	15	2100
108	4	20	207	110	435	1051	263	16	2106
109	2	9	94	50	242	476	119	7	1000
110	2	10	103	55	266	524	131	8	1100
111	6	33	338	180	872	1714	429	26	3598
112	42	236	2378	1267	6135	12183	3022	185	25442
113	7	37	376	200	969	1904	477	29	4000
114	16	93	939	500	2422	4761	1193	73	9997
115	7	38	385	205	993	1952	489	30	4100
116	10	57	573	305	1477	2904	728	45	6100
117	5	30	308	164	794	1562	391	24	3278
Totals	117	663	6693	3565	17165	34065	8503	519	71290
Exurbia	1	9	25	122	353	977	88	1	1576
Americus County									
1	4	15	40	114	758	1567	213	12	2723
2	8	32	88	251	1668	3447	468	26	5988
3	10	43	118	335	2224	4595	624	34	7983
4	9	37	102	290	1921	3969	538	30	6896
5	0	1	4	11	76	157	21	1	271
6	1	3	7	20	135	279	38	2	485
7	1	5	13	38	253	522	71	4	907
8	2	9	25	71	473	977	133	7	1697
Totals	35	145	397	1130	7508	15513	2106	116	26950

Crime Analysis Bulletin

MEMORANDUM

TO: Planning Task Forces
FROM: Central Crime Analysis, Oceana Police Dept.
SUBJECT: Crime Analysis Bulletin

The following details regarding crimes in the various wards are provided to assist task forces in making appropriate decisions regarding strategic and tactical policies for crime control and response in each of the city's areas.

HOMICIDE

Citywide, there may be one or two serial killers operating. The mode of operation (MO) of attacks on nurses suggests this possibility, and more than three of the prostitute deaths may be linked. In the case of the prostitutes, the killings are likely to involve drugs, also. It appears that no single approach will have an impact on either the number of homicides or their clearances. *The factor most related to the increase in homicides is competition in the drug trade*.

WARD
NO.

101 Case is probably family-related.
104 Two acquaintance, one drug-related.
105 Two drug buys gone sour, a street robbery killing, a Triad gang turf disagreement.
106 One related to gambling seamen in a bar, two others in a knife fight. Other victims: a homeless man, one careless wanderer from a yacht (possibly seeking drugs).
107 One glitterati case: bank president's wife in 12-room condo. A murdered prostitute. A street robbery killing.
108 One child abducted, strangled near lagoon; two drug-related. A rape-killing of a jogger.
109 A widow and her nurse-companion, together; probable panic burglary killing.
110 A secretary working late, possible serial rape-homicide. A tourist at an ATM.
111 One family violence; one child, near stadium, a sex crime. Three nurses leaving Medical Center. An abduction from West Side Mall.
112 Three prostitutes (similar MO), a cab driver, a police officer who walked in on a robbery, a train passenger who wandered too far from the train station; three children, stadium abduction sex crimes. Two cases in stadium during soccer games, one a robbery. All the rest in or near the Hi-Lo housing project, including a security guard; drive-by shootings; some resulting from rapes, muggings, armed robbery, theft, burglary. Many related to drug trade competition.
113 Three family violence; two prostitutes, either serial cases or drug trade; a

double shooting in the workplace.

114 Two nurses leaving City Hospital after midnight; three family or neighborhood violence; a few street robberies that were resisted. Drive-by shooting. One child, sex crime. Two outside night clubs. Others drug-trade related.

115 Family violence fatality; convenience store robbery deaths; drive-by shooting.

116 Four prostitutes, one suspected drug competition, one tavern fight gone too far. Four children, abuse or sex crimes.

117 South Mall abduction, two shootings in the workplace (airport and mall), drug dealer found in trunk of car at airport, robbery at mall ATM.

RAPE

Reason to believe there are several serial rapists working the city, possibly including some cases reported as homicides. Also child sex-abusers, some of whom may have killed their victims.

WARD
NO.

101 Mostly date-rapes, but also two baby-sitters, one maid, one child.

102 Date-rape.

103 Baby-sitter.

104 Some in victims' homes or workplace; several raped in their cars after parking or on entering their cars, others dragged into abandoned houses while walking home from jobs in 105-110.

105 Eight restaurant and cocktail waitresses; Chinatown residents walking near homes and workplaces; residents in homes, female drivers kidnapped in their cars. Several women who left bars with new acquaintances.

106 Most victims were brought to 106 from other areas and raped; six employees of industrial firms in area; three prostitutes assaulted, robbed and raped. Five female patrons of taverns, after leaving. One child, attacked and left in 106.

107 Maids, a cook, several baby-sitters, two secretaries, residents in the parking ramps of condos, convenience store clerks, a cab driver, several date-rapes, Medical Center staff walking home.

108 Stranger-rapes of four at Lovers' Lane, after their dates were disabled; date-rapes; two prostitutes robbed and raped; visitors to park. Two children abducted, raped, released.

109 One housekeeper and her elderly employer at her home, both assaulted and robbed; elderly widows in their homes, also robbed and assaulted. Five cases linked, others uncertain.

110 Two physicians, one lawyer, a stock broker, a CPA, and three secretaries at their places of employment. Two cab drivers.

111 Date-rapes, three residents in their homes by phony repairmen; six in stadium parking lot; nine Medical Center staff, most incidental to drug-robberies, several patients; the remainder street-related. One child.

112 Many date-rapes, nurses from Medical Center, Stadium patrons in parking

ramps and lots; travelers abducted from periphery of Railroad Depot. Stranger rapes of numerous residents of Hi-Lo in their homes, in parking lots, stairwells, elevators, corridors, on roof, in central compounds. Residents of flats to west of Hi-Lo, in homes, cars, vacant lots and houses. Sixteen children.

113 Patrons leaving bars. One child abducted from mall. Cab drivers, convenience store clerks. Date-rapes.

114 Hospital staff, including nurses, in connection with drug robberies and abducted from cars and parking lots. Date-rapes; several abductions from cars at traffic signals; some in homes of victims, some incidental to burglary, two by phony salesmen. Two children. Pedestrians pulled into vacant buildings.

115 Many of the following: date-rapes, stranger rapes in homes, pedestrians abducted to vacant buildings; residents raped by burglars, prowlers, phony salesmen, tradesmen. Several children.

116 Date-rapes. Kick-in robberies and rapes. Burglary rapes. Some taken there and attacked, some patrons leaving bars, employees of industrial offices, prostitutes robbed/raped. Four children left there after attacks.

117 Flight attendants, other airline and airport employees and travelers in parking ramp; mall patrons car-jacked while leaving parking ramp and lots at night.

Robbery

Ward
No.

101 Kick-in robberies in homes. Convenience stores, banks, one by hitchhiker picked up. ATM patrons. Small businesses. Pedestrians.

102 One kick-in robbery in home, a mall payroll, patrons of mall in parking ramp, pedestrians, small businesses. ATM patrons.

103 Holdup of cocktail lounge at yacht club, separate robbery of a late-night gambling party on a cabin cruiser in slip. Kick-ins at two homes. Cab driver.

104 Numerous hits on convenience stores, small shops, cab drivers, pedestrians, drivers stopped at signals, delivery trucks, pizza-deliverers. Violent hits on crap-games. Many drug customers and street dealers. Numerous autos taken.

105 Sixteen drug hits at hospital, many at restaurants and bars near closing time, several business payrolls, many patrons leaving restaurants and bars, drivers waiting at signals, numerous pedestrians, cab drivers, delivery people, prostitutes; violent hits on gambling rooms, massage parlors, porn movie cash boxes, patrons of porn shops, B-joints (patrons and staff). At least two-thirds drug-related. Many autos taken in robberies.

106 Working-class taverns late at night (cash register and bottle goods), payroll on docks, a shipment suspected to be contraband, several seamen for their wages on leaving ships, cab drivers, truck drivers, hookers, crap games, massage parlors. Numerous drug-competition cases.

107 Several in condo ramps, street robberies of pedestrians near park, store payrolls, many stores for end-of-day cash, gas stations, convenience

stores, drivers stopped at signals (autos taken), cab drivers, late-night workers leaving (in buildings, on street, at cars, in lots, ramps, at bus stops). Many affluent targets in 107.

108 Mostly targets of opportunity at night, some concession stands, golfers in lot after too many drinks at the "nineteenth hole," many couples at Lovers' Lane (some including rape or aggravated assault and auto theft).

109 Robberies of elderly residents on streets, in homes by fake sales people; students and faculty on campus, often in university buildings, in area surrounding arena. Some motorists, autos included.

110 Stores, office personnel, small merchants, banks, wholesale jewelers in upper floors of office buildings, payrolls, daily cash intakes, etc. Individuals on streets, parking lots, on buses and even commuter trains and platforms. Autos taken also.

111 Medical Center staff and patients; residents in every circumstance, mall merchants, stadium patrons, small stores and businesses, delivery people, school children at knife-point for their lunch money. Drug cases.

112 Stadium patrons in parking ramps and lots, Arena and Railroad Depot patrons who stray from lighted areas. Every person or enterprise with a thing of value is vulnerable, every kind of object is used as a weapon, but many robberies are unarmed. Drug cases thrive.

113 Targets of opportunity, such as taverns, mall businesses, convenience stores, mall patrons, pedestrians, drivers stopped at signals, cab drivers, students, transients.

114 Convenience stores, small businesses, City Hospital staff and patients, pedestrians, motorists, drive-ins of all kinds, banks, S&Ls, kids for their lunch money (near 115 and 112 boundaries). Mostly cash and jewelry taken. Drug cases.

115 & 116 Every person, enterprise, household with something of value can be targeted. Numerous pedestrians (including children for bikes, athletic equipment, school money, basketball shoes, etc.). Taverns and their patrons, business offices (payrolls, cash intake, small change, personal belongings), pedestrians.

117 Parking lots, ramps. Airport concessions late at night, one armored car stickup (payroll). Mostly money, jewelry, luggage. Some robberies of "drug mules."

Aggravated Assault

Ward No.

101 Spouse abuse, cocktail lounge fights, neighbor quarrels, labor problem at mall, high school students tussling, basketball brawl. Increasing numbers of traffic fights. Drug deal squabbles.

102 Same distribution as 101.

103 Spouse abuse, mostly out-of-hand party on boat.

104 Tavern fights, family, school violence, gang fights, ethnic and racial violence. Skinhead attacks. Traffic fights. Drug deal fights.

105 Tavern fights, ethnic, racial, neighborhood boundary violence, gang fights. Skinhead attacks. Asian extortion gang attacks on Asian sex-oriented businesses. Traffic fights. Street drug-selling violence.

106 Labor strife, tavern fights; injuries to transients, homeless, alcoholic derelicts. Attacks on and by seamen, dock workers and local residents who work there. Drug-deal fights.

107 Family violence in Parkview Heights, labor problems in three major high-rise construction projects, a few skinhead attacks. Traffic fights. Street muggings of affluent at night.

108 Nighttime attacks on park patrons, two golf fights, one skinhead attack, signs of ethnic/racial confrontations. Possible drug deals.

109 Attacks on elderly, students on campus, patrons of arena, some burglary-related. Campus drug trade related.

110 Traffic/parking fights, same labor problems as 107, some skinhead attacks and confrontations, abortion-rights confrontations leading to assaults, attacks on homeless and alcoholic street people.

111 Many related to stadium events, traffic fights, parking fights in mall, neighbor fights, family violence, school violence, skinheads, cycle gangs, abortion clinic violence. Drug trade turf battles.

112 Unceasing in Hi-Lo housing area: high ethnic/racial tensions in this high-density, low-cost housing project. Ethnically and racially integrated by policy; includes all recent in-migrant population groups, most new to living in a large city. Victims include all age groups, from children to the elderly. Tavern, pool hall, video arcade violence. Drug-related violence of all kinds. Traffic fights. Spills over into Stadium and Railroad Depot. Ethnic gang activity, boundary disputes.

113 Related to taverns, traffic, racial tensions, neighbor disputes. Skinhead incidents. Many drug trade related.

114 Essentially a combination of 112 and 113. Tenement housing is not hi-rise, so less concentration.

115 & 116 Similar to 114. Plenty of ethnic gang activity, boundary disputes. Skinhead attacks at fringes of area. Huge amount of drug trade violence.

117 Security-gate incidents, parking fights at airport and mall, attack on airline counter staff regarding cancelled flight, traffic disputes, acquaintance attacks.

Residential Burglary

Targeted property differs from place to place, consistent with the value and accessibility of the goods taken. The primary pattern is that fencible property is targeted. However, coin collections, art works and some other items are being offered for resale to original owners (ransom). Some complete household "moveouts" by van while residents are traveling.

Resale of stolen property is thought to be occurring through pawn shops, flea markets, garage sales, and a variety of second-hand selling techniques. Most burglars assumed to be drug users.

Business Burglary

Safe jobs, furs, truckloads of appliances, train-cars of commodities, shipping containers from warehouses, wholesale jewelry offices in 107 and 110, payrolls

Seemingly peaceful park in 108.

and receipts being held overnight in store/factory safes. Drugs from pharmacies, clinics, doctors' offices, hospitals. Every kind of commodity from every kind of premise. Most burglars assumed to be drug users.

Larceny Over $100

Everywhere in city. Victims from children (bikes, stereos, shoes) to elderly (including a wheelchair). Most thieves assumed to be motivated by need for drug money.

Motor Vehicle Theft

Distribution as shown in chart. All locations vulnerable; however, increasing thefts from mall lots and ramps, airport ramps, medical center and hospital lots and ramps, zoo/park lots, and an increased penetration of the Parkview Heights condo ramps. Increasing numbers of cars stolen in connection with robberies at traffic signals, in parking lots and ramps, outside homes. Intelligence is that cars are being stolen for:

- chopping, selling parts at junk yards
- repainting, reselling locally or within state
- repainting, renumbering, shipping from port to other lands
- transportation for the evening
- use in robberies (with stolen plates)
- nationwide syndicate for retitling, painting, reselling
- stealing/reselling on order, by type and color of vehicle

Organized shipment of stolen vehicles by freighters is centered in Ward 106. Asian and Latino gangs are suspected to be dominant.

Arson

Motive bases noted: Profit (insurance, professional arsonist), revenge, crime concealment, psychological excitement, vandalism.
Distributed as shown in table, by ward, randomly among these categories.

Oceana Traffic Accident and Enforcement Data

	Fatal and Personal Injury Accidents	Convictions for Hazardous Violations	Enforcement Index
Previous Year	11,400	43,320	3.8
Grant Year*	10,100	88,800*	8.8
Following Year	11,200	52,640	4.7

*Grants for a DWI task force and STEP demonstration project augmented all traffic enforcement operations for one year, reflected in the decrease in collisions, increase in convictions for hazardous violations, and the enhanced enforcement index. For that year there was a full-time traffic analysis staff and technical assistance from traffic specialists at the university. the STEP grants set the following multi-year goals for Oceana's traffic program:

- Enforcement index of 20
- An approximate "standard" of one hazardous violation summons per car per watch
- Less reliance on radar enforcement

There is at present no traffic analysis unit, and most of the resources of the DWI task force and STEP project have been allocated back to the patrol force. Radar is back in heavy use, not necessarily in hazardous violation enforcement, and not supported by traffic analysis.

There is no information regarding traffic accidents and enforcement for Americus County. The newly elected sheriff considers this a priority matter, to be corrected as soon as feasible.

Table 14: Crime Cleared by Arrest

	U. S. Percentages	City of Oceana Percentages	Town of Exurbia Percentages	Americus County Percentages (Pcts 1-4)	Americus County Percentages (Pcts 5-8)
Tot Pt 1 Cleared	21.6	22.4	21	17.8	18.2
Violent Crime	45.6	47.7	44	38	38.9
Property Crime	18.1	19.6	17	15.5	15.5
Murder	67.2	75.2	100	59.8	61.2
Rape	52.8	55.8	65	44.4	45.5
Robbery	24.5	27.2	21	21.7	22.2
Agg Asslt	57.3	60.4	48	48.1	49.2
Burglary	13.8	14.1	12	11.3	11.5
Larceny	20.5	21.8	21	17.4	17.8
Veh Theft	14.6	15	20	12	12.2
Arson	14.9	15.2	100	12.1	12.4

Table 15: Costs of Detention for Additional Arrests
(@ $35/arrestee/day)

Additional Daily Arrests	**10**	**30**	**50**	**100**
Assuming average of one day detention	$ 350	$ 1,050	$ 1,750	$ 3,500
Cost Per *Week* Assuming avg. of one day detention	$ 2,450	$ 7,350	$ 12,250	$ 24,500
Cost per *Week* Assuming avg. of three days detention	$ 7,350	$ 22,050	$ 36,750	$ 73,500
Cost Per *Week* Assuming average of five days detention	$12,250	$ 36,750	$ 51,250	$122,500

Two Residential Areas at Opposite ends of Economic Spectrum

Parkview Heights Condominium District
Ward No. 107
Oceana

A two-mile strip of opulent, luxurious condominiums and apartments, only one block wide (400 feet), in an unbroken line between the west side of the part and the west commerce district of Tract 107. It is a structural boundary between tracts 107 (in which it is located) and 108, which contains the park, zoo, and golf course.

The apartments are bounded by a street on their west side but face directly on the park on their east side—no street.

- 24 apartment-condo complexes in a line, each 400 feet square
- Average elevation: 10 stories; range 6–30 stories
- Average apartment complex: 4,000 square feet; range of sizes:
  - 2,000 sq. ft. (60 apts. per floor, per complex)
  - 3,000 sq. ft. (40 apts. per floor, per complex)
  - 4,000 sq. ft. (30 apts. per floor, per complex)
  - 6,000 sq. ft. (20 apts. per floor, per complex)
  - 8,000 sq. ft. (15 apts. per floor, per complex)
- 120,000 square feet of apartment space per floor, average building
- Average: 800 parking spaces per building in interior ramps
- Entire two-mile strip of building contains:
  - 7,200 apartments, all luxury grade
  - 28.8 million square feet of residential space
- Population density in Parkview: 93,000 per square mile
- Total population in Parkview Heights strip: 14,000

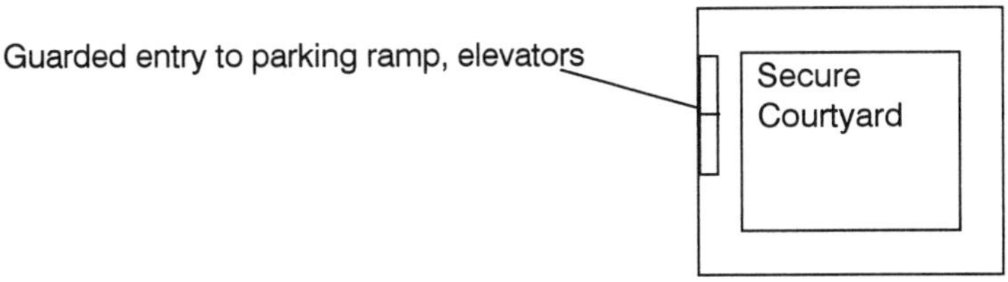

Hi-Lo Housing Project

Located in Ward 112, Hi-Lo is the brief form of the official name of this Hi-Rise, Lo-Cost Public Housing Project, federally funded.

DESCRIPTION: 36 square blocks, six blocks on a side

DIMENSIONS: Each block of apartments is:

- 400 feet square
- Ten stories high

EACH APARTMENT BLOCK CONTAINS:

- 400 apts—900–1,500 sq. ft./apt.
- 3,400 residents (estimated)

TOTAL HI-LO PROJECT CONTAINS:

- 14,400 apartments
- 122,400 residents
- 8.5 residents per apt (average)

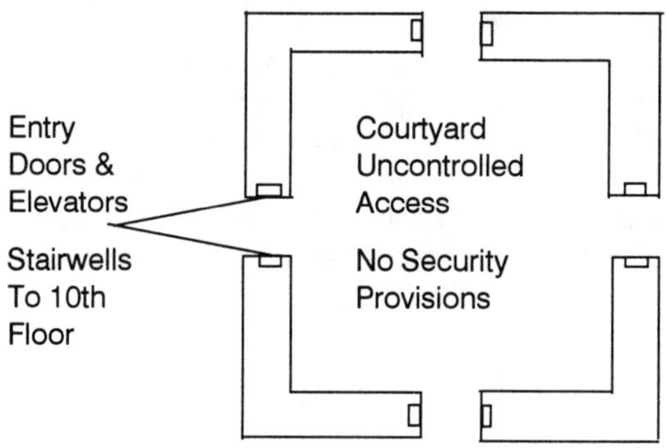

A grim discovery in Hi-Lo.

Geo-Demography and Racial Demography of Metro Area

Table 16: Oceana Geo-Demography

Ward	Sq. Miles	Percent Resdential	Resident. Sq. Miles	Pop.	Pop. per Sq. Mile	Pop. per Residence	No. of Homes
101	6.14	93	5.7	33,500	6,140	4.5	7,440
102	4.27	90	3.8	4,780	1,258	3.5	1,365
103	4	98	3.9	2,580	662	4	645
104	3.7	65	2.4	35,375	14,700	8	4,420
105	1.15	60	0.7	35,000	50,725	6	5,830
106	9.22	11	1	20,000	19,800	5.5	3,640
107	0.76	14	0.1	15,225	140,500	3	5,075
108	1.67	1	0.01	120	12,000	2	60
109	2.9	70	2	9,610	4,735	3.7	2,600
110	0.9	25	0.2	12,000	53,300	2.5	4,800
111	2.5	78	1.9	26,080	13,375	4	6,520
112	2.77	70	1.9	170,100	87,680	8	21,260
113	3	93	2.8	36,130	12,950	4	9,035
114	3.2	65	2.1	80,000	38,460	6	13,330
115	3.42	98	3.4	40,000	11,940	4	10,000
116	3.6	65	2.3	49,000	20,940	5.5	8,900
117	6.8	1	0.06	500	8,330	4	125
Totals	60	57	34.4	570,000	16,580	5.4	105,045

Table 17: Exurbia Geo-Demography

Square Miles	5
Percent Resdential	99
Residential Square Miles	4.95
Population	25,000
Population per Square Mile	5,050
Population per Residence	4.3
Number of Homes	5,814

Table 18: Americus County Geo-Demography

Precinct	Sq. Miles	Percent Resdential	Resdential Sq. Miles	Pop.	Pop. per Sq. Mile	Homes, Ranches	Pop per Residence*
1	25	88	22	90,726	4,124	15,620	5.8
2	35	57	20	133,063	6,653	22,400	5.9
3	40	50	20	145,160	7,258	34,000	4.3
4	30	33	10	114,918	11,492	10,374	11
5	58	17	10	18,144	1,814	5,500	3.3
6	75	6.7	5	24,193	4,838	2,700	8.9
7	75	6.7	5	36,291	7,258	3,300	11
8	65	7.7	5	42,338	8,468	5,200	8
Totals	403	24	97	604,833	6,235	99,084	6.1

*Population per residence is very high in some precincts because of large dormitory-type facilities for farm workers, ranch-hands and fisheries workers.

Table 19: Metro Geo-Demography

Locale	Area in Sq Miles	Pop.	Density/ Sq. Mile
Oceana	60	570,000	9,500
Exurbia	5	25,000	5,000
County	403	604,833	1,500
Metro Total	468	1,199,833	2,564

Table 20: Oceana Racial Demography

Ward	Total Pop.	Non-Hisp White	Non-Hisp Afr Amer	Hispanic All Races	Asian & Pac. Islnd	Native American	Other
101	33,500	33,200	70	165	47	13	5
102	4,780	4,720	8	38	13	1	0
103	2,580	2,470	7	83	20	0	0
104	35,375	32,590	976	576	1,113	108	12
105	35,000	18,154	13	14	15,705	106	1,008
106	20,000	12,000	2,020	5,200	200	40	540
107	15,225	14,685	150	280	110	0	0
108	120	70	24	17	5	2	2
109	9,610	9,430	60	80	40	0	0
110	12,000	5,770	2,250	2,160	1,640	70	110
111	26,080	16,380	2,200	4,690	2,080	30	700
112	170,100	38,400	80,700	45,200	700	500	4,600
113	36,130	27,459	3,071	3,757	217	145	1,481
114	80,000	56,800	10,800	8,320	480	320	3,280
115	40,000	30,400	3,400	4,160	240	160	1,640
116	49,000	33,240	8,165	5,096	294	196	2,009
117	500	380	42	52	3	2	21
Total	570,000	336,148	113,956	79,888	22,907	1,693	15,408
Percent	100	59	20	14	4	0.3	2.7

Table 21: Exurbia Racial Demography

Race	Pop.	Percent
Non-Hispanic White	24,750	99
Non-Hispanic African American	50	0.2
Hispanic All Races	75	0.3
Asian & Pacific Island	100	0.4
Native American	0	0
Other	25	0.1
Total Pop.	25,000	100

Table 22: County Racial Demography

Precinct	Total Pop.	Non-Hisp White	Non-Hisp Afr Amer	Hispanic All Races	Asian & Pac. Islands	Native American	Other
1	90,726	90,652	719	5,354	977	2	3,022
2	133,063	117,410	921	7,853	2,365	82	4,432
3	145,160	119,383	10,550	8,567	1,762	63	4,835
4	114,918	88,499	11,977	6,782	3,770	62	3,828
5	18,144	16,330	44	1,071	95	0	604
6	24,193	19.447	258	1,428	94	2,160	806
7	36,291	27,320	3,788	2,142	190	1,642	1.209
8	42,338	24,639	3,202	2,498	10,589	0	1,410
Total	604,833	493,680	31,459	35,695	19,842	4,011	20,146
Percent	100	81.6	5.2	5.9	3.28	0.663	3.33

Table 23: Metro Area Racial Demography

	Total Pop.	Non-Hisp White	Non-Hisp Afr Amer	Hispanic All Races	Asian & Pac. Islands	Native American	Other	% of Met. Pop.
Oceana	570,000	336,148	113,956	79,888	22,907	1,693	15,408	47.5
Exurbia	25,000	24,750	50	75	100	0	25	2.1
County	604,833	493,680	31,459	35,695	19,842	4,011	20,146	50.4
Metro Tot.	1,199,833	854,578	145,465	115,658	42,849	5,704	35,579	100
Percent	100	71.2	12.1	9.6	3.6	0.5	3	

Table 24: Asian, Hispanic Ethnicities

	Totals	Percent
Total Asian	22,907	100
Chinese	6,186	27
Filipino	5,269	23
Japanese	3,207	14
Korean	2,978	13
Indian	1,603	7
Vietnamese	2,978	13
Other Asian	228	1
Pac. Islands	458	2
Total Hispanic	79,888	100
Mexican	36,748	46
Cuban	23,966	30
Puerto Rican	7,989	10
Other Hisp	11,185	14

Table 25: Nativity and Language Ability

	Pop.	Native of State	Born Diff State	Foreign Born	Other Lang Than Eng Spoken	Little/No English Spoken
Oceana	570,000	273,600	222,300	74,100	119,700	57,000
Percent	100	48	39	13	21	10
Exurbia	25,000	9,500	15,320	180	100	0
Percent	100	38	61	1	0.4	0
County	604,833	308,465	247,981	48,387	72,280	30,242
Percent	100	51	41	8	12	5

Profiles of Key Political Figures and Organizations

Mayor and City Council of Oceana

Mayor Tara Warfield's platform includes reforming the police department. She agrees with the state criminal justice planning agency that there should be better coordination between the Oceana PD and the Americus County Sheriff's Department, but her first priority is to modernize, streamline and economize. She has just appointed a new chief of police from outside and thinks of the department as a political liability and far too expensive for the service it provides. Her Honor was formerly corporation counsel for Pope Brewing Co. and is a friend of Lucretia Pope, who owns the biggest business in the city. She is extremely business-minded but also knows where the votes are and courts all constituencies.

Ward 101

Miles Gorton, Marketing Manager, Argyle Phosphates. Politically moderate. Special Forces Vietnam veteran. Rotary, Lions, Chamber of Commerce. Pro-life; fiscal moderate. "Annex Exurbia, maybe the whole county." Hates traffic enforcement, especially radar. Reported for spouse abuse by a 911 call, he threatened responding officers.

Ward 102

Aaron Haenosch, advocate of property owners, with emphasis on issues of interest to white, elderly, retired residents. Politically conservative, but pro-choice. Fiscal conservative. Pet peeves: "abandoned" cars, burned-out street lights, unkempt properties, unknown pedestrians in his ward.

Ward 103

Lucretia Pope, President and Board Chair of Pope Brewing Company. Third generation executive-owner of the biggest single industry in the city. Vivacious, popular society personality; chairs the Symphony Board, member of University Board of Regents. Unpredictable politically, but pro-choice. "Forget the county, but maybe annex Exurbia." Likes cops, but dances with Bull Dog Bodine.

Ward 104

Genevieve Jacobi-Davis, teacher in the public school system and officer in the Federation of Teachers. Serious, broad-spectrum issues person, but special advocate of educational system, teachers and kids. Politically and fiscally liberal, favors public spending programs, school meals, public transport, expanded library and museum. Pro-choice. Thinks city's schools would do better without added burden of county's problems.

Ward 105

Meng Tzu Lin, President of the Asian Business Owners' Association and patriarch of Chinese family dating back to the 1850s. Meng is an effective spokesman for Asian business people; many Asian Indians, Japanese, Koreans, Filipinos and Vietnamese consider him to overrepresent the interests of the Chinese but vote for him. No public view on abortion; fiscal conservative. Isolationist except for Asians living in Precinct 8 of the county.

Ward 106

LaToya Kateshia Jones, former attorney for the Tavern-Keepers' Association, gadfly; popular with liberals, small business owners, taxi drivers. Supported by unions of dock workers, barge crews, warehousemen, other industrial and transportation workers.

Has represented adult bookstores, massage parlors, revoked liquor licensees, vending machine distributors, the Gay Rights Union, and whistle-blowers in industry. Liberal, pro-choice; fiscal liberal, in favor of city-county cooperation.

Ward 107

Dr. Jacob Steinmeier, Chairman of the Board for a high-tech manufacturer of diagnostic, surgical and biomedical engineering equipment. Speaks with technical authority. Extreme social and political conservative. Pro-life. Believes only home owners should vote, only parents should pay school taxes, health insurance is socialistic. Owns a complete block of apartments in Parkview Heights. Police radio in personal car, shoots Olympic target guns on police academy range. Sees huge conflict of interest between Oceana and Americus County, no grounds for cooperation.

Ward 108

Sierra Nevada Greenpeace, relentless advocate of environmental and wildlife issues. Recently introduced citywide bike and jogging path construction bill and a bikers' rights resolution. Pro-choice; fiscal liberal. "The county? Why not clean it up, along with the city?"

Ward 109

Charlie Marx, Ph.D., a radical sociologist at Metro State University. Dr. Marx considers the police to be the running dogs of the rich, oppressors of the working class. Advocates city ownership of all basic utilities and services. His support base includes many faculty, students, elderly liberals and increasing numbers of poor residents in the rundown, one-time silk-stocking district. Pro-choice; fiscal radical. "Let's keep the county rednecks out of our city."

Ward 110

Lorton Simmons, executive in major computer manufacturing corporation which employs 8,000. Wants to renew core of the city, revive working class housing near his plant, attract more industry back to city. Favors high sales taxes, but proposes five-year incentive rebates of taxes for new industries. Pro-life. Willing to cooperate with the county.

Ward 111

Pete Cjakowski, country-western singer, supported by the large working-class population of 111. Reloads his own ammunition, shoots with the police team, monitors dispatch in his personal car and at home, is often seen responding to major incidents in 111. Police groupie. Outspokenly pro-life; fiscal conservative; regards county as "my kind of people—cowboys," would not mind its industrial tax base for the city.

Ward 112

Malcolm "Brothers" Santoro, black Hispanic social worker turned political leader. Led the "Jobs for Brothers" campaign, and the move to get bilingual teachers in every school. Has support in Hispanic and African American sectors. "Sure, the 112th produces lots of offenders, but it's also home to the greatest number of victims." Pro-choice; fiscal liberal; too busy to think about the county.

Ward 113

Rosario Magdato Flynn, Filipino-Irish "melting-pot militant," who has worked hard to establish a coalition of the working-class whites and minority groups in his Ward. Represents the richly mixed, socially disorganized fears and

Dr. Charlie Marx harangues City Council.

concerns of the large, densely populated southwest side of Oceana. Pro-life privately, pro-choice in office; fiscal liberal; feels he also represents working class of county.

Ward 114

Lupe Reyes, veteran political figure and realtor. Represents a working-class district, plans to run for mayor soon. League of United Latin American Citizens (LULAC) and broad-based support. Pro-choice in public, pro-life as a Catholic lay leader. Fiscal conservative. Cooperates with county.

Ward 115

Sandor Lucas, conservative hard-hat welder supported by white working-class residents. Antagonistic toward racial minorities who want bilingual education and other public programs. He says, "Work for it the way my old man did, when he came here from Hungary. He din't know no English neither." Religiously pro-life; fiscal conservative, except for workmen's comp. Regarding cooperation, he says, "Sure, we'll work with the county, if they shut down the bimbo joint on that island."

Ward 116

Jody Harris, African American political leader supported by southside ethnic and racial minorities. Referred to as the "Southside Attitude Man." *Very* tough, powerful. Pro-choice; fiscal liberal. More worried about Oceana than working with the county.

Ward 117

B. D. Bodine. Known to all as "Bull Dog" Bodine since a fellow ground support pilot in Vietnam exclaimed on network news that "he hit those Vietcong positions like a bull dog." Awarded the Distinguished Flying Cross. Leader of airline pilots' association. "Pro-life, pro-choice, hey, we all got to live together." Fiscal moderate. Cooperate with the county: "Why not?" Most popular Council member. Paints the town with Lucretia Pope.

Town of Exurbia Government
Town Manager

Curtis Quick, who recently completed his Master's Degree in City Management, is in his first job, and will advance quickly in his profession. The meager police salaries in his town worry him, as he loses officers to Oceana and the county. But the entire town budget is paltry because of the weak property tax base, lack of big business and industry, and lack of a sales tax.

Exurbia's Town Council

(All members elected "at large" on nonpartisan ballots)

Position 1

Lyman Tortes, general practice attorney. Well known in the courtrooms of the metro area, but not a mogul. Shares general view that Exurbia must be protected from the big city and needs help from the county. Fiscal conservative; pro-life.

Position 2

Loretta Lindquist, queen of the realtors in Exurbia. Sees her town as a haven from the vileness of the big city and the "country" atmosphere of the county. "Exurbia is just right for good, decent people." Fiscal liberal; pro-choice.

Position 3

Jocko Lightfoot, retired NFL running back, TV sports anchor in Oceana. A local African American who made it big, he integrated Exurbia in its early days. Popular, quiet, middle-class guy. Fiscal moderate, but shifting left. Pro-choice.

Position 4

Jason Probus, actuary for a large insurance corporation in Oceana. Extreme fiscal conservative who lives in Exurbia to escape Oceana's high property taxes and outlandish social programs. Believes any extra revenue should go to the police. Pro-life.

Position 5

Errol Stanley Falconer, novelist and occasional visiting professor at Metro State. Quite liberal in fiscal policies and never saw an educational program he did not like. Thinks Exurbia schools need an uplift, more funding, more creative programs in the arts. Pro-choice.

Americus County Commission
County Administrator

"Roughneck" Hogan, retired CEO of Oriental Petroleum and owner of 480 acres of prime citrus groves. Ran for the office because "I needed something to do with my time" after retiring. Believes the secret of successful administration is "knowing how to run your board of directors. Just stay ahead of 'em." Fiscal conservative; pro-choice ("for those people down there in the city"). "We don't need the city's problems. Fence 'em in down there."

Precinct 1a Commissioner

Winston Chesterfield, big time land developer. Planning to build a mall to compete with the opulent Northside Mall, and some huge subdivisions. Looks on citrus groves and grazing land as just waiting for a chance to earn serious money. Has talent and contacts for packaging big venture capital for his projects. Growth-oriented, pro-zoning for residential and commercial land uses. Fiscal wheeler-dealer; pro-life. Will work with the city or anyone else.

Precinct 1b Commissioner

Schmuel "Schmooze" Rosengarten, retired garment manufacturer from New York City. Campaigns with, "I promise you life *can* be a rose garden if you stick with me." Represents very large population of northern, predominantly Jewish retirees and snow-birds in his fine residential neighborhoods. Pro-choice; fiscal moderate. "Sure, we'll work with the city."

Precinct 2a Commissioner

Reverend Justin Shackelford, leader of Moral Nation Encampment, a conservative survivalist enclave in far north county. Preaches against evils of the big city and its "encroachment on the God-fearing folks who till the good earth." Rails against land development, population encroachment on rural land and zoning. Outspokenly pro-life; fiscal arch-conservative. Cooperate with the city? "We don't deal with the Devil."

Precinct 2b Commissioner

Sheila "Hugs" Honey, public relations professional whose clients include the very large, bustling and prosperous Love Island, an adult theme park where thousands of singles "Take a land cruise on Love Island." The other nationally known theme park just across the water on another island in Oceana Lake continues trying to oust this business from Americus County. Hugs insists Love Island is a great draw for young single tourists. She is detested by Commissioner Shackelford and returns the feelings. Fiscal conservative; strongly pro-choice. Would cooperate with the city, where she has many clients.

Precinct 3a Commissioner

Bobby Cratchett represents the working class and lower-middle classes in this southwest suburban bedroom community. Fights for low-density, single-family zoning throughout the precinct: "We may be poor, but we keep it wholesome for our wives and kids." Agrees with Rev. Shackelford that Love Island is an abomination that threatens Oceana Legend Isle and family values in the county. Fiscal moderate; pro-life; hates the city and its emigrants.

Precinct 3B Commissioner

Rooney Toones, vice president of world famous Oceana Legend Isle, the second biggest payroll in the metropolitan region and a magnet for national tourism. Wants vice squad to raid Love Island. Pro-choice; fiscal moderate; loves the city and all those people who visit his theme park.

Precinct 4A Commissioner

Carlos "Jimmy" Jimenez, activist for wide-spectrum Latino interests. Support from VFW, American Legion, LULAC, Vietnam vets in general. Much decorated Vietnam vet, battlefield commission in Air-Cav unit. Double amputee. Generally respected figure in the metro region. Pro-life Catholic layman, pro-choice politician. Fiscal moderate; believes in working with the city, where he has strong Latino political links.

Precinct 4B Commissioner

Miles Atwood, retired head of the Railway Porters' Brotherhood. An old, charismatic labor leader who got into civil rights and then politics. Pro-choice; fiscal moderate. Political links to city. Powerful but aged black statesman.

Precinct 5A Commissioner

Jack "Dozer" Jackson, owner of huge construction firm which builds malls, airports, factories, subdivisions, why not whole cities? Zoning is fine if he defines the zone. Pro-life; fiscal wheeler-dealer, whatever works. City and county are all one big community that needs things built.

Precinct 5B Commissioner

Thomas "Bull" Mix, rancher who represents the real country perspective in north county. Believes every yard should have a few head of cattle and a horse. A Brangus breeder who says people are like cattle: "They breed true—all you got to know is where they started from. Zoning? No. Development? *Hell*, no. Keep 'em out." Pro-choice ("Too much breedin' downtown"); fiscal conservative.

Precinct 6A Commissioner

Limerick "Limey" Groves, dynastic citrus heiress and Citrus Growers' Association power. Sees herself as agrarian counterpart to Lucretia Pope, who is a friend. For generations her family controlled West County, and she is outraged that people born elsewhere should have any political say in West County. Pro-choice; fiscal conservative. Believes in keeping Oceana's emigres out; "If you weren't born here, you don't belong here."

Precinct 6B Commissioner

Ernesto "Picker" Pizarro, union organizer of agricultural workers, native of El Salvador who migrated from Texas's Rio Grande Valley to Americus County some years ago. He fights for the stoop laborers and crop pickers. Brash, handsome and attractive for his political potential. Pro-choice; fiscal liberal.

Precinct 7A Commissioner

Toby Maddox, represents South County industry, primarily the phosphate industry in the seventh. He believes upscale housing in South County would disrupt the ease of big phosphate operations. "Keep it rural, industrial, unzoned." Pro-life. Fiscal arch-conservative. Hold the city at bay; require passports.

Precinct 7B Commissioner

Joe Canoe-To-Catch-Rice lives at the east end of the Shawnee Reservation, where it adjoins Potawatomi land, both of which protrude into Precincts 6 and 7 of Americus County. His Algonquian language fluency enables him to represent both the Potawatomi and Shawnee residents of West County. He mediates between the Bureau of Indian Affairs police and the sheriff's department constantly on overlapping jurisdictional matters. No public view on abortion; fiscal liberal. The city? "I take care of my people, wherever they are."

Precinct 8A Commissioner

Roscoe Beach, fourth generation shrimper. Runs as "a true son of a shrimper," whose interest in the 8th is Southport Village and the fishing/shrimp fleet docks. "Two issues: don't let the Vietnamese shrimpers destroy the wholesale seafood system—stop 'em from selling off the docks—and head off Asian migration into the 8th." Pro-life; fiscal conservative. "What city?"

Precinct 8B Commissioner

Tran Van Dong, former general in the Army of South Vietnam, repatriated during the fall of Saigon and praised for his support of the American war effort in his country. Owner of shrimping and fishing fleet, seafood-packing plants, import-export businesses. Insists shrimpers be allowed to sell right off the dock, opposes wholesalers' control policies. Tough, competitive, connected. Pro-life; fiscal conservative. Links to Asians in the city.

Law Enforcement Organization Data: Police Chiefs and Sheriff

Police Chief Miguel "Mike" Duro has just been appointed in Oceana, having come from the senior staff of another, larger city. He is known to be reform-minded and ethical, tough but popular with his subordinates. He has ties to PERF, the Commission on Accreditation and IACP's Committee on Intergovernmental Cooperation. His main concern is to persuade his mayor, Tara Warfield, that policing can't be improved without careful analysis.

Jack Tracy is Chief of the Exurbia Police Department, having come up through the ranks since the incorporation of the town eight years previously. His budget is meager, based on the limited tax base of his bedroom community. Most of Exurbia's crime problems stem from displacement of crime from Oceana by that city's larger, better funded agency.

Sheriff Randall Scott is newly elected, having run on a modernization platform for Americus County. He has worked in county, city, and federal law enforcement and served as a Provost Marshal in the U.S. Army. He is on the Professional Standards Committee of the National Sheriff's Association, a carryover from his previous position as undersheriff in another large county. The Oceana PD, Exurbia PD, and Americus County SD have largely avoided each other over the years. Although the mayor and county administrator recently pledged closer cooperation and coordination of law enforcement services for the future, their core political concerns are within their own jurisdictions. Sheriff Scott, Chief Tracy, and Chief Duro have committed themselves to a policy of closer cooperation, but many members of their departments remember past days of competition, interference and general discord among the three agencies. Some of them don't see how they can overcome all of that, and many of them see no reason even to try.

The Oceana PD has adopted fairly modern techniques; however, the recently defeated sheriff of Americus County, who had been in office for 28 years, had neglected to maintain the department's resources at a level commensurate with the rapidly-growing workload demands of his urbanizing, industrializing county. By the time he lost the election, his staff had given up trying to meet demands for law enforcement services and assumed they would never build that fully designed pre-trial detention center to eliminate the severe overcrowding of the existing jail and correctional farm.

Americus County Correctional Administrator

Samantha Slamm, "Sam the Slamm," is a professional correctional administrator in the Americus County Sheriff's Department. She is African American and holds an M.A. degree in Corrections, earned while working the dog watch (midnights) in the Department of Corrections. Her aspiration is to build the new pre-trial detention facility, the plans for which reside on her desk. She has quietly done all she can to generate political support for the construction but has had to defer to the false economies of the aging sheriff who was recently defeated for re-election. She now sees an opportunity to build this state-of-the-art county detention facility.

State Criminal Justice Planning Representative

Paul Plumber, former planning director of a major metropolitan police department, earned his B.S. in Systems Science. His agency advocates regionalization of law enforcement services and cooperative metropolitan information bases and programs. Paul has a priority list of regionalization projects, including pool recruiting for law enforcement, crime analysis database, centralized communications center, major crime investigations unit, area-wide central records bureau, computerized warrant file, computerized prison release address files, and many others. He is dedicated, driven, and sometimes impatient. Although he talks like a technocrat, he struggles hard for cultural pluralism in planning for the future criminal justice system response to crime and disorder.

Americus County Jail Division Database

The long-time sheriff, who recently left office, believed civilians had no place in law enforcement, as reflected in his own office staff, field operations, investigations, and civil divisions. Only the jail division employed substantial civilian staff, because of its requirement of medical, nursing, counseling and other non-enforcement services, many requiring formal credentials.

Even in the jail division, the former sheriff resisted civilian staffing, preferring to contract for non-enforcement services in many cases. Thus sworn deputies continue to be assigned to many clerical and support service positions throughout the law enforcement and civil process areas of the department.

The jail division just completed its fifth year of increases in workload demands without corresponding increases in system capacities or human resources. The cumulative effect of these workload increases has resulted in a jail division which is holding approximately 40 percent more pre-trial and sentenced inmates than it was designed and authorized to hold.

As in the past the jail division has operated two major facilities: the Americus County Jail, and the Correctional Center, also known as the Prison Farm. A grant enabled the jail division to establish, for the first time, a community correction unit during the year. This minimum-security facility accommodated only a small number of sentenced inmates during the year, but it is hoped this facility can be expanded because the ratio of inmates to staff is being maintained at more than twice that of the jail, and half again the ratio for the farm facility. Community corrections, however, will not ease the jail and farm crowding significantly, even if it is expanded to its full potential. Only the construction of a pre-trial detention facility will raise ACSD's detention capacity to the authorized standard.

INMATE POPULATION

Following is the daily average count of the two main facilities and the grant operation during this past year:

	MALE INMATES	FEMALE INMATES	TOTAL INMATES	PERCENT OF TOTAL
Jail	955	130	1,085	39%
Farm	1,275	174	1,449	52%
Community Corrections	212	29	241	9%
TOTALS	2,442	333	2,775	100%

In contrast to this pattern, a nearby county last year maintained 24 percent of its inmates in community corrections status, and 37 percent of its inmates in its equivalent to Americus County's farm facility, a more cost-effective pattern than Americus County can maintain.

STAFFING OF JAIL DIVISION

	JAIL	FARM	CC UNIT	TOTAL JAIL DIV.
Administrator (Captain)	1			1
Captains	2	3	1	6
Lieutenants	9	8	2	19
Sergeants	47	37	3	87
Officers	241	195	17	453
Counselors	5	8	4	17
Nurses	19	9	1	29
Chaplain	1	1	-	2
Civilian, Support	5	9	2	16
TOTALS	330	270	30	630
INMATE RATIO TO STAFF	3.3	5.4	8.0	4.4

SYSTEM INTAKE

Total booked	60,920
Misdemeanors	39,183
Felonies	20,839
Federal	—
Civil	897
Violation: probation/parole	906
Other (fugitive, etc.)	413
Total Re-books	29,263
Total add-on charges	6,062
Total I.D. Prints	72,136
D.U.I. Arrests	4,570
Chemical tests administered	3,129
Urinalysis tests	420
Refusals of tests	1,310
Blood tests	97
Public inebriates	522

SYSTEM RELEASES

Notice to appear	10,830
Surety bonds	9,747
Cash bonds	2,530

Other bonds (ROR, etc.)	4,620
Total bonds	27,727
Undersentence transfers	11,742
Temporary housing transfers	13,010
Transfer to DOC	5,424
Released to other jurisdict.	2,780
Escapes	7
Medical treatment walk-offs	131

Jail Division Operations

Meals served	1,306,867
Staff	70,536
Working inmates	156,673
Non-working inmates	1,037,973
Medical	41,685
Average cost per meal	$1.30
Crisis intervention screening	63,704
Medical treatments	35,047
Transfers to Medical Center	3,525
Mental health interviews	6,343
Dental referrals	745
Commissary items	417,879
Drug and alcohol treatment	1,267
Educational classes	983
Contact visits	5,016
Tours	80
Library distributions	25,347
Laundry—items washed	281,607
Vehicles—total mileage	232,106

Chaplain's Office

Inmate contacts	22,717
Staff contacts	355
Inmate worship services	400
Inmate emergency services	225
Number of volunteers	35
Hours volunteers worked	2,365

General Policy Analysis Reference Information

The following pages are taken from the Kansas City Response Time Study, which was conducted in the early 1970s by William Bieck, the distinguished crime and operations analyst. They represent law enforcement's first hard empirical grasp of police response time and its significance for the clearance and successful prosecution of serious crimes.

The time-distribution graphs simply depict the amount of crime and service demand from 7:00 A.M. each day to 6:59 A.M. the next. Given the amount of variation from one day of the week to the next, and the influence of weather, etc., these graphs must be considered approximations. They are nevertheless useful for general resource allocation estimates.

The probability-of-arrest graphs show the fall-off of arrest probability as the minutes pass, up to a half-hour from time of the report. Involvement crimes refer to those in which the victim is directly involved, implying the probability of a delay in calling the police. Response-related arrests refer to those which involved a call to the police and a dispatched patrol response. All arrests include not only those involving calls to the police and a dispatched patrol response, but also on-view discovery arrests by officers, silent alarm responses, and others such as stakeouts, etc.

This material is considered useful primarily in setting policies regarding resource allocation, prioritization, and the feasibility of crime response measures.

Table 26: Violent Crime by Shifts

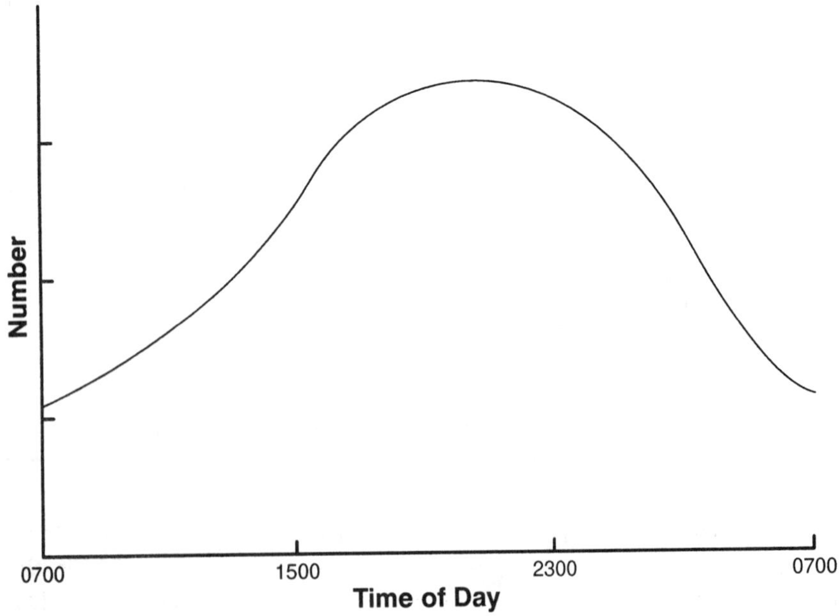

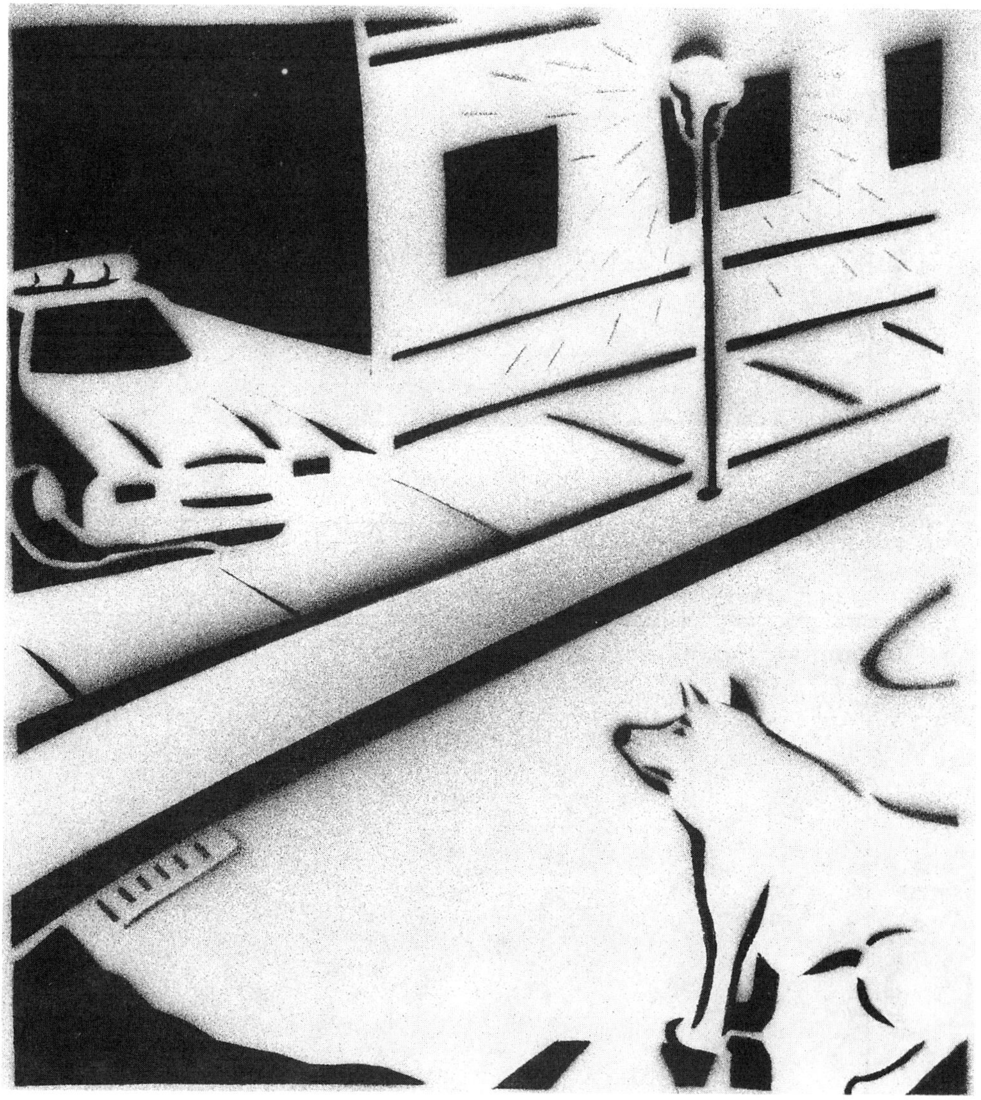

Dog Watch

Table 27: Nonviolent Crime by Shifts

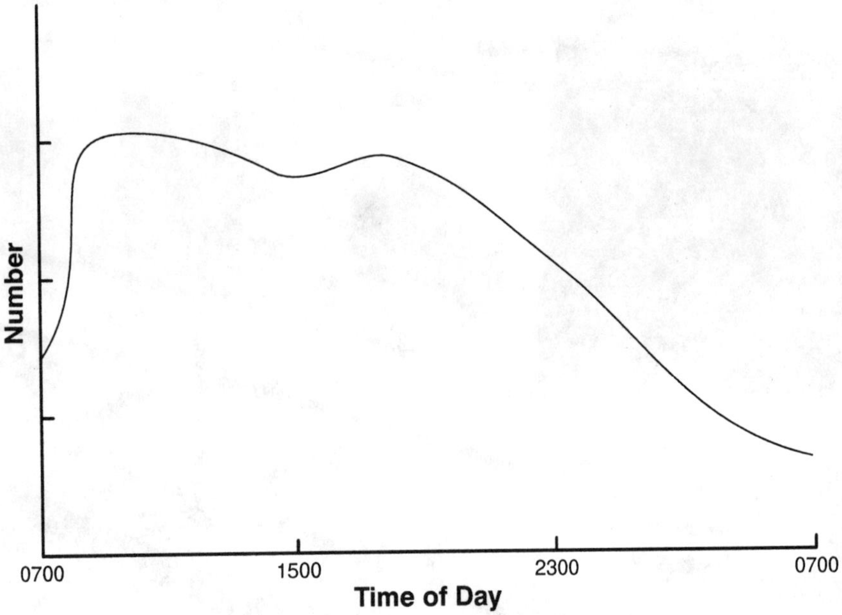

Table 28: Part II Crime by Shifts

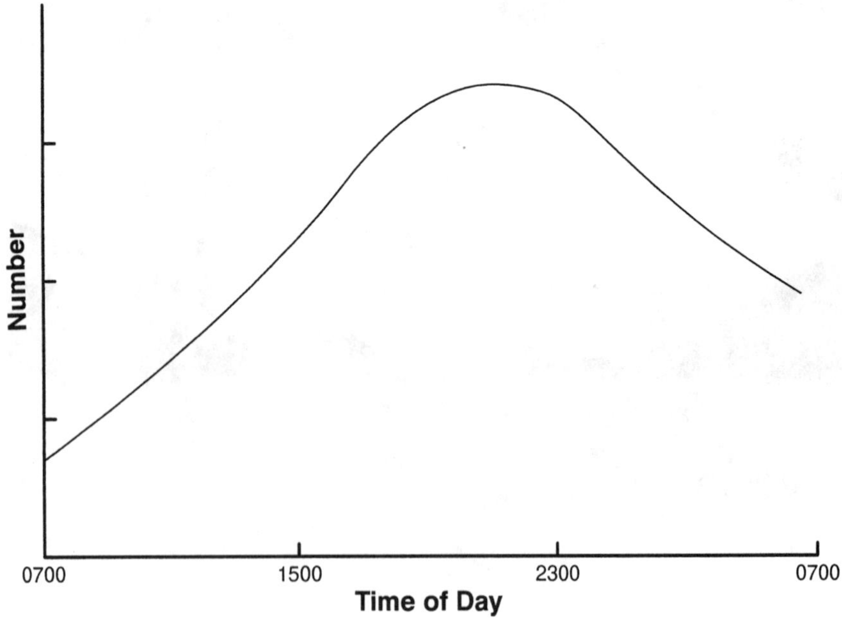

Table 29: Total Calls for Service by Shifts

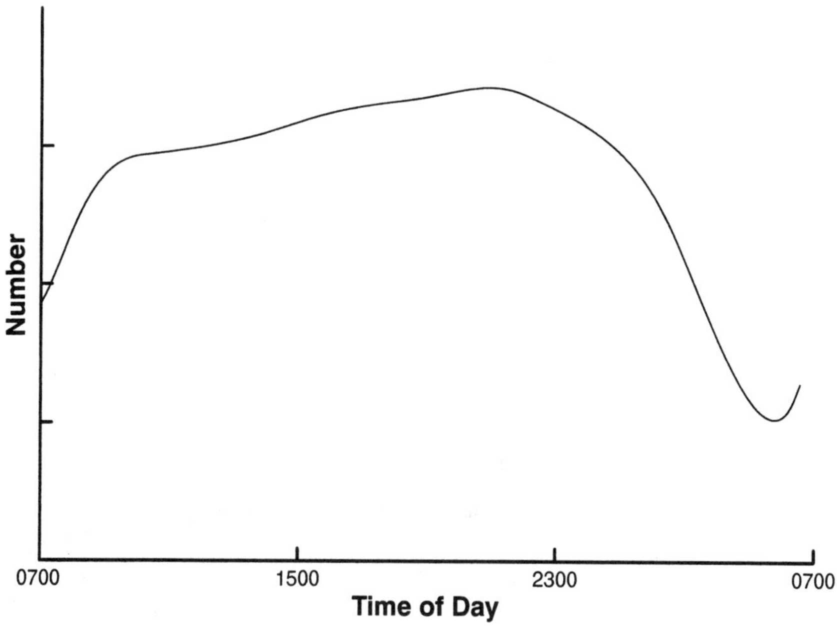

Table 30: Probability of Arrest: Part I Involvement Crimes

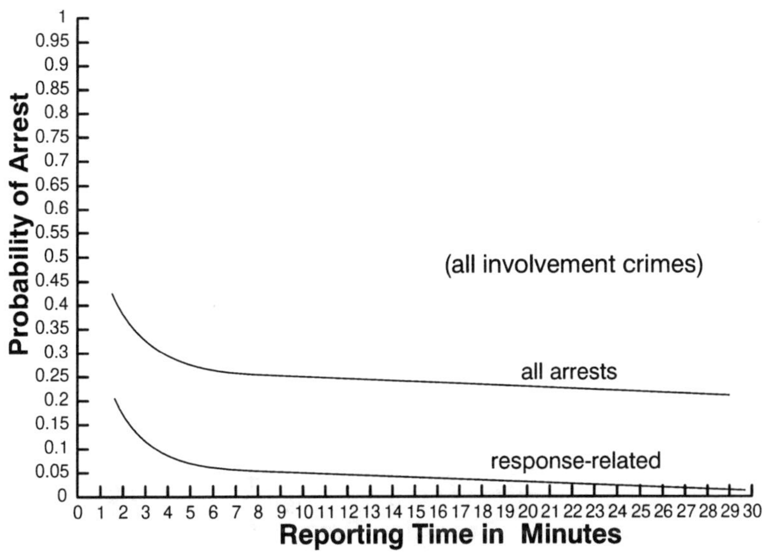

Probability of an arrest or a response-related arrest for Part I involvement Crimes at reporting times of 0 to 30 minutes.

Table 31: Probability of Arrest: Part I Involvement, Violent, Nonviolent

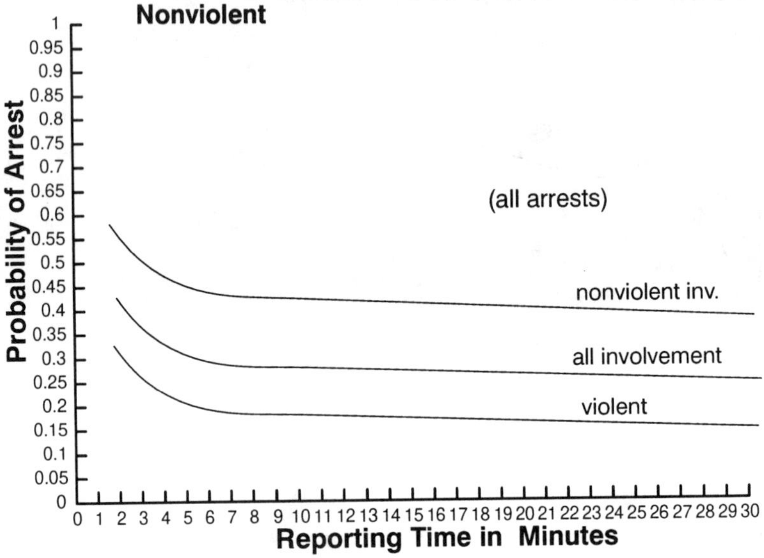

Probability of an arrest for Part I involvement crimes, violent crimes and nonviolent involvement crimes at reporting times of 0 to 30 minutes.

Table 32: Probability of Arrest: Part I Response-Related

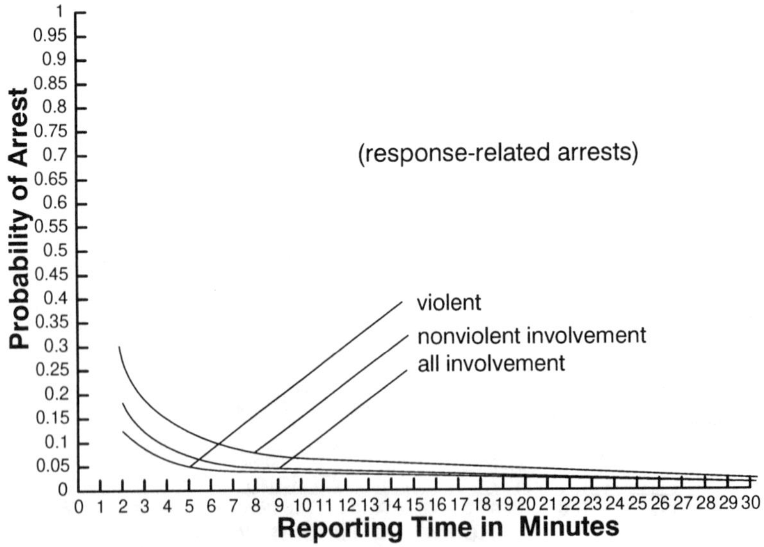

Probability of a response-related arrest for Part I involvement crimes, violent crimes and nonviolent involvement crimes at reporting times of 0 to 30 minutes.

Table 33: Probability of Arrest: All Violent Crimes

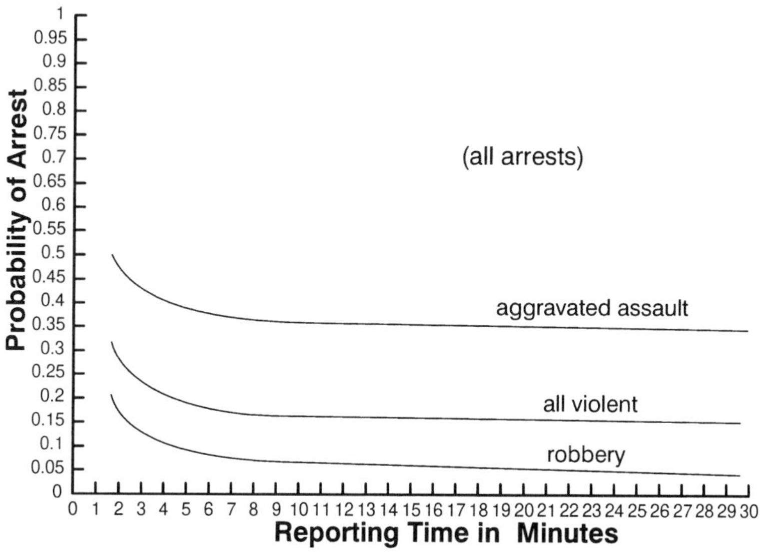

Probability of an arrest for all violent crimes, robbery, and aggravated assault at reporting times of 0 to 30 minutes.

Table 34: Probability of Arrest: Response-Related Robbery, Aggravated Assault

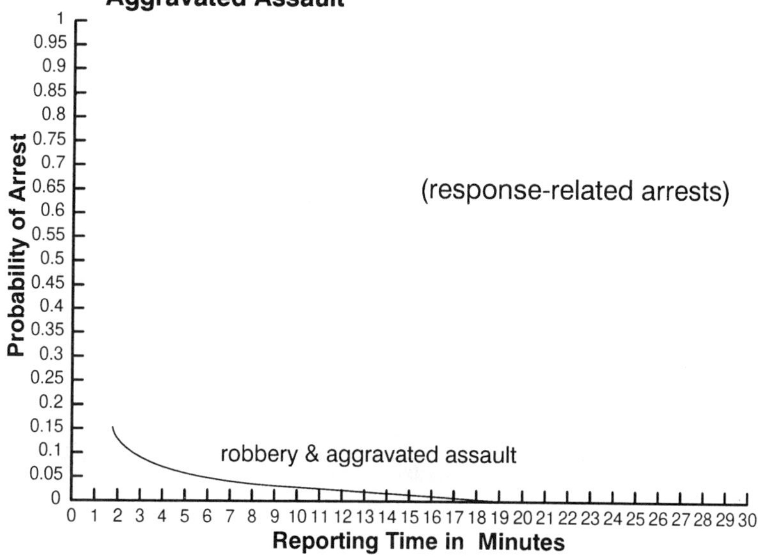

Probability of a response-related arrest for robbery, and aggravated assault at reporting times of 0 to 30 minutes.

Table 35: Probability of Arrest: Response-Related Part I Nonviolent, Involvement

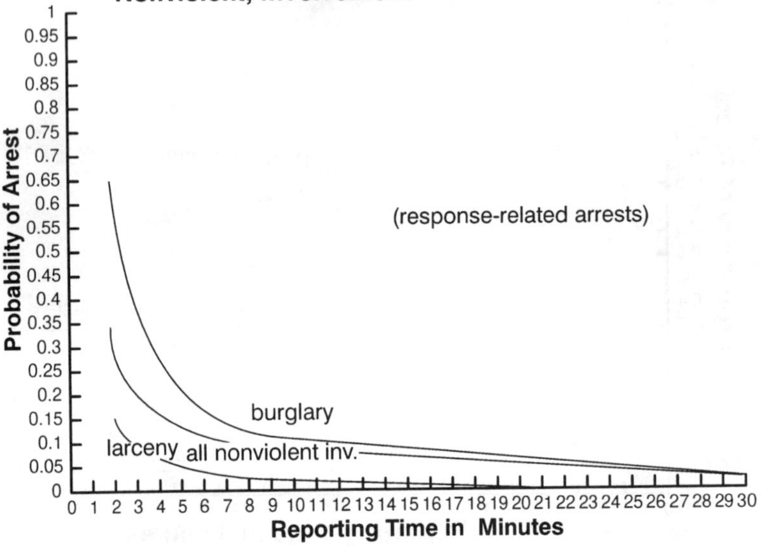

Probability of a response-related arrest for all Part I nonviolent involvement crimes, involvement burglary and involvement larceny at reporting times of 0 to 30 minutes.

Table 36: Probability of Arrest: Response-Related Part I Involvement

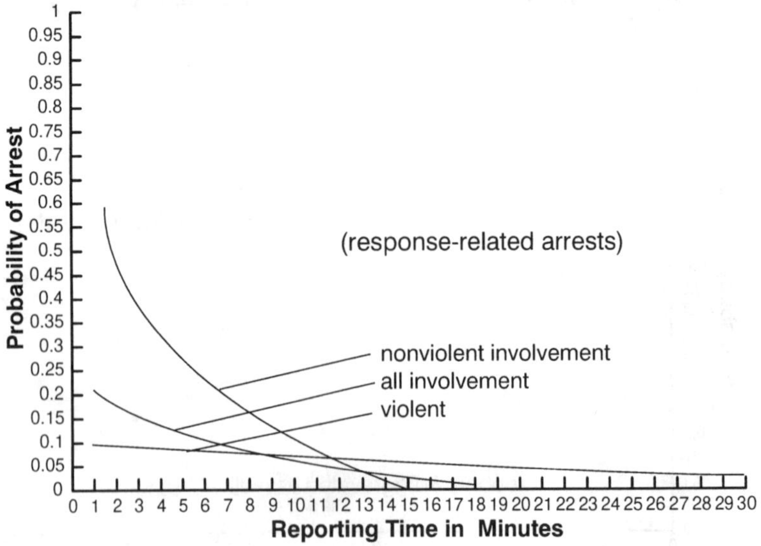

Probability of a response-related arrest for Part I involvement crimes, violent crimes, and nonviolent involvement crimes at travel times of 0 to 30 minutes.

Table 37: Probability of Arrest: Response-Related Involvement Burglaries

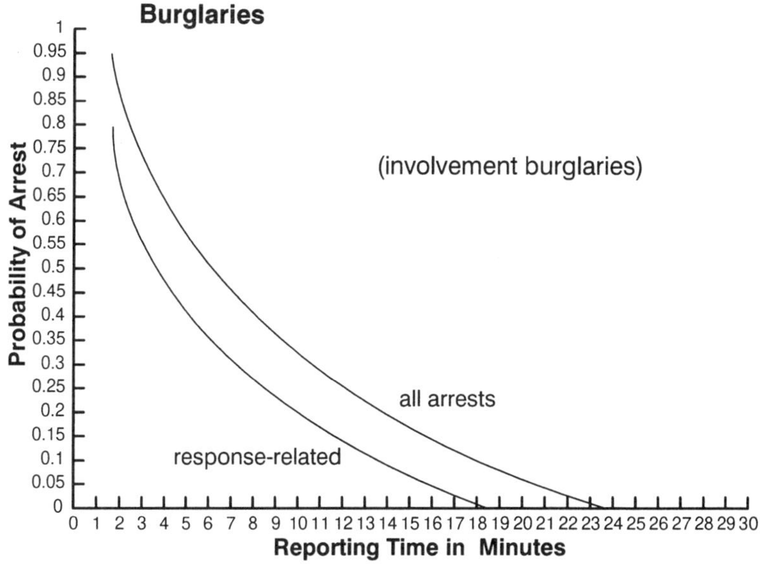

Probability of an arrest or a response-related arrest for involvement burglary at travel times of 0 to 30 minutes.

Table 38: Probability of Witness Availability: Part I Involvement Crimes

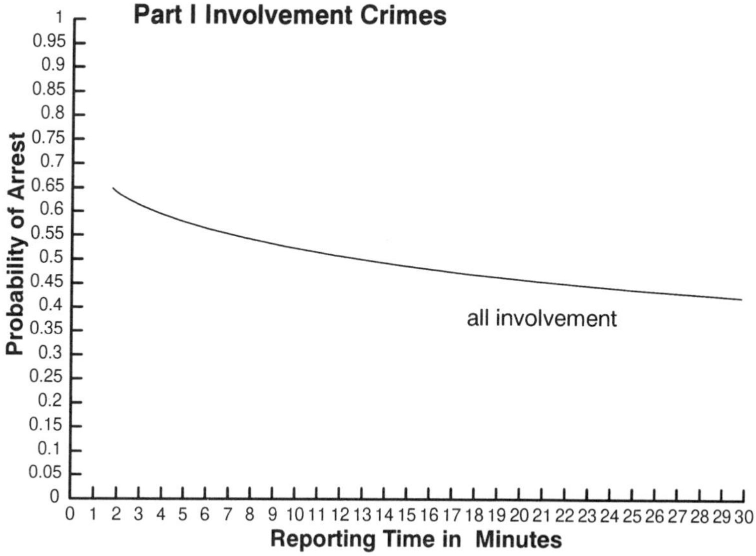

Probability of witness availability for Part I involvement crimes at reporting times of 0 to 30 minutes.